"Grace is one of the [. . .]
the riches of God's l[. . .]
provides us in *Grace* [. . .]
of grace that leads to liberty. In *Grace Works!* you will find grace
as it should be taught and practiced; it refreshes, encourages,
and points us to Christ. God lavishes his grace on sinners; you
will sense it washing over and renewing you again and again
in the pages of *Grace Works!*"

—**Dominic A. Aquila**, President, New Geneva Theological
Seminary, Colorado Springs

"Douglas Bond is a 21st-century watchman on the wall, courageously warning the church against works-oriented distortions of the gospel. Following in the footsteps of Paul, Calvin,
Luther, the Puritans, and Spurgeon, this book rightly exalts the
sovereign free grace of God as the sole source of our salvation.
To God be the glory."

—**Lonnie Arnold**, Pastor, Hilltop Bible Church, Tacoma,
Washington

"God's grace is our only hope. Christ came full of grace—and
people crucified him. The world does not like grace. Sadly,
insofar as sin remains in believers, we too have a surprising
distaste for God's grace. Douglas Bond's book is a bold call
to cling to Christ alone as our only righteousness. In brief,
straight-shooting chapters, he diagnoses the tendency of even
the most biblical churches to drift into legalism. This is a key
book for everyone who loves the church of Christ."

—**Joel R. Beeke**, President, Puritan Reformed Theological
Seminary, Grand Rapids

"Anyone familiar with Douglas Bond's other works will know
him as a great storyteller. This book is about the greatest story
of all: the gospel. Issuing from the faith of a recipient of God's

good news and the care of a shepherd, any wounds inflicted here will be those of a friend. Grace is not the enemy of works but the only proper source. It's amazing how many ways we can get that wrong—usually, as Doug argues, by incremental and often imperceptible changes. There is a lot of wisdom in this book, but none greater than the wisdom that Christ is and gives us in his gospel."

—**Michael Horton**, J. Gresham Machen Professor of Systematic Theology and Apologetics, Westminster Seminary California

"Grace works! What a concept! So simple, yet so neglected in our churches today. Douglas Bond opens our eyes to the power, beauty, and necessity of grace alone from regeneration to glorification and sounds a clear warning trumpet against the 'moralistic therapeutic deism' that dominates pulpits today."

—**Tito Lyro**, Pastor, The Bible Presbyterian Church of Olympia, Washington

"*Grace Works!* clearly shows how an emphasis on grace differentiates Christianity from all the works religions invented by man. Douglas Bond also explains well what happens when we decide the cake God gives us needs our own frosting: we get a sugar rush now and a stomachache later."

—**Marvin Olasky**, Editor-in-chief, WORLD News Group

"Douglas Bond has written here his most important book on the most important controversy in the world: the gospel. With his usual verbal dexterity and ease, Bond not only drives out the demons of our remaining Pelagianism but fills our hearts with the work of our Savior and Lord. Read this book and be changed, because Jesus changes everything."

—**R. C. Sproul Jr.**, Chair of Philosophy and Theology, Reformation Bible College, Sanford, Florida

Grace Works!

Grace
Works!

(And Ways We Think It Doesn't)

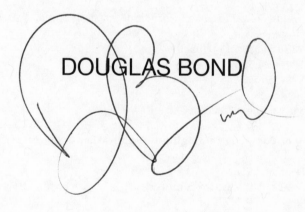

DOUGLAS BOND

P&R PUBLISHING
P.O. BOX 817 • PHILLIPSBURG • NEW JERSEY 08865-0817

Unless otherwise indicated, Scripture quotations are from *ESV Bible* ® (*The Holy Bible, English Standard Version* ®). Copyright © 2001 by Crossway Bibles, a publishing ministry of Good News Publishers. Used by permission. All rights reserved.

Scripture quotations marked (NIV) are from the HOLY BIBLE, NEW INTERNATIONAL VERSION®. NIV®. Copyright © 1973, 1978, 1984 by International Bible Society. Used by permission of Zondervan Publishing House. All rights reserved.

Scripture quotations marked (KJV) are from the King James Version.

Italics within Scripture quotations indicate emphasis added.

ISBN: 978-1-59638-743-0 (pbk)
ISBN: 978-1-59638-744-7 (ePub)
ISBN: 978-1-59638-745-4 (Mobi)

Printed in the United States of America

Library of Congress Cataloging-in-Publication Data

Bond, Douglas, 1958-
Grace works : (and ways we think it doesn't) / Douglas Bond. -- 1st [edition].
    pages cm
Includes bibliographical references.
ISBN 978-1-59638-743-0 (pbk.)
1. Grace (Theology) I. Title.
BT761.3.B66 2014
234--dc23
                              2013049333

*For all those honest enough to admit
that they have sometimes thought
grace might not actually work*

"The safest road to hell is the gradual one—the gentle slope, soft underfoot, without sudden turnings, without milestones, without signposts."
—C. S. Lewis

"Satan's stratagem is that he does not attempt an avowed destruction of the whole gospel, but he taints its purity by introducing false and corrupt opinions."
—John Calvin

"We must exercise the utmost caution lest we allow any counterfeit to be substituted for the pure doctrine of the gospel."
—John Calvin

Contents

Foreword

I WAS RECENTLY READING a book by an influential American pastor who made the argument that people both inside and outside the church are seeking happiness; therefore, the task of the church is to give them happiness. Failure so to do will lead to irrelevance, collapse in church attendance, impotence in outreach, and a general inability to connect with the wider culture.

The argument sounds plausible on first reading. After all, surely nobody of sound mind seeks to be unhappy or to find unhappiness? Yet there are a number of serious flaws with the case for happiness. The first is that it roots the meaning of life in the narrow felt needs or immediate desires of the individual. Second, it assumes the church is here to meet those needs and desires. Both are dangerously erroneous assumptions.

The man who walks into the doctor's office wanting a painkiller for his headache might actually need to have a brain tumor removed, and the doctor who simply gave him an analgesic would be delinquent in his duty and be jeopardizing the health of the patient. Thus it is with human beings and the church. Of course human beings want to be happy, but happiness is not their most pressing need, nor is it one that can be directly addressed in the manner in which we might ourselves desire. Further, it is not the church's task to pander to human desires and ambitions on this front; rather it is for the church to make people face the reality of their condition, to offer a precise diagnosis, and to propose an appropriate and adequate cure. Too often "happiness" and its pursuit is a way of escaping reality, not facing up to it.

In this book, Douglas Bond points to the real need which human beings have: not a need for happiness but a need for grace. Fallen men and women are in and of themselves utterly inadequate to stand before God. Every thought, word, and deed places them under divine judgment. It might make us happy to ignore this fact or to pretend it is not really there, perhaps even to trick ourselves into believing we might live forever. But time's winged chariot moves swiftly, and there comes a point where this world will pass away, along with all its temporary distractions, pleasures, and placebos. At that point, only grace—the grace of God manifest in and constituted by the person and work of the Lord Jesus Christ—will avail for anything at all. Ironically, therefore, only grace can bring true and lasting happiness.

Read this book and take its message to heart. It is an antidote to the superficial gospels of happiness and pleasure, which compete for your attention. Here are words of the truth that will last even beyond the—your—grave.

Carl R. Trueman
Paul Woolley Professor of Church History
Westminster Theological Seminary
Glenside, Pennsylvania

Acknowledgments

I AM DEEPLY INDEBTED TO so many for what I have attempted to communicate in this book; many of their names occur repeatedly in the footnotes. I'm ever grateful for P&R Publishing and the editorial staff for their patience with me and for publishing so many of my books, and I am especially grateful for the editorial skill and endurance of Amanda Martin on this book. Marvin Padgett gave me the initial jolt to begin work on this book some years ago. Greg Bailey helped significantly to shape the early organization of it. The intrepid Spear family, my faithful and sometimes brutal local editors, made important suggestions, including contributing the study guide questions at the end of each chapter. Clark Edwards assisted in topical research, unearthing some of the Puritan gems that are found in the book. Pastor Tito Lyro read the manuscript and made many helpful and detailed suggestions for its improvement. Always and ever, I owe my mother, Mary Jane Bond, a great debt for instilling a love of books and reading in my childhood, and for her encouragement and her loving critique of everything I write.

Introduction

WHILE I WAS GIVING a lecture on church history and the various corruptions of the gospel that have crept in throughout the centuries, my cell phone started warbling in my pocket. I glanced at the caller. It was the Director of Editorial at P&R Publishing, one of the most likeable people I know. I stepped out and took the call.

In his enthusiastic Southern drawl he said, "You've just got to write a book about this." I groaned. Other times when publishers had initiated book ideas, it had meant stormy times ahead for my imagination. After that dreaded phone call, I was like Gollum and Sméagol, arguing with myself, berating myself with reasons why writing this book was such a bad idea: "I write history and fiction. I'm a storyteller, not a theologian. If this book needs writing so much, leave it to the experts."

Next, I reminded myself of how C. S. Lewis had his demon Screwtape dry up his patient's spiritual life by getting him to write a book about it.[1] Just when I'd convinced myself to get no closer to this book than I would to nuclear waste, counterarguments would shout in my ear. "It's the gospel that's at stake," said one. I'd always wanted to believe that departures from the gospel only happened to others. Then, while reading John Newton, author of the hymn "Amazing Grace," I heard him lament that in his day "errors abound on all sides, and every truth of the gospel is either directly denied or grossly misrepresented."[2]

1. C. S. Lewis, *The Screwtape Letters* (New York: Macmillan, 1982), 60.
2. John Newton, *Selected Letters of John Newton* (Edinburgh: Banner of Truth, 2011), 115.

This made me uneasy. What Christian has not heard preaching that sounds more like misrepresentation than proclamation of the pure doctrine of the gospel? Who among us has not heard a sermon that felt like it was leading us into By-Path Meadow, the stony pitfalls leading us to Doubting Castle and Giant Despair?

Newton's words made me uneasy because I too had heard these things. I'd heard sermons that sounded less and less like justification by grace alone, through faith alone, in Christ alone. I read on. Newton proceeded to extol how laudable it was "to contend for the faith once delivered to the saints; we are commanded to contend earnestly for it, and to convince gainsayers."[3]

In fear and trepidation, I succumbed. Though I hate controversy, here it is; I've written a book birthed in the very dust and grit of it. In doing so, however, I want to hear, and I want my readers to hear, what Newton wrote in a letter to a friend zealously setting out to contend for the free grace of the gospel. "Few writers of controversy," Newton cautioned, "have not been manifestly hurt by it. Controversies are productive of little good. They provoke those whom they should convince, and puff up those whom they should edify."[4]

Which makes me again want to abandon the project altogether, dump the manuscript over the rail, return to my genre, maybe take up basket weaving. I'm keenly aware of how dangerous writing this book is, and I so desire to flee that danger.

It's dangerous because it can so easily make me critical and superior, proud and self-righteous, pedantic and smug; it sets me up to "flatter [my] own superior judgments,"[5] as Newton put it. And it so easily puts me in the mode of tut-tutting at the

3. Ibid.
4. Ibid.
5. Ibid.

16

speck in my neighbor's eye while ignoring the 2x12, obvious to everyone else on the planet, protruding from my own eye. Knowing this, entering the fray feels like being fitted for new neckwear: a millstone.

On deeper reflection, though this book was *birthed* in controversy, it really isn't intended to be about it. It is far more a book about rediscovering the loveliness of Christ. Hence, I hope that readers who get to its last page won't think it's about controversy at all. My hope is that you will close the book bedazzled with the Savior, slack-jawed in wonder at a gospel of grace that works, that accomplishes all that our gracious Redeemer said it would.

To get there, however, I will explore the various ways we doubt that grace actually works, the various ways the Enemy distorts and corrupts the free grace of the gospel, and the various ways we become willing participants in his relentless scheme to redefine the gospel.

This is also a book about an overarching message of church history. Just as there is an impulse in every generation to corrupt the gospel, there is equally an overwhelming historical consensus about what the gospel of grace actually is. Hence, it is a call for generational vigilance to guard the pure doctrine of the gospel against Satan's strategy to insinuate false and corrupting opinions about the gospel, to the ruin of the church and her children.

Moreover, this book about grace is also a book about peace and unity—gospel unity. In that spirit, I'm forced to expose the various rivals to grace that have crept into the church in her past and to unmask corruptions threatening to destroy the gospel in every generation. And here's where the danger creeps in. I'm compelled to give examples of gospel deviations sounding from pulpits today.[6] This book is emphatically not, however,

---

6. In writing this book I have found it necessary to illustrate my concerns by quoting from sermons and other statements given by ministers in Bible-believing,

an exposé on individuals or churches. That would entirely defeat my purpose. My purpose is to help Christians realize that gospel corruptions don't just happen in other churches, to other ministers, to other institutions, to other families, to other people's children. Without constant vigilance to protect the pure doctrine of the gospel, as church history relentlessly demonstrates, it will happen to us.

Lastly, though most of my heroes are theologians and preachers, I'm neither; I'm a storyteller and willingly leave the theological intricacies to the experts. In the interest of equipping the saints, this book ranges widely in the fertile soil of my heroes, the best theologians dead and alive, men who unmask counterfeits and placard the Savior.

The conclusions I draw will not be tidy formulas, or simplistic how-to strategies, or lists of more rules about the rules. None of that works. The conclusion is grace, because only grace works. Only the Prince of Peace breaks down dividing walls and unifies his church around grace itself, grace that's not a thing but a person, Jesus Christ.

As I put pen to paper, "set for the defense of the gospel," as Newton wrote, it's my desire to be clothed with the "meekness, humility, and love" of Jesus, the qualities that "correspond with the precepts of the gospel."[7]

Read on, and hold me to it.

---

reformational, and theologically aware churches and denominations. I have made every effort to faithfully represent their wording and context, and I have reproduced unwritten conversations to the best of my memory and ability, and with as much accuracy as possible.

These quotations are used for one reason only: to demonstrate how distortions of the gospel may creep into the thinking of any individual or into the message in any church. But since most of us are sure it won't happen in our church or denomination, I decided it would be best not to give specific citations for these illustrations so readers won't dismiss these as some other church or minister's problem. We *all* are inclined to corrupt the gospel.

7. Newton, *Selected Letters.*, 112–13.

PART 1

The Unanimous Testimony
of Church History:
It Will Happen to Us

1

From Grace to Disgrace

FLYING HOME FROM UGANDA after two busy weeks of teaching, I was eager for an overnight layover in Amsterdam. Africa is a fascinating continent, but I was weary and hungry—and looking forward to Dutch cleanliness and orderliness. As we made our approach to the runway, I admired the beautifully ordered farms and the tidy layout of the city laced with narrow waterways. In my frame of mind, those canals seemed to sparkle in the sunlight like streets paved with gold.

While teaching in a remote area without running water or electricity, I had spent several nights in a Ugandan mud hut; it would be good to get back to civilization. It was a sunny Saturday afternoon, and my colleague and I were eager to find a good meal and explore Amsterdam. After all, it was a city that since 1578 had been a bastion of the Reformation, a city once filled with thousands who had been set free from the bondage of their sins by the regenerating power of the Spirit of God.

Once in the city, it was impossible not to be charmed by the warm evening, the old-world stone houses with Dutch gables, the tantalizing smells of flowers and pastries that hung in the air, and all about us the tall, fair-haired, smiling, affluent people strolling the narrow cobbled streets or dining and drinking together on their canal boats.

And then I halted. A medieval church loomed above the street, and though it appeared now to have been converted into a boutique shop, its gothic arches, stained glass windows, and hand-chiseled stonework arrested my attention. I had to get a photograph. But there was a problem. The street was so narrow that even with a wide-angle perspective, I couldn't capture it. So I backed up, pressing myself tightly against a shop window. That was better. But just as I depressed the shutter on my camera, I heard and felt someone tapping gently on the window I was leaning against. I turned.

Most of us have heard about the notorious red-light district in Amsterdam. I came to the conclusion on that visit that there is not a clearly contained district—stay out of it and you'll be fine; it seemed to extend its brazen tentacles throughout much of the central city.

On the other side of the window I was leaning against, only inches away, posed an alluring young woman, smiling and offering her body to me. What flashed into my mind were the Scripture's warnings against the prostitute: "Do not desire her beauty in your heart" (Prov. 6:25). She could not have been a day older than my eldest daughter, early twenties at the most, and my heart almost broke. This poor, deceived, entrapped woman was some father's daughter. How had she come to this?

Which set me on a course of thinking: How had Amsterdam come to this? How had a country like the Netherlands, brought by the Spirit of God so overwhelmingly under the influence of the gospel of free grace 450 years ago, how had it come to this? There were no doubt prostitutes in Reformation Amsterdam, but in the gospel-saturated world that it then was, prostitution was clearly seen, known, and censured as a vice. Not so today.

It's not only legalized sex-for-hire peddled by live manikins in street-level windows; Amsterdam is known for its sweeping embrace of legalized hallucinogenic drugs, sex slavery and child pornography, gun running, same-sex marriage, abortion on demand, and state-sponsored euthanasia. How had it come to this?

Calvin's Geneva

After college I worked on a Swiss dairy farm—a sturdy, rustic place—farmed for generations by a Christian family with roots in Calvin's Reformation in nearby Geneva. On August 1, after milking the cows, we cleaned up and drove the twenty minutes to Geneva to celebrate Swiss Independence Day.

I had studied Reformation history in college and had devoured works of John Calvin in those years. Under Calvin's preaching and pastoral ministry, Geneva had become the spiritual and theological capital of the Reformation. Refugees from all over Europe flooded to the city to hear Calvin preach. "Man's only righteousness," he declared from the high pulpit in Saint-Pierre, "is through the mercy of God in Christ, which being offered by the Gospel is apprehended by faith."[1]

Walking the promenade along the lake with thousands of revelers that evening, I found it hard to imagine Calvin proclaiming the imputed righteousness of Christ in Geneva. The "tearing wolves" of the city had returned. Drunkenness, indecency, and debauchery were as commonplace as cowbells, alpenhorns, and fondue. Enter the church where Calvin preached, and today one hears clerics still claiming to be reformational Christians but declaring a message mangled by centuries of ministers fudging and tweaking with the central doctrines of the gospel preached by Calvin long ago. It's tragic. But it's not just the Netherlands and Switzerland.

Knox's Scotland

After several years as a refugee in Europe, John Knox returned to Scotland and declared Geneva "the most perfect

1. John Calvin, *Commentaries on the Epistles of Paul the Apostle to the Romans*, trans. and ed. John Owen (Grand Rapids: Baker, 1996), xxix–xxx.

school of Christ since the days of the apostles."[2] I wonder what he would call it today. Knox returned to Scotland in 1559, there to lead one of the most wide-encompassing revivals the Western world has known. There may have been more true Christians per capita in sixteenth-century Scotland than in any country at any time in history.

When John Knox stepped into the pulpit in 1560 and proclaimed the gospel of grace alone, through faith alone, in Christ alone, thousands repented and turned to Jesus Christ. Knox, so fearful of mishandling the gospel in the pulpit, said of his preaching, "I quake, I fear, and tremble."[3] He declared that in his calling, "I sought neither preeminence, glory, nor riches; my honor was that Christ Jesus should reign."[4] And so King Jesus was proclaimed throughout Scotland during his lifetime and in the years immediately after his death, and the Church of Scotland grew and flourished.

Visit Scotland today, however, and you will be deeply perplexed. Not long ago I had the privilege of sitting down for lunch (it may have been haggis, nips, and tatties) in St. Andrew's with David Robertson, pastor of St. Peter's, Dundee, where Robert Murray McCheyne preached Christ in the nineteenth century. Not only was the Spirit of God poured out in a great revival there, but also as a result Scotland sent missionaries around the globe to proclaim the gospel to unreached peoples in China, Africa, India, and the Pacific Islands. "Today, Scotland leads Europe in drug and alcohol abuse," David told me, "and Dundee has the highest rate of substance abuse in Scotland."[5] He went

2. John Knox, cited in D. G. Hart, "The Reformer of Faith and Life," in Burk Parsons, ed., *John Calvin: A Heart for Devotion, Doctrine, and Doxology* (Lake Mary, Florida: Reformation Trust, 2008), 50.

3. John Knox, cited in Iain Murray, *John Knox: The Annual Lecture of the Evangelical Library for 1972* (London: Evangelical Library; Edinburgh: Banner of Truth Trust, 1973), 22.

4. Ibid.

5. David Robertson, conversation with author, Doll House Cafe, St. Andrew's, Scotland, April 2008.

on to describe the moral free fall of the country, the devastating effect on the family, the escalating rate of suicide, and in general the dismal condition of Scottish society and the church.

From the glorious revival beginning in 1560 when churches all over Scotland were filled with grateful worshipers, eager to hear the gospel of grace, church attendance in Scotland has been in steady decline for decades. Fewer than eight people out of a hundred attend church with any regularity, and the decline in attendance continues to plummet.

In 1996 I sat in the parlor of the venerable William Still in Aberdeen, Scotland, listening in wonder as he gave glory to God for the gospel blessings on his flock there and on dozens of missionaries—loved, prayed for, and supported by his congregation—proclaiming Christ throughout the world. Pastor Still's widely influential gospel ministry with little doubt was the high watermark of Scottish Christianity in the twentieth century. What remains in the Church of Scotland today, however, is a small huddle of men faithful to the gospel, clinging for life to a sinking ship. In its last gasps, the church for which Knox laid the foundation, the Church of Scotland, voted to install an openly homosexual minister, one who had divorced his wife, abandoned his children, and was living openly in a homosexual relationship.

It gets worse. There are a handful of faithful ministers in the Church of Scotland, but when one of them, David Randall, minister at Loudoun Parish in Newmilns, courageously stated that for its decades of defection from the authority of Scripture the Church of Scotland is apostate and is blaspheming the Holy Spirit, he was the one called up on charges of apostasy.

Apparently a Church of Scotland minister can break his marriage vow to his wife, leave her to care for the children, take up with a male lover, and yet step into the pulpit of his church and be a minister in good standing. But when my friend

Pastor Randall speaks out against it, he is the one brought up on charges. One wonders if there could be a more glaring illustration of ecclesiastical irony. But it's not just the Netherlands, Switzerland, and Scotland.

Edwards's New England

When John Winthrop preached his sermon "A Model of Christian Charity" on the decks of the *Arabella*, flagship of the Massachusetts Bay Company fleet in 1630, and declared the Puritan community a "Wilderness Zion" and a "city on a hill," he could not have in his wildest dreams envisioned what New England has become today.

The decline began earlier than most of us want to admit. With the Half-Way Covenant in 1662, people who had no credible profession of faith in Christ were invited to the Lord's Supper. In short order Christ was reduced to a great moral example to follow, but was rejected as the Divine Son of God, the only Lord and Savior of sinners. The result was an erosion of the gospel that devolved into the rationalism and hostile unbelief endemic in the next centuries.

Today New England is the most irreligious, unbelieving region in the United States, with fewer people attending church—any church—than anywhere else in the country.

The compelling question is: how did it come to this?

For Discussion

1. Read Galatians 3:1–3 and 5:7. Discuss the verbs Paul uses and what they reveal about the problem he sees in the Galatian church.

   O foolish Galatians! Who has bewitched you? . . . Let me ask you only this: Did you receive the Spirit by works of the law or by hearing with faith? Are you so foolish? Having begun by the Spirit, are you now being perfected by

the flesh? . . . You were running well. Who hindered you
from obeying the truth?

2. Read Heidelberg Catechism 60 and discuss what it declares
about how we are made righteous before God.

   Q. How are thou righteous before God?

   A. Only by a true faith in Jesus Christ; so that, though my
   conscience accuse me, that I have grossly transgressed
   all the commandments of God, and kept none of them,
   and am still inclined toward all evil; notwithstanding, God,
   without any merit of mine, but only of mere grace, grants
   and imputes to me, the perfect satisfaction, righteousness
   and holiness of Christ; even so, as if I never had had, nor
   committed any sin; yea, as if I had fully accomplished all
   that obedience which Christ has accomplished for me;
   inasmuch as I embrace such benefit with a believing heart.[6]

3. What other cities have had great times of revival and gospel
proclamation but are now almost devoid of gospel witness?
What were features of those revivals, and what led to the
unbelief that marks those places today?

Pray earnestly for your pastor and elders that they would
be faithful to the all-sufficiency of Christ and the gospel
of free grace.

---

6. The confessions and catechisms quoted in this book can be found in *Historic
Creeds and Confessions,* edited by Rick Brannan (*Christian Classics Ethereal Library,*
http://www.ccel.org/ccel/brannan/hstcrcon.txt) or at Ligonier Ministries (http://www
.ligonier.org/learn/topics/creeds-and-confessions/).

2

It Won't Happen in My Church

I LOVE READING church history, but when I read about great times of spiritual triumph in the past, a nagging uneasiness starts working in the back of my mind. That uneasiness turns to outright despair when I learn about the seemingly inevitable decline and defection that results in the generations following great moments of progress for the gospel.

It seems so wrong that it doesn't last. Pure things should last. "Love is not love which alters when it alteration finds," Shakespeare put it. "It is an ever fixed mark."[1] But the gospel's influence over a particular country, or city, or family seems never to remain as an ever-fixed mark in that country, or city, or family. I find this deeply discouraging.

We want a gospel that lasts, don't we, a grace that works? One that doesn't alter when it alteration finds. What good is the triumph if it's followed by equal or greater falling away? And it's not just a Dutch problem. It's ubiquitous. Name the country that has had a great revival in past centuries, then visit it today. Ready yourself for grave disappointment. Or name the institution of higher learning founded in the past on the gospel: Harvard, Yale, Princeton—the list goes on—and in the vast majority of cases you will find scorn and open hostility to the gospel in that institution today.

1. William Shakespeare, "Sonnet 116," *The Penguin Book of Sonnets*, ed. Carl Withers (New York: Penguin Books, 1943), 61.

It Won't Happen to Us

Herein lies the grave danger. So odious is error to us that we're inclined to detach ourselves from these examples of decline. "This only happens to other people," we tell ourselves. It only happens in other places, in other people's churches, to other people's ministers and institutions. Surely we've grown out of this today; our churches and institutions will remain faithful, surely they will.

No doubt the Dutch, Swiss, Scots, and New England colonists somewhere along the way began saying this to themselves. Declaring ourselves to be impervious to defection from the truth, however, does not make us so. On the contrary. Telling ourselves this about our church actually lulls us away from vigilance and into complacency—which is precisely where the Enemy wants us.

No church is exempt. No preacher is exempt. No family is exempt. And there is no greater danger than when we believe we are immune to the Loadstone Rock of decline and decay.

I realize I am painting a pretty grim picture here. But if it is an accurate one, what do we do about it? Do we give up in despair? Must we simply resign our church to the vicissitudes of history, to ending up like virtually every wreck of a church or institution whose triumph is but a faint quaver of vitality on the timeline of the past? Or do we whistle still more loudly in the dark, assuring ourselves that it just won't happen to us?

"I See Nothing!"

In our hatred of strife and controversy and in our love of peace and unity, we Christians sometimes play the ostrich. We hope controversy and gospel attack will just go away; we bury our heads in the sand and pretend it won't happen to us. We imagine that the best defense against error is to be like Sergeant Schultz in the old *Hogan's Heroes* situation comedy. "I see nothing!" he repeatedly assures himself—

when there is, indeed, a great deal going on under his nose. Schultz's self-talk strategy makes for entertaining comedy, but it does not make for an effective defense against the Enemy of the gospel.

Christ commended the church at Ephesus for vigorously contending against false teaching, even for doing so in Christ's name (Rev. 2:1–7). But he had this against them: they had abandoned their first love (2:4). There's the rub. The great danger when false teaching rears its ugly head in the church—as it will do—is that in our zeal to test that teaching and root out the false, we too can lose our love for other Christians. Anyone who has been in a church split knows how enervating, how soul-killing controversy and strife become when Christians are at each other's throats, each side certain that this is the hill they were meant to die on.

What is Satan's strategy when Christians are at odds with each other? On the one hand, he wants to get us to lose our love for one another in our zeal to uphold the truth. On the other hand, he wants us to hate controversy so much that we are willing to fudge the truth in order to maintain visible unity, a sort of *Pax Romana*, a charade of peace, a peace at any price, a peace that offers up truth as a burnt offering.

Satan wants one or the other, because either of these errors diverts our attention away from the object of his attack: the truth. One faction is ready to sacrifice the doctrinal truths of the gospel on the altar of unity. Those on the other side, in their very zeal to uphold the truth, have done violence to that truth by losing their first love for one another—and thereby for Christ himself.

I suspect Satan may be a bit more anxious about the first group as a threat to his schemes—they're so concerned for the very truth he wants to corrupt—so he may work all the more earnestly to shift their attention away from the truth and to the hatred he wants them to have for one another. So predisposed are we to finding fault with our brothers, it's probably not a very strenuous task for him. A narrow-eyed suggestion here, a nod and a nudge there, and we're certain our pastor or elder or seminary professor is apostate. And we put on our theological brass knuckles and go to work.

Satan breathes easier, however, if we just capitulate to the new teaching, if we tell ourselves we're sure the man teaching us means well, if we convince ourselves that a scholar of his theological training and connections could never get things wrong, if we console ourselves with how ridiculous it would be for our pastor to be a false teacher. But what Satan absolutely does not want us to be is Bereans (Acts 17:11) who are on our guard, who diligently and earnestly search the Scripture to see if what we are hearing matches up with what the Bible declares to be true. This he hates.

For Discussion

1. Read the passages below and discuss how God's gift to us and our call to love others keep us vigilant in upholding the truth.

   But God, being rich in mercy, because of the great love with which he loved us, even when we were dead in our trespasses, made us alive together with Christ—by grace you have been saved—and raised us up with him and seated us with him in the heavenly places in Christ Jesus. (Eph. 2:4–6)

   By this we know love, that he laid down his life for us, and we ought to lay down our lives for the brothers. (1 John 3:16)

2. Discuss the "grand exchange" of the gospel described in Belgic Confession, article 20:

God therefore manifested His justice against His Son when He laid our iniquities upon Him, and poured forth His mercy and goodness on us, who were guilty and worthy of damnation, out of mere and perfect love, giving His Son unto death for us, and raising Him for our justification, that through Him we might obtain immortality and life eternal.

3. In chapter 2, how does the author show that we can do damage to the truth while setting about to contend for the truth?

Pray today, and often, for your church to have holy zeal in contending for the truth, and at the same time grace in loving one another as Christ loves his people.

3

Satan's War Strategy

"SATAN'S STRATAGEM," wrote Calvin, "is that he does not attempt an avowed destruction of the whole gospel, but he taints its purity by introducing false and corrupt opinions." Once we acknowledge that there really is a war on and face up to the Enemy's strategy, "we must exercise the utmost caution lest we allow any counterfeit to be substituted for the pure doctrine of the gospel."[1]

Calvin knew that the Devil is too clever to come at the church with frontal assaults on the gospel. The fiend knows we'd see him coming. Rather he's patient, slow, incremental, and he loves making us think that our plausible new interpretation is at long last getting at the burden of the text, that we have achieved the spiritual and theological high ground. Managed by the Deceiver, error will always sound reasonable, sophisticated, intellectual, urbane—whatever it takes to convince us it's true. The Devil is very skilled at his craft; he's been fine-tuning it for millennia.

Moreover, for this war, Satan doesn't need to commission outside assassins. He works most effectively from within the church, employing homegrown allies. He works by stealth within the gate suggesting "false and corrupting opinions." It is war, and we must train our minds, our hearts, and our ears

1. John Calvin, *Commentary on Galatians*, trans. and ed. John Owen (Grand Rapids: Eerdmans, 1974), 97.

to hear the "plausible arguments" (Col. 2:4) and the cunning rhetoric that tampers with the gospel (2 Cor. 4:2).

Therefore, we must exercise the greatest vigilance within the church, where he most perniciously works. Francis Schaeffer often quoted words attributed to Martin Luther, "Where the battle rages, there the loyalty of the soldier is proved."[2] Where does it rage today? Where it always has. Church history is the chronicle of cunning attacks on and departures from the gospel. Because it so often works this way, the task of Christians in every age requires informed, unstinting vigilance.

Men, Not Angels

Zealous for maintaining the purity of the gospel against the inevitable onslaught of the Enemy, Reformer John Knox developed a plan to equip everyone in Scotland to test what they heard in the pulpit. Knox wrote that since "God hath determined that His Church here on earth shall be taught not by angels but by men," it was essential for the country to develop a system of universal literacy to equip the average person—rich and poor, male and female—to be on their guard against false teaching in the pulpit. It was as if Knox were placing a built-in system of checks and balances so that no preacher could arrogate his views above what the Bible taught. For Knox "virtuous education and godly upbringing of the youth of this realm"—that is, Christ-centered education—was necessary for maintaining the purity of the gospel.[3] Knowing his own frailties, Knox wanted an entire country of Bereans.

Being a Berean, however, means taking your stand, planting your flag, and readying yourself for war. "You may not be interested in war," Trotsky once said, "but war is interested

---

2. Attributed to Martin Luther in Francis Schaeffer, *The Great Evangelical Disaster* (Westchester, IL: Crossway Books, 1984), 333. The quotation originates in Elizabeth Charles's work *Chronicles of the Schönberg-Cotta Family*, published in 1868.

3. John Knox, cited in R. A. Houston, *Scottish Literacy and the Scottish Identity* (Cambridge: Cambridge University Press, 1985), 5.

in you."[4] Most Christians are not interested in slugging it out over doctrine, and we wonder why so many Christians disagree about so many things. Why can't we just get along? We're not interested in war; we want peace and unity in the church. Deceiver that he is, the Enemy can use even our desire for unity to disarm us for his attacks at the vitals of doctrinal truth. In this war, let's be sure we have due respect for our Enemy; the Devil deserves credit for being single-minded. He has one thing, and one thing only, in his crosshairs: the purity of the gospel.

Floods and Fire Hoses

The Deceiver wants us to roll our eyes and guffaw at how ridiculous it is that our church could teach a counterfeit gospel. My guess is he loves throwing out the notion that we're making mountains out of molehills; I wonder if it's not his favorite cliché. But the last thing he wants is for us to "exercise the utmost caution lest we allow any counterfeit to be substituted for the pure doctrine of the gospel."[5]

The Enemy is never more persuasive than when he insinuates plausible arguments within Christian theology and the preaching and practice of that theology in the church. He comes at the church from many angles, but I wonder if a favorite method might be to get us preoccupied with legitimate practices and ordinances in Christian worship.

He loves getting us "running around with fire extinguishers whenever there is a flood,"[6] as C. S. Lewis puts it, and encouraging us to make our latest discovery about liturgy, the sacraments, educating our children, or clerical robes appear to be the central dogma of the church. As he aims his arrows

---

4. Leon Trotsky, cited in George F. Will, "The Doctrine of Preemption," in *Imprimis* 34, no. 9 (September 2005): 2.

5. Calvin, *Commentary on Galatians*, 97.

6. C. S. Lewis, *The Screwtape Letters* (New York: Macmillan, 1982), 118.

at justification by faith alone, I suspect he delights in getting theologians and pastors to harangue each other about the efficacy of baptism and the Lord's Supper. He probably is little concerned with the fact that Christ himself instituted these as means of grace. He's just interested in nudging us on so that before we realize it, we've allowed the means of grace to trump the object of grace, Jesus Christ.

By this and dozens of other deflections, he gets us running around attempting to hold back floods with fire hoses and to put out fires with blowtorches. The last thing he wants is for us to keep the main thing the main thing. When he's succeeded in shifting our attention away from the person and work of Christ in the gospel, as he did in Amsterdam, his task is nearly done. Instead of earnest, Christ-loving, gratefully enchanted, and adoring Christians, the church will then produce generations of Pharisees or rebels.

He's probably fine with the church becoming more concerned about the moral decline in society just so long as we suckle the next generation on a gospel that includes a tiny bit of moral self-improvement. And he never wants us to realize that it's happening. He will positively encourage us to believe that it's the other guys who have it all wrong. We never could.

Moreover, the Devil knows that when we add just a little bit of law to balance out all that grace in the gospel—to help keep the kids in line—we won't actually get law keeping, not from the heart; we'll produce congregations—young and old—filled largely with nominal, externally conforming moralists, who will virulently deny it. And he is hell-bent on making certain that we do not realize that we have imbibed a justification that is dependent to some degree on our sanctification. I suspect he strains every infernal sinew to make certain we never wake up and realize that we have done violence to the good news of salvation by grace alone, through faith alone, in Christ Jesus alone.

38

Grace That Works

Satan, I imagine, had a jolly time wrecking the church in Amsterdam, Geneva, Scotland, and New England, and he no doubt is excited about the prospects of doing the same in your church. It must have been entertaining for him to see the gradual slackening of the hand of theologians and preachers as they revised their message for their hearers, or for their scholarship, or as they sought to make the gospel compatible with entertainment, or science, or politics, or philosophy. I envision him barely able to contain his glee as he watches church leaders supplant the "pure doctrine of the gospel" with a plausible-sounding counterfeit.

Church history proves that Satan's strategy works—that is, it works when he gets us to doubt that the pure doctrine of grace actually works.

If our churches, families, institutions, and ministries are going to endure, it will only come about as we rediscover how wretched, poor, and needy we are, and as we rediscover every generation that only grace works. That rediscovery will find us on our knees and on our faces intoxicated with the love of God in Christ Jesus our only Redeemer, Savior, and Friend. And, as promised, that scandalously free good news will bear the fruit of heartfelt, grateful, and loving obedience, fruit that is produced and nurtured by the grace that really does work.

But Satan is hell-bent on doing his best—little by little—to make sure we think it doesn't.

For Discussion

1. Reflect on 2 Timothy 3:15–17 and Ephesians 6:12, and discuss from the chapter how being a Berean is different from being intellectually superior:

   How from childhood you have been acquainted with the sacred writings, which are able to make you wise for salvation through faith in Christ Jesus. All Scripture is breathed out by God and profitable for teaching, for reproof, for correction, and for training in righteousness, that the man of God may be complete, equipped for every good work. (2 Tim. 3:15–17)

For we do not wrestle against flesh and blood, but against the rulers, against the authorities, against the cosmic powers over this present darkness, against the spiritual forces of evil in the heavenly places. (Eph. 6:12)

2. Read 1 Corinthians 1:27–31 and discuss what occurs when we try to make the gospel compatible with entertainment, science, politics, or philosophy.

But God chose what is foolish in the world to shame the wise; God chose what is weak in the world to shame the strong; God chose what is low and despised in the world, even things that are not, to bring to nothing things that are, so that no human being might boast in the presence of God. And because of him you are in Christ Jesus, who became to us wisdom from God, righteousness and sanctification and redemption, so that, as it is written, "Let the one who boasts, boast in the Lord."

3. Read Belgic Confession, article 22, and discuss the antidote that will cause churches, families, institutions, and ministries to endure.

We believe that, to attain the true knowledge of this great mystery, the Holy Spirit kindles in our hearts an upright faith, which embraces Jesus Christ with all His merits, appropriates Him, and seeks nothing more besides Him. For it must needs follow, either that all things which are requisite to our salvation are not in Jesus Christ, or if all things are in Him, that then those who possess Jesus Christ through faith have complete salvation in Him.

Consider which ministries you support financially. Create a prayer list of them and regularly pray for an enduring spirit to prevail in maintaining the pure doctrine of the gospel—of salvation in Jesus Christ alone.

PART 2

"Grace Won't Work without Works":
*And Other Ways We Distort
the Gospel*

4

The Gospel at Thirty-Five Thousand Feet

I DON'T PARTICULARLY enjoy flying, and especially not when there's lots of snow, high winds, and the inevitable flight delays that accompany nasty winter weather. So it was with a sigh of relief that I emerged in one piece from a sardine-can turboprop plane after a blustery flight from Sheridan to Denver, a flight that had felt more like I was riding a bucking bronco in a Wyoming rodeo.

Settling into my seat on my connecting flight to Seattle, I pulled out *Modern Reformation* magazine and thumbed through the pages to where I had left off reading. It had been an engaging article on the Great Commission, but no sooner had I begun reading than a big fellow took the seat next to me, turned, and asked, "Business or pleasure?"

My magazine poised in reading position, I half turned. To my shame, I thought I had the sure way to silence him. "I suppose you'd call it business. I was speaking at a men's *Bible* conference." His interest didn't flag as I had expected, so I added, "And I just preached a sermon this morning at First Baptist Church in Sheridan, Wyoming." That ought to shut him up, I thought.

But it didn't. Manuel proved to be a chatty British Petroleum construction worker who hailed from Colorado Springs, and he seemed at first curious to know what I had preached and taught. So I began giving him a summary of forty-two chapters of the book of Job, then started explaining to him how the sufferings and testing of Job pointed to Christ and the gospel of grace.

Manuel listened politely for a few minutes and then began telling me about a high-voltage, near-death experience he had had and then about the theological ideas he had developed from that experience. As he became more animated, it became clear to me that he had come to have an intractable faith in his homegrown theology.

Sidelines or Front Lines

As I listened, I thumbed through my magazine full of stimulating articles on the Great Commission. I almost laughed out loud at the irony—and at my own folly. Here I was with an opportunity to be used as an instrument of the Holy Spirit, to actually participate in the Great Commission, and I had preferred to sit on the sidelines, to bury my face in the theory of sharing the good news.

I closed my magazine. For an hour and half I listened to Manuel's sincere but deeply befuddled experiential theory of death and meeting God. "It's all about free will," he said enthusiastically. "We each of us are going to be faced with a choice, and we have to be ready to choose love and not hate, good and not evil, God and not Satan."

As I listened, I prayed for the Spirit to give me wisdom—and that Manuel would take a breath so I would have an opportunity to speak. At last he paused, and I began probing how he defined all those terms he used, especially good and evil, God and Satan. "It's up to each of us to define them according to our own feelings and experience," he said, as if reciting from a Postmodernism 101 textbook.

So I proceeded to share with him what the Bible declared to be true about the holiness of God and about my profound unholiness, how much I had offended God's will and way, how right it is for God to be angry with me, and how desperately lost I am. Next I began to explain how God sent his Son, Jesus, and what it was he came to do; how only through the atoning sacrifice and righteousness of Jesus Christ could we be rescued from the just condemnation we are under for our sins. "Jesus put it this way," I told Manuel. " 'I am the way, the truth, and the life; no man comes unto the Father but by me.' "

Manuel replied, "Oh, I agree with that totally."

I attempted to show him the incompatibility of agreeing with Jesus' exclusive declaration and believing that salvation is up to each individual's feelings and experience. How could Jesus be right and everybody's free ideas that directly contradict what Jesus said be right at the same time? "I believe in a very open God," said Manuel, "and there are many ways to him."

"But Manuel, how can you agree with Jesus' words, when he declares by the authority of God himself that the Son of God alone is the way, the truth, and the life, and that no one comes to the Father but through Jesus?"

He returned to his mantra about there being many ways to God. I tried to help him see that his theory about good and evil and finding his own way to God didn't work in the real world—for example, in the world of aeronautical engineering. If the designer of the Airbus jet in which we were suspended thirty-five-thousand feet above ground had designed this jet the way Manuel had designed his theology—based on his free will, his individual feelings about lift and thrust, or about there being many equally legitimate theories of gravity and flight—we'd all be doomed.

He agreed with me—he was a very agreeable fellow—but I could tell he was beginning to get frustrated with the conversation; it wasn't exactly ending with us singing in perfect harmony. He then went confidently back to his assertion that there are many ways to God and so Jesus' way was also a valid one. And then he returned to his favorite point: everything finally came down to man's free will and us choosing the right way.

Every Other Religion

I attempted to show him how every religion in the world is like what he had described to me: man doing something (choosing the right way), earning the favor of a deity, performing to receive a reward in turn for the good works done to win the favor of the god.

Manuel's interest was waning, so I prayed for the folks around us who could scarcely have avoided hearing our conversation. And then I attempted to show him the beauty of the Christian gospel, that instead of God requiring us to sacrifice ourselves to win his favor, he stooped down in Christ and sacrificed himself to redeem sinners, to ransom the lost, to rescue the unworthy from the clutches of death—not just near-death—a terrifyingly real death that every one of us has coming to us for our rebellion against the will and way of the one true God who made us.

It was Manuel's turn to get engrossed in his magazine. As the plane landed in Seattle and we parted, he said, "I feel like we may meet each other on the other side someday." I told him I would like that and would pray to that end.

All of which got me thinking about the importance of getting the gospel unshakably right—and the eternal danger of fashioning a gospel in our own image.

For Discussion

1. Read 1 Peter 3:18 and discuss how this succinct statement of the biblical gospel differs from every other religion in the world:

> For Christ also suffered once for sins, the righteous for the unrighteous, that he might bring us to God, being put to death in the flesh but made alive in the spirit.

2. Read Belgic Confession, article 21. Discuss the difference between the Belgic Confession's theology of salvation and Manuel's experiential ideas about salvation.

> Wherefore we justly say with the apostle Paul that we know nothing save Jesus Christ, and him crucified; we count all things but loss and refuse for the excellency of the knowledge of Christ Jesus our Lord, in whose wounds we find all manner of consolation. Neither is it necessary to seek or invent any other means of being reconciled to God than this only sacrifice, once offered, by which he hath perfected forever them that are sanctified.

3. Role-play how you would answer someone who believes there are many ways to God. Draw from conversations you have had with unbelievers and discuss other biblical texts that help explain the true gospel to people caught in this common error.

Pray for specific evangelists and for those you know who travel a great deal, that they would have opportunities to engage others in the truths of the gospel, actively and winsomely represent Christ to those whom they encounter, and speak words of pure gospel.

5

Getting the Bad News Right

WHAT IS THE GOSPEL? Sure, my seatmate Manuel was pretty confused about things, but most everybody knows what the gospel is, right? We're inclined to think this might be altogether too simple of a question. Though there may be some things that are so obvious they need no definition, the gospel is not one of them.

The gospel is so counterintuitive, such enormously good news in a world of bad news, that we're sure we must have misunderstood its message. If it seems too good to be true, we tell ourselves, it must be so. I hear confusion about the gospel every day from my students, and these are kids who grew up in Christian homes, go regularly to church and youth group, and go on summer mission trips to share the gospel. But many of them are deeply confused about just what that gospel is.

Describing the widespread misunderstanding of the gospel, Jerry Bridges tells of a conversation he had with church leaders organizing a speaking engagement for him. Though Bridges was to be addressing a large group of evangelical Christians, the organizers put it bluntly, "The people here don't know what the gospel is."[1]

In 1993 there was a survey taken on the floor of the largest Christian publishing annual event in the world. Surrounded by

---

1. Jerry Bridges, *Disciplines of Grace: God's Role and Our Role in the Pursuit of Holiness* (Colorado Springs: NavPress, 2006), 45.

Christian publishers, Christian authors, Christian bookstore owners, Christian distributors of Christian literature—when the results were tallied, only one out of sixty people was able to give an adequate definition of the gospel.[2] What is more, there was a clear pattern to people's misconceptions of the gospel: the vast majority of answers—remember, these were professing Christians—included some measure (often a pretty substantial measure) of our fitness, merit, and good works.

I suspect that these people's basic flaw in their understanding began with not fully understanding the bad news—just how lost and undone we are in our sins.

The Bad News Is Worse Than We Think

Before the good news of the gospel makes any sense at all, we must first hear the bad news. And it could not be worse. It is horrendously bad news, and if we doll it up or sugarcoat it, we'll never see the need for the good news.

There's been a cosmic change in our standing and nature since God the Holy Creator of all things made Adam and Eve in his own image and declared them "very good" (Gen. 1:31). In defiance of God's revealed will, man chose to rebel against the will and way of God, thereby plunging the entire race into sin and the misery of separation from the God who made us.

Any honest person who reads the news knows that there's something gone badly wrong in the world. The new atheism notwithstanding, the vast majority of people in the world believe there is some kind of god out there and that we're not on the best of terms with him.

Just as every good novel has a controlling idea, so every religion has a controlling idea, and it goes something like this: humans fall short of the will of the god(s) and must get busy and appease the god's anger and win and keep winning his favor by being good. This idea is so universal that even people

2. Ibid.

who want others to consider them nonreligious assume that religion ought to work this way.

Works and Rewards

Arguing against the unconditional love and grace of God taught in the Christian gospel, psychology professor Jean M. Twenge asserts that "the good works you perform and the way you treat others" is the traditional and better way to "define a proper spiritual outlook and its rewards."[3] In other words, she thinks that grace and the free gift of God's love in the gospel is not such a good idea, that doing good works and getting rewards for doing them is the way religion ought to operate. For Twenge the message of the gospel is too counterintuitive. It makes no economic sense to give people something so valuable for free. They just won't appreciate it. They'll feel entitled, and they certainly won't treat their neighbors very nicely. No, for Twenge good works and rewards for good performance make better sense. And the gospel? It just doesn't make sense at all.

Compare the Bible to every other religion and we discover that it too has a controlling idea: God is holy, just, and perfect, but man is an intractable rebel against the will and ways of God. But here is where the Christian gospel begins its departure from every other religion. Whereas the other religions tell us that the human problem with the gods is pretty bad, the gospel tells us it's far worse than that: "None is righteous, no, not one" (Rom. 3:10).

There's nothing hazy and impressionistic about it. In bold, clear lines, the Bible paints a picture of human beings as corrupt, foolish, mean, selfish, hateful, envious, which all too often escalates into barbaric cruelty and violence. If we are honest with ourselves, the seeds of the most heinous acts are germinating in each one of our hearts. No one picks up a club

3. Jean M. Twenge, *Generation Me: Why Today's Young Americans Are More Confident, Assertive, Entitled—and More Miserable than Ever Before* (New York: Free Press, 2006), 35.

and bludgeons his neighbor to death without first despising him for dumping grass clippings over the fence.

A Zoo of Lusts

When C. S. Lewis began honestly to examine his own heart, he said, "I found what appalled me; a zoo of lusts, a bedlam of ambitions, a nursery of fears, a harem of fondled hatreds. My name was legion."[4]

There's no getting around the fact that we are lovers of what we should hate, and haters of what we should love. And like it or not, what the Bible says about us is acted out every day, not only in what we read in the news but in our own desires, words, and deeds.

At the same time as the Bible says this about us, it reveals to us a God who is the very opposite of us. He is holy, just, and good. In a word, he is perfect. And because he is perfect he cannot look on sin, which means he cannot look on us. There is a vast chasm between human beings and the perfectly holy God who made us. What's more, the hopeless condition we're in affects everybody. "For all have sinned and fall short of the glory of God" (Rom. 3:23). We all of us fall short. There's no nonsense in the Bible about some people being good and some being bad; we're all bad. And not only do we not measure up to the glorious perfection of God, we cannot measure up (Rom. 8:7). Sinners that we are, nothing we can do is sufficient to appease God's wrath and win his favor.

Another expression of our sinfulness emerges in our resentment at the very fact of it. We're quick to accuse God of being too tough on us, of being too harsh. His standard is too hard. Why doesn't he just lighten up a bit? I've long thought that Jesus' words, "Be perfect as your heavenly Father is perfect" (Matt. 5:48), read in isolation from the good news,

---

4. C. S. Lewis, *Surprised by Joy: The Shape of My Early Life* (New York: Harcourt, Brace, Jovanovich, 1987), 124.

constitute the scariest verse in the Bible. Martin Luther came to the place where he admitted that he hated God for his holy requirement of perfection from us. "This word is too high and too hard that anyone should fulfill it," he wrote.

> This is proved, not merely by our Lord's word, but by our own experience and feeling. Take any upright man or woman. He will get along very nicely with those who do not provoke him, but let someone proffer only the slightest irritation and he will flare up in anger, if not against friends, then against enemies. Flesh and blood cannot rise above it.[5]

But that doesn't mean we don't keep trying to win God's favor by our efforts. Luther told of his own desperate labors to appease God's wrath, "I was a good monk, and I kept the rule of my order so strictly that I may say that if ever a monk got to heaven by his monkery it was I. If I had kept on any longer, I should have killed myself with vigils, prayers, reading, and other work."[6]

Only when we, like Luther, come to know how impossible it is for us to keep God's law, how futile it is for us to think we can win God over by our efforts, never mind how sincere or strenuous, will we be ready to hear the good news.

As true as it is that "all have sinned and fall short of the glory of God," Paul hastens to tell us in the next verse that hopelessly unworthy sinners "are justified by his grace as a gift, through the redemption that is in Christ Jesus" (Rom. 3:23–24).

For Discussion

1. Read Psalm 53:2–3 and discuss what the controlling idea of the gospel is concerning God and man? Share with one

5. Martin Luther, cited in Roland Bainton, *Here I Stand: A Life of Martin Luther* (Nashville: Abingdon, 1980), 34.
6. Ibid.

another how you first came to understand your own lost condition.

> God looks down from heaven
>> on the children of man
> to see if there are any who understand,
>> who seek after God.
>
> They have all fallen away;
>> together they have become corrupt;
> there is none who does good,
>> not even one.

2. Before the gospel makes sense, what must each person come to understand? Consider Belgic Confession, article 23, in your discussion.

> If we should appear before God, relying on ourselves or on any other creature, though ever so little, we should, alas! be consumed. And therefore every one must pray with David: O Jehovah, enter not into judgment with thy servant: for in thy sight no man living is righteous.

3. How is the gospel counterintuitive? Discuss examples of how you have confused the radical nature of the gospel in your own experience. Role-play answering the question, "What is the gospel?"

Pray for those you know, or authors you admire, who are in the business of writing books, and those who publish books, that they will not shrink from proclaiming the bad news and that their words will be true and faithful in proclaiming the good news grounded in Jesus Christ and in the Word.

6

Getting Grace Right

THE LATE MEXICAN NOVELIST Carlos Fuentes, though
no friend of Christianity, wrote of the "epochal shift" in theology
for native cultures in the Spanish Conquest: "One can only
imagine the astonishment of the hundreds and thousands of
Indians who asked for baptism as they came to realize that
they were being asked to adore a god who sacrificed himself
for men instead of asking men to sacrifice themselves to gods,
as the Aztec religion demanded."[1]

The good news of the gospel is such stupendously good
news because God completely and perfectly fulfills what his
holiness requires; Christ "sacrificed himself for men." God's law
required obedience—perfect, unremitting obedience. No exceptions, no mitigating circumstances, no discounts, no rebates,
no compromises. The law bluntly pronounces the bad news:
blessings if we obey and curses if we fail to obey (Deut. 27–28).
And we all miserably fail to obey.

But that's where the good news comes to our rescue. Paul
declares that "Christ is the end of the law for righteousness
to everyone who believes" (Rom. 10:4). Christ took our place,
paid our legal debt, bore our guilt and punishment on himself,
and imputed to us what God in his holy perfection required of

1. Carlos Fuentes, cited in Robert Royal, "Columbus and the Beginning of the
World," *First Things* 93 (May 1999): 37.

us, what we were utterly incapable of offering—perfect obedience. And all based solely on Christ's performance, not ours.

"It is only in the gospel of Jesus Christ," wrote Tim Keller, "that you get the verdict before the performance."[2] Every other religion requires performance before the verdict. But in the gospel, Christ stooped down and perfectly obeyed for us, as our substitute. Jesus the righteous one was righteous in our place. By the grace of the gospel, performance will follow, but in justification the verdict is already in: we are forever righteous in Christ. That is immeasurably good news!

God's Good News

Pagan Anglo-Saxons, when they first heard the good news, had no category for such a radical story and no word to describe it, so they were forced to invent a new word. They combined the word *gōd* (meaning "good") and *spel* (meaning "news") to refer to God's rivetingly spellbinding story. Centuries later, Bible translator William Tyndale employed the Anglo-Saxon word *gospel* to translate the Greek New Testament word *euangélion*, from which we get words like *evangelism* and *evangelist.*

In this good news story, God sent his Son, Jesus, to pay our debt—fully, perfectly—to appease God's wrath and "burst the gate of hell,"[3] to bear the curse of the law we deserved and thereby win for us the favor of God. Free as this grace is to us, however, it came at a horrendously great price. It cost Jesus everything. Sally Lloyd-Jones summed up the gospel and what it costs this way: "It's not about trying, it's about trusting. It's not about rules, it's about Grace: God's free gift that cost him everything."[4] German Lutheran hymn writer

2. Timothy Keller, *The Freedom of Self-Forgetfulness: The Path to True Christian Joy* (Chorley, England: 10Publishing, 2012), 39.

3. Charles Wesley, "Christ the Lord Is Risen Today," *Trinity Hymnal* (Atlanta: Great Commission, 1990), 277.

4. Sally Lloyd-Jones, *The Jesus Storybook Bible: Every Story Whispers His Name* (Grand Rapids: Zondervan, 2007), 340.

Johann Heermann perfectly captures what the redemption of sinners cost the Son of God.

> Who was the guilty? Who brought this upon thee?
> Alas, my treason, Jesus, hath undone thee.
> 'Twas I, Lord Jesus, I it was denied thee:
> I crucified thee.
>
> Lo, the good Shepherd for the sheep is offered;
> The slave hath sinned, and the Son hath suffered;
> For man's atonement, while he nothing heedeth,
> God intercedeth.[5]

The grand exchange of this salvation in its entirety is God's doing; unmerited, undeserved, no bargaining, no conditions, absolutely a free gift, paid in full by the precious Son of the Almighty himself. Sinners don't get it by any merit, and we don't keep it by any merit (Jude 1:24). Jesus truly did pay it all, period, plus nothing.

Believing the gospel, however, is not just about believing some theoretical ideas. It is about owning up to our hopeless condition and falling at the feet of a Person, coming to and believing in the perfections and righteousness of Someone else, Someone who took the place of sinners, who took my place, bore my guilt and punishment in himself. What is more, it is believing that he alone is God the Savior of sinners and that he did all this for me.

The apostle John concluded his gospel account by telling us that the whole world could not contain the full account of all that Jesus said and did while he was here on earth: "But these are written so that you may believe that Jesus is the Christ, the Son of God, and that by believing you may have life in his name" (John 20:31).

---

5. Johann Heermann, "Ah, Holy Jesus How Hast Thou Offended," *Trinity Hymnal* (Atlanta: Great Commission, 1990), 248.

But can it really be that free? Where's the fine print? The free grace of the gospel just doesn't make sense; it doesn't make economic or moralistic sense. It defies all our sensibilities about proportionate exchange. We think we do this and we get that in exchange, a *quid pro quo*, but there is absolutely no place in the gospel for this way of thinking. Free grace is a scandalous message, and any proclamation of the gospel that does not come across as such is not only a distortion of the message, it is no longer good news.

Wages and Rewards

Nevertheless, we continue to think of the gospel in terms of a partnership: we do something good and get a reward for doing it. Misreading our Bibles contributes to this error: "The wicked earns deceptive wages, but one who sows righteousness gets a sure reward" (Prov. 11:18). Alas, it is possible to hear passages like this one used to silence what Romans 6:23 means. "The wages of sin is death, but the free gift of God is eternal life in Christ Jesus our Lord." Worried that too much grace might lead to loose living in their congregations, some preachers seem to feel that Paul needs some help with the wording here. "Both masters pay wages," one preacher put it. "Sin's wages, however, are death; God's wages are eternal life." However sincere the motives, this kind of rephrasing unearths precisely the *opposite* of the plain meaning of Paul's words.

Paul's meaning is clearer yet when we compare Scripture with Scripture. A few pages later in Romans, Paul illustrates how silly it is for us to think that God gives us eternal life as a wage we've earned; he poses the laughable question, "Who has given a gift to [God] that he might be repaid?" (Rom. 11:35). This confusion even in conservative pulpits underscores how in our suspicion of the radical nature of the gospel we default back to thinking that we earn at least some part of our salvation by duty-doing faithfulness.

The Meaning of the Law

In the London theatre adaptation of Victor Hugo's *Les Misérables* (and the major motion picture), longest running musical in the world, ruthless chief of police Jauvert, the quintessential self-righteous legalist, touts his theology with the quip, "Honest work, just reward; that's the way to please the Lord."[6] While ex-convict Jean Valjean is a veritable slave of the strict legalities of the law code, barred from escaping the stigma of having been a convict, Jauvert is relentless in hunting him down until he has made Jean Valjean feel the full weight of the law's demand for his offense.

Though no Christian or theologian, Hugo finds himself inadvertently indebted to biblical imagery as he attempts to portray the free, unmerited gift of grace. He has the kindly bishop protect the desperate and embittered thief Valjean from the police, and presses him to take, along with the silver cups he stole, the silver candlesticks as well. But as the brilliant production unfolds, theological cracks begin forming.

What becomes clear is that every character is on his own chosen self-salvation enterprise, one that operates at best on the assumption that God above gives salvation to those who have paid back their debt to society, reformed their lives, and earned it. But this is neither what Paul says nor what the rest of the Bible tells us about the radical difference between earning salvation by works or having it given to us as a free gift by faith.

> For what does the Scripture say? "Abraham believed God, and it was counted to him as righteousness." Now to the one who works, his wages are not counted as a gift but as his due. And to the one who does not work but believes in him who justifies the ungodly, his faith is counted as righteousness,

6. Herbert Kretzmer, "Fantine's Arrest," *Les Misérables*, (Milwaukee: Hal Leonard Corporation, 1987).

just as David also speaks of the blessing of the one to whom God counts righteousness apart from works:

> "Blessed are those whose lawless deeds are forgiven,
>   and whose sins are covered;
>   blessed is the man against whom the Lord will not count
>   his sin." (Rom. 4:3–8)

What the covenant of grace teaches about salvation is that it is not the result of wages earned, not "Honest work, just reward; that's the way to please the Lord." The reason the gospel is good news is precisely because we don't get a just reward for our sins, or for our perceived good works. We get the free gift of God, which is eternal life through Jesus.

Crowning His Own Gifts

But some will hasten to protest, basing their protest on a Bible verse they think contradicts grace. The gospel has to at least be partly about being rewarded for doing good things; after all, the Bible says, "Do good, O LORD, to those who are good" (Ps. 125:4). Isolated from the whole, this text and others like it do sound like tit-for-tat theology: we do good, then God rewards us with good as a result. Misapplied, passages like this one become a corrosive to justification by faith alone.

In his rules about prayer, however, Calvin makes clear that "by such expressions [biblical writers] mean nothing else but that by their regeneration itself they are attested as servants and children of God to whom he promises that he will be gracious."[7] He goes on to declare that in statements like these, the one praying "does not set the value of prayer according to the merit of works. . . . His assurance his prayers will be answered rests solely upon God's clemency, apart from

7. John Calvin, *Institutes of the Christian Religion*, ed. John T. McNeil, trans. Ford Lewis Battles (Philadelphia: Westminster Press, 1960), 3.20.10.

all consideration of personal merit."[8] At the last, unworthy sinners that we are, we "take the person and disposition of a beggar."[9] The problem may go deeper. When we misconstrue and misapply texts like these to include some merit on our part, it may be a symptom of our misunderstanding of the Psalms, perhaps of the whole Bible.

Early French Reformer Jacques Lefèvre d'Étaples wrote a helpful introduction to his expositions on the Psalms, written "with the assistance of Christ, who is the key to the understanding of David. *He is the one about whom David spoke.*"[10] If David is speaking true words in Psalm 125:4, then comparing his words ("Do good, O LORD, to those who are good") with Jesus' true words on the same topic is essential to finding clarity; Jesus said, "No one is good except God alone" (Mark 10:18). If both David's and Jesus' words are true, then only by becoming united with God in Christ can anyone become good.

Moreover, there are still greater problems with lifting out Psalm 125:4 and turning it into an argument for some degree of works righteousness; doing so fails to reckon with its immediate context, the trustworthiness of the Lord who "surrounds his people, from this time forth and forevermore" (125:2). This graciously encircling God alone is good, and he alone by his free gift makes his children good forevermore. And then, wonder of wonders, he rewards us for the divine goodness he has worked for us (justification) and continues to work within us (sanctification)! This verse is no call for patting ourselves on our backs; it's a clarion call to fall on our knees in adoration of the prodigal generosity and divine goodness of God.

Imagine it! Jesus takes the damning wages we've earned by our sins and freely gives us his eternal reward. Yes, believers

---

8. Ibid.
9. Ibid.
10. Jacques Lefèvre d'Étaples, cited in Martin I. Klauber, "Reformer on the Run," *Christian History* 71 (July 2001): 21. Emphasis mine.

in Jesus get rewards, but they are gifted rewards, the merits of Christ extravagantly imputed to us. The justifying rewards we get are unmerited—redemption and forgiveness accomplished and applied by the unbounded goodness of God alone. Hence, it is equally true that the rewards gifted to us for sanctified obedience are God "crowning his own gifts,"[11] as Augustine called it.

Since we can never begin to pay the debt of undeserved love we owe to such a Savior as this, what do we do?

> Therefore, kind Jesus, since I cannot pay Thee,
> I do adore thee, and will ever pray thee
> Think on thy pity and thy love unswerving,
> Not my deserving.[12]

For Discussion

1. Read Philippians 3:8–9 and discuss why Paul so carefully contrasts law and faith. Discuss why the author might be using the word *scandalous* when describing the free grace of the gospel.

   Indeed, I count everything as loss because of the surpassing worth of knowing Christ Jesus my Lord. For his sake I have suffered the loss of all things and count them as rubbish, in order that I may gain Christ and be found in him, not having a righteousness of my own that comes from the law, but that which comes through faith in Christ, the righteousness from God that depends on faith.

2. "Believing the gospel . . . is not just about believing some theoretical ideas. It is about . . . falling at the feet of a

---

11. Augustine, *Of Grace and Free Will*, trans. Peter Holmes, *Logos Virtual Library*, accessed May 1, 2014, http://www.logoslibrary.org/augustine/grace1/06.html.
12. Heermann, "Ah, Holy Jesus."

Person . . . believing in the perfections and righteousness of Someone else." Read Belgic Confession, article 21, and discuss the difference between rejecting a set of theoretical ideas versus rejecting a Person who has paid the ultimate price for our salvation.

Therefore, He restored that which he took not away, and suffered, the righteous for the unrighteous, as well in His body as in His soul, feeling the terrible punishment which our sins had merited; insomuch that his sweat became as it were great drops of blood falling down upon the ground. He called out: My God, my God, why hast thou forsaken me? and has suffered all this for the remission of our sins.

3. Look up, compare, contrast, and discuss the following verses: Psalm 50:23; Romans 10:3–4; 11:35–36; Galatians 5:16–18, 22–24; 6:7; and Revelation 19:8b. Our default setting is to think we contribute to our salvation and to single out verses that appear to point to our effort.

Pray for your pastor this week as he prepares his sermon. Pray for his encouragement and his awed worship at the feet of a Person; pray for his ability to understand and interpret Scripture in light of Scripture, to make much of Christ and magnify his finished work on our behalf.

7

Objections to Free Grace

SOMETHING IN US RECOILS at such a message. If grace is really that free, won't the gospel be confused with cheap grace, an easy-believism, and thereby produce loose-living professors who presume on grace?

"The doctrine of justification by faith," wrote W. Stanford Reid, "particularly if it has the word 'alone' attached to it, causes problems in many minds."[1] Reid described how some church people became so suspicious of the doctrine that they became neonomians, requiring so many layers of good works that a Christian's sanctification became not the evidence of but a condition of their justification. But it's not just neonomians from the past who are afraid of too much grace. Reid described the extent of our distaste for the doctrines of grace when even "some Reformed theologians could term the doctrine of justification by faith alone as 'easy believism.'"[2]

The Bible addresses these important questions—but not necessarily the way we think it should. Surely the Bible will balance out grace with a message that keeps grace in bounds. But not so. When declaring the grace of the gospel, the Bible uses expansive, wide-sweeping language. "Where sin

---

1. W. Stanford Reid, "Justification by Faith according to John Calvin," *Westminster Theological Journal* 42:2 (Spring, 1980) (Galaxie Software), 291.
2. Ibid.

increased, grace abounded all the more," as Paul extravagantly puts it in Romans 5:20.

Paul's way of describing the free, unmerited character of grace abounding all the more in excess of sin compels us to raise objections. If people think that grace is that expansive, that it covers such vast sinning, won't folks just sin more and presume on grace to cover their sinning? We wonder if Paul should not have used such a comparison, sin abounding and grace abounding still more. Isn't that a bit indiscreet of him?

People were actually saying these kinds of things about the gospel Paul was preaching. In our mind's eye we can almost see them doing it. "Why not do evil that good may come?—as some people slanderously charge us with saying" (Rom. 3:8). What is so helpful to us in these objections is that they show us that Paul's gospel message leads inexorably to these kinds of slanderous objections. Nothing could be more logical. We can almost hear the critics lining up. "If you teach that Christ by his grace can cover the most heinous of sinners, folks will run out and commit heinous sins. Figure it out, Paul!"

A message like this from Paul will always raise the objection of those whose greatest fear is antinomianism. But Paul's hypothetical and inspired objections give us still more clarity on just what it was he meant in his message. He really was preaching a gospel of scandalously free grace, because, intractable enemies of God that we are, that's the only kind of grace that works.

God's Enemies

"For if while we were enemies we were reconciled to God by the death of his Son, much more, now that we are reconciled, shall we be saved by his life" (Rom. 5:10). Paul here uses the reference to Christ justifying us while we were enemies to show the absolute unconditionality of Christ's justifying work. It was not based on prior fitness. Enemies deserve nothing from a just God except his righteous condemnation. Yet while we were enemies Christ reconciled us by his life and by his death. If it were any other way, enemies that we are, we would be without hope, utterly lost. But Paul is declaring a salvation that is for sinners; it's not for self-righteous folks, but scandalously for sinners.

Skim down a few paragraphs and we see another revealing objection. "What shall we say then? Are we to continue in sin that grace may abound?" (Rom. 6:1). Such an objection only makes logical sense if the gospel of grace is as scandalously free as Paul declares it to be. His reply is grounded in the redeemed sinner's union with Christ in the finished work on the cross and in the empty tomb. "By no means! How can we who died to sin still live in it?" (6:2). And a few verses later in his argument he reasserts the very message of radical grace that had given rise to the objection in the first place. "For sin will have no dominion over you, since you are not under law but under grace" (6:14).

God's Free Will

A few pages later in his sustained explanation of the gospel, Paul quoted from the prophet, "Jacob I loved, but Esau I hated" (Rom. 9:13; cf. Mal. 1:2–3); he then poses an objection that we will naturally make to the electing love of God in the gospel: "What shall we say then? Is there injustice on God's part? By no means!" (9:14). In other words, his teaching on the sovereign prerogative of God's free grace will raise the objection in our minds that it sounds like God is being unjust.

If this objection was based on a misunderstanding of what Paul had been trying to say, there could not be a better opportunity to correct the misunderstanding. He might have clarified with something like this, "No, I didn't mean that God is that sovereign over things. I just meant that he left both guys to their own free will and, hey, one guy chose to believe and the other chose not to believe." But this is emphatically not what Paul says. He presses the point and argues for the freedom of God's will to have compassion on whom he wants to have compassion (9:15): "So then it depends not on human will or exertion, but on God, who has mercy" (9:16). This is a radically free mercy indeed, and according to Paul this is the mercy of the gospel.

After teaching that God "has mercy on whomever he wills, and he hardens whomever he wills" (9:18), Paul poses yet another objection that we will naturally raise to God's radically free grace. "You will say to me then, 'Why does he still find fault? For who can resist his will?'" (9:19). This kind of objection would never be raised by an anemic grace, by a gospel where Jesus only paid most of it,[3] where God sat passively in the heavens wringing his hands in hopes that we sinners might get around to deciding to believe in him. But this objection makes perfect sense if Paul is teaching a radical grace, a grace that eviscerates reward and punishment based on our performance. Here he is saying that grace that is as free as he has described it will make us ask how God can blame us for our sins. If he is so sovereign over salvation that he gives it freely to whomever he wills, then how can he justly punish those who don't believe it?

Paul answers his own objection by calling us to our knees in worship at the feet of a glorious Sovereign who has richly prepared from all eternity both Jews and Gentiles to be objects of his prodigal mercy (9:23). God is free to make known the riches of his mercy on unworthy sinners as he chooses, and Paul's response to the high wonder of such a radical grace is always worship, heartfelt, humble, on-our-face worship.

3. See appendix B for my version of a hymn if Jesus only paid most of it, if salvation was up to our free will or anything in us.

Conditional Election

Church history chronicles creative ways we try to diminish or redefine Paul's message, ways we attempt to add conditions to what he is saying about electing love. A recent scholarly effort goes something like this: "The Bible only rarely speaks of election, and when it does it is referring to God loving and choosing a group, the covenant community, Israel or the church. But we're not supposed to think it's actually about God loving and choosing individuals. It's about him choosing the group and if you're in the group, and if you keep the conditions required of the group, then you're elect."

This redefining of Paul's doctrine has a name; it's called *covenantal election*. But we should always beware when experts start redefining terms for us. Let's be very clear; covenantal election has another name, one very familiar to historical theology: it's called *conditional election*. Relabeled, this latest spin on election says, "Fulfill the conditions—obey the law, be faithful to the conditions of the covenant—and you will be saved. Well, maybe you'll be saved—that is, if you continue to keep the conditions."

Notice, however, that no one would think to raise the objections that Paul's theology inevitably raises. This kind of election is perfectly fair: keep the conditions and God rewards you according to your efforts. Nothing unfair-sounding about that. But there's nothing wonder-producing about it either.

Imagine me telling my wife that I love her because I love her whole group, all women. Not a good leadoff at a Valentine's dinner date. Imagine how it would warm her heart to hear me tell her that I chose her to be my wife, but on certain conditions; as long as she keeps those conditions I will keep her as my wife. And then try to set that down in poetry and sing about it.

71

While John Wycliffe called predestination "the principle grace,"[4] we often treat it as a moldering skeleton in the closet and cast about for ways to shroud it or bury it altogether. Our distrust of our heavenly Father's electing grace may simply be the primal symptom of our distrust of the free grace of the gospel.

Partnership theologies by whatever name will never thrill us. They never leave us empty to be filled only by the merits of Jesus. Only electing, unconditional love, with all the conditions perfectly fulfilled by the free mercy of our Substitute, will produce slack-jawed wonder in our hearts. Only the exclusive, pure, intoxicated (Prov. 5:19), unstoppable love the Bridegroom has for his bride, his body the church, enthralls our hearts and inflames our passion for the Savior.

Fixing Grace

Christian theology is littered with many other efforts to remove some of the scandal of the free mercy of God in the gospel. It's as if we think we need to improve on Paul, tidy things up a bit so the kids won't rebel. We're just certain that this salvation deal has to depend at least to some degree on our will and work. So we construct explanations to fix the scandal. We say things like, "Vast portions of Holy Writ speak of salvation as a responsible partnership where God acts and we cooperate in covenant with him, where we determine our destiny by our faith and our obedience."

Alas, all our efforts to fix the scandal of free grace only serve to smash it to pieces; they result in a salvation by synergism, a blending of man's work with God's work. In these efforts we work away at crafting a gospel that is designed to remove the need for the objections Paul raises to his teaching.

4. John Wycliffe, quoted by Gary J. Hall, *John Wycliffe: A Light Shining in a Dark Place, Archive*, accessed December 13, 2013, http://archive.org/stream/JohnWycliffe ALightInADarkPlace/JohnWycliffe_djvu.txt.

No one would ever raise any of these objections to a message that said, "We determine our destiny by our faith and our obedience." Paul raises them precisely because the gospel of free grace inevitably leads to these kinds of objections.

Here is a test: If our understanding and proclamation of the gospel of grace does not evoke these objections, we can be certain that, whatever we call ourselves confessionally, we are no longer teaching Paul's gospel. If our way of teaching grace does not lead to Paul's extravagant and scandalous way of putting things, we have allowed "false and corrupt opinions"[5] to diminish the gospel. But a diminished gospel is no longer good news, and it doesn't work.

Grace Works

It is only the pure doctrine of the gospel of free grace that actually works, that is actually capable of solving our problem. The magnitude of our lostness requires a magnanimous grace, one that is unlimited in effect, one that is mighty to save, a grace that works—and keeps working.

For sinners who know the bad news, the gospel truly is good news. Jesus really did deliver us from the curse of the law. He really did pay it all. He really did wash us clean in his precious blood, and he will make good on his promises. He will bring us home to God.

The good news recalibrates everything. Whereas I used to love my sins and worship myself, now I fall at the feet of my Savior; I love him; I adore him; I fix my eyes on him in love and gratitude and wonder—and I sing!

> Let us love and sing and wonder;
> Let us praise the Savior's name;
> He has hushed the law's loud thunder;

5. John Calvin, *Commentary on Galatians*, trans. and ed. John Owen (Grand Rapids: Eerdmans, 1974), 97.

He has quenched Mount Sinai's flame;
He has washed us with His blood;
He has brought us nigh to God.[6]

Rescued from a blasphemous life of slave trading, John Newton knew he was a great sinner, and he knew that Jesus was a great Savior. In short, he knew about the amazing grace of the gospel. In this hymn he thrills us with wonder at the work of our precious Savior, who alone does what the law could never do.

Nevertheless, we persist in thinking we need to obey the law to win and keep God's favor. Though it is central to the proclamation of the bad news, nothing does more to corrupt the pure doctrine of the gospel than when we include even a tiny bit of "the law's loud thunder" in the proclamation of the good news.

For Discussion

1. What are ways we show that we are intractable enemies of God? What is Paul's response to the high wonder of God's radical grace, and what does this mean to our own holiness? Discuss thoughts from the chapter and from Romans 3:28, 31:

   For we hold that one is justified by faith apart from works of the law. . . . Do we then overthrow the law by this faith? By no means! On the contrary, we uphold the law.

2. Read Belgic Confession, article 24, and discuss the various objections to free grace that you have made yourself or have heard others make. If free grace abounds, will sin abound more?

6. John Newton, "Let Us Love and Sing and Wonder," *Trinity Hymnal* (Atlanta: Great Commission, 1990), 172.

74

Therefore it is so far from being true that this justifying faith makes men remiss in a pious and holy life, that on the contrary without it they would never do anything out of love to God, but only out of self-love or fear of damnation.

3. Why does the "sovereign prerogative of God's free grace" elicit such resistance in today's church environment? List and discuss indicators that the gospel sometimes preached today may not be the same message as Paul's.

Pray that God will give us humble hearts and then break down our natural resistance to God's sovereign grace. Pray also for a deeper trust in the power of Christ's sanctifying work in us as we desire "holiness without which no one will see the Lord" (Heb. 12:14).

PART 3

Why Keeping Grace and Works
in Order Matters:
*More Ways We Allow Law
to Creep into Gospel*

8

Trust *and* Obey?

"SO LET ME GET THIS STRAIGHT," said the anxious young woman, "we're justified by faith and by works. Is that right?" Bewildered by the sermon she had heard at her church the night before, she was in earnest. After growing up in the Baha'i faith, now in her mid-twenties, she had recently become a Christian, but she was deeply troubled by what she had heard in that sermon. She was not alone in her confusion.

What was I to tell her? Find another church, one that stands with Martin Luther and the Reformers who rediscovered justification by faith alone in the sixteenth century. That ought to fix the problem. But that precisely was the problem. She had heard that sermon in a church that claims to stand for justification by faith alone and the gospel of free grace. What had happened? Was it just bad listening on her part? Or had she heard a conflicted message, a confusing distortion of law and gospel in that sermon? So I listened to the sermon.

Faith and Obedience

What I discovered about this intelligent young woman was that, though a baby Christian, she was a very good listener. After her minister made the obligatory affirmations of justification by faith alone, she heard him wrap up his series on the law with this: "But it does not for a moment set aside the fact that those who trust the Lord and those who obey his commandments and those only will reach the promised land, will gain God's blessing and favor in the world and after death in the world to come."

How do we sort out what ministers mean when they declare words like these from the pulpit? We start with grammar. The indefinite pronoun *it* in the above sentence has to have an antecedent, and there is only one grammatical option. *It* has to refer back to the justification by faith the minister had been affirming. When we hear any preacher or teacher tell his congregation that justification by faith must also be accompanied by works of obedience in order to gain God's blessing and favor, we have just been offered another gospel, not the pure doctrine of the gospel.

But what about trusting and obeying? Aren't we supposed to trust *and* obey?

> Trust and obey, for there's no other way
> To be happy in Jesus[1]

as the Sunday school song goes, right?

Wrong. Serious error arises when trusting *and* obeying are required as concurrent actions the sinner must do in the context of his justification. Trusting is not sufficient— which is the same as saying that faith alone is not sufficient; you must also obey the law to win God's final favor. Which requires us flatly to deny what Paul without equivocation insists, that "by works of the law no one will be justified" (Gal. 2:16).

Furthermore, in this context, it was unclear at best what a preacher meant by "trusting the Lord." In this syntacti-

---

1. John H. Sammis, "Trust and Obey," *Trinity Hymnal* (Atlanta: Great Commission, 1990), 672. It is worth noting that it would be an exercise in futility to argue that this lyric remotely represents the high watermark of Christian hymnody.

cal construction, what is it we're trusting the Lord to do? It clearly cannot mean trusting in Jesus' imputed righteousness, trusting him to perfectly obey the law in my place. So we are left with the unequivocal assertion that we must "obey [God's] commandments." After hearing a message like this one, we're left with only one way of thinking: justification doesn't actually save me; trusting in the Lord doesn't actually save me; I still must obey the law to win God's favor and be saved.

There's no other way to slice it; this is a message that dismantles the foundational declaration of the gospel— "The just shall live by faith." It is small wonder this new Christian was utterly bewildered. "We're saved by faith *and* by our works?" Given what she had heard in the sermon, it seemed a very *apropos* question to ask. But the faithful gospel preacher will never leave his flock anxiously asking this question.

In his book *Christ-Centered Preaching*, Brian Chapell anticipates the danger of this kind of confused preaching and warns men when preaching the law: "Sermons on the law will not inadvertently teach that God's acceptance depends on our righteousness."[2]

When the flock hears any message giving the impression that "those who obey his commandments and those only will gain God's blessing and favor," they are being led away from the gospel of grace; they are being taught to turn their eyes away from the Savior's obedience and to their own obedience. Perplexed by such preaching, hearers have no option but to conclude that their acceptance with God depends in some measure on their keeping of the law. This is not good news; this is very bad news, and, as it should, it deeply troubled this young woman.

2. Brian Chapell, *Christ-Centered Preaching: Redeeming the Expository Sermon* (Grand Rapids: Baker, 2008), 305.

Bait and Switch

Christ has already and once for all time procured the blessing and favor of God for us. If he hasn't, then the words of the psalmist, "his steadfast love endures forever"—repeated twenty-six times in Psalm 136, so we are sure to get the message—are nothing more than

> A tale
> Told by an idiot, full of sound and fury,
> Signifying nothing.[3]

There is no bait and switch in the gospel. If we are justified by faith alone, but this justification doesn't procure the favor of God for us, then the gospel is a cruel jest. If my justification finally depends upon my performance, my faithfulness to obey all God's regulations, then all hope is lost, all confidence is removed.

What I heard as I listened to that same sermon was an erudite but confused message, flawed in several ways, but most glaringly by diluting the gospel with the law. It was a sermon from the law of Moses, but it did everything but drive this young woman to Christ (Gal. 3:24), who alone kept the law perfectly for her and imputed to her an alien righteousness. On the contrary, it left no other conclusion than that finally what mattered was her obedience to God's moral law. Yes, God would be gracious on the judgment day and would accept her sincere though partial obedience, but the bottom line was that he would judge her by her works.

Make no mistake about it. Salvation *does* finally depend on perfect obedience to God's law. Justification is not the product of God's leniency, of his cutting us some slack, diverting his eye at our imperfections, and meeting us part way. No,

3. William Shakespeare, *Macbeth*, 5.5.26–28.

justification is the glorious result of perfect justice, of the momentous exchange, the just dying for the unjust: Christ satisfying the wrath of God by making peace through the blood of his cross—for sinners who always fall short of his glory (Rom. 3:23). This is the good news, the gospel. "The gospel always demonstrates that God's perfect law and His love were fulfilled on the cross of Christ."[4]

Whatever faint glimmers of the gospel heard in that sermon series had been effectively squelched into silence by a message trumpeting a badly mistaken application of "the law's loud thunder."[5]

For Discussion

1. If we're trusting the Lord for our salvation, and we're trusting to some degree in our obedience, what then are we trusting the Lord to do? Discuss what happens when we think our obedience affects God's acceptance of us.
2. Read and discuss Hebrews 9:13–15. What does the writer of Hebrews say can alone purify "our conscience from dead works to serve the living God"?

For if the blood of goats and bulls . . . sanctify for the purification of the flesh, how much more will the blood of Christ, who through the eternal Spirit offered himself without blemish to God, purify our conscience from dead works to serve the living God.

Therefore he is the mediator of a new covenant, so that those who are called may receive the promised eternal inheritance, since a death has occurred that redeems them from the transgressions committed under the first covenant.

4. Robert Norris, "Preaching Grace," *Tabletalk*, May 2010, 24–25.
5. John Newton, "Let Us Love and Sing and Wonder," *Trinity Hymnal* (Atlanta: Great Commission, 1990), 172.

3. The author wrote in this chapter: "Justification is the glorious result of perfect justice, of the momentous exchange, the just dying for the unjust." Though we know ourselves to be utterly tainted by sin, how does God's perfect justice lead us to ultimate comfort? Discuss in light of Westminster Larger Catechism 38:

Q. Why was it requisite that the Mediator should be God?

A. It was requisite that the Mediator should be God, that he might sustain and keep the human nature from sinking under the infinite wrath of God, and the power of death; give worth and efficacy to his sufferings, obedience, and intercession; and to satisfy God's justice, procure his favor, purchase a peculiar people, give his Spirit to them, conquer all their enemies, and bring them to everlasting salvation.

Pray today for seminary professors. Pray that they will teach future pastors to understand God's holiness and justice aright, and how God by grace through Christ alone purifies the sinner's conscience through the gospel.

9

Three Uses of the Law—
Not Four

"THERE IS NO POINT on which men make greater mistakes," said Charles Spurgeon, "than on the relation which
exists between the law and the gospel." Remembered as the
Prince of Preachers, Spurgeon went on to show how dizzying
can be the various ways preachers make these mistakes, and
concludes that all who do so "understand not the truth and
are false teachers."[1]

If we are to avoid the inevitable decline into false teaching and unbelief tragically demonstrated in church history,
we must exercise the greatest care in understanding the right
relationship between law and gospel. This begins with making
sure we understand the three biblical uses of the law.

Uses of the Law

Protestant theologians have long understood and articu-
lated three uses of the Mosaic law in preaching: the pedagogic
use, the civil use, and the didactic use.[2] What do these mean?
I like the way Paul Tripp lays out so clearly and simply the

1. Charles H. Spurgeon, *New Park Street Pulpit* (Pasadena, TX: Pilgrim Publica-
tions, 1975), 1:285.
2. John Calvin, *Institutes of the Christian Religion*, ed. John T. McNeil, trans.
Ford Lewis Battles (Philadelphia: Westminster Press, 1960), 2.8.6.

first two uses of the law: "Rules reveal and restrain sin, but they have no power to rescue us from sin."[3] The father of Elizabethan Puritanism, William Perkins, put it similarly four hundred years earlier, "The law exposes the disease of sin and stimulates and stirs it up. But it provides no remedy for it."[4]

Therefore, the first use of the law is to expose just how sinful we actually are compared to God's holiness, thereby revealing our desperate condition and our great need of some other righteousness than our own. Lutheran hymn writer Matthias Loy (1863) captured in perceptive verse how it is that the law reveals our hopeless condition:

> The law is good; but since the fall
> Its holiness condemns us all;
> It dooms us for our sin to die
> And has no pow'r to justify.[5]

Loy proceeds from the first use of the law, revealing and condemning us for our sin, to the second use of the law, restraining the evil of unbelievers in civil society:

> When men the offered help disdain
> And willfully in sin remain,
> Its terror in their ear resounds
> And keeps their wickedness in bounds.[6]

But it is confusion about the third use, the didactic use, where we can go fatally astray. The third use of the law shows Christians God's holy will and how to live out their gratitude

---

3. Paul Tripp, conversation with author, Getting at the Heart of Parenting conference, Bellevue, WA, January 11, 2012.

4. William Perkins, *The Art of Prophesying* (1592; repr. Edinburgh: Banner of Truth Trust, 1996), 54–55.

5. Matthias Loy, "The Law of God Is Good and Wise," *Trinity Hymnal* (Atlanta: Great Commission, 1990), 150.

6. Ibid.

for the free, unmerited grace poured out on them in the gospel. The hymn writer got the third use correct as well:

> To those who help in Christ have found
> And would in works of love abound
> It shows what deeds are his delight
> And should be done as good and right.[7]

The hymn writer understood what is so easily misunderstood. When preaching casts the first use of the law—exposing our inability to obey it—into the shade by an inordinate application of the third use of the law—showing us what pleases God in our sanctification—we go badly off the rails. A message that does this will leave us bewildered, like the young woman troubled by the sermon on the law that forced her to conclude that she was justified by faith and by her efforts to obey the law. But this kind of obedience motivated by fear is a million miles from the "works of love" which God works in us by the free grace of his Spirit in gospel sanctification.

Notice closely that not one of the three uses of the law has anything to do with our gaining the favor or blessing of God. Nevertheless, because none of us fully grasps the magnitude of our offense against God and his law, we are predisposed to think we can actually obey his law. Since my default mode is to believe that when I obey I am accepted by God, my heart will always go back to this kind of thinking unless I "deliberately and repeatedly set it to gospel mode."[8] It is for this reason that the church so tirelessly returns to a distorted gospel, one that so easily switches everything around. Still calling ourselves Christians, and still insisting we believe in justification by faith alone, back we go into the

7. Ibid.
8. Timothy Keller, *The Prodigal God* (New York: Dutton, 2008), 115.

darkness and futility of trying to keep God's law, not out of love and gratitude, but out of fear and duty, out of a desire to win or maintain God's favor.

Good Intentions

A well-intentioned preacher, wanting to see moral upright-ness in his congregation, can easily and unintentionally shout down the first use of the law with the third use. His inten-tions notwithstanding, the practical effect will be to give the impression that the law demands our obedience and that when we read the Old Testament and hear the law's imperatives (the things the law demands for us to do), we'd better muster our resolve and try very hard to do them—or else.

A minister, rightly desiring to see holiness in his con-gregation, can so easily slip into a work-work mode. Armed with holy intentions, he may then find himself pummeling his flock with the third use of the law while holding back a bit on the extravagant message of free grace. But unless he is first showing his congregation how the law damns them, how utterly incapable they are of winning or keeping God's favor by their obedience, he will encourage his people to return to their default mode, to believe that they must obey to win God's favor. Before his flock can hear aright the will and way of God in their sanctification, he must deliberately and repeatedly show them that the law "dooms us for our sin to die and has no pow'r to justify."

If we allow law keeping to creep in the tiniest degree into our thinking about justification, we misunderstand the holiness of God, the totality of our depravity, and the utter impossibility of our doing what God's law justly demands. If we are not first embracing this bad news, there can be no embrace of the good news. And it's only by the change wrought in us by the good news that we can offer heartfelt and grace-enabled obedience.

Ministers in Amsterdam in the generations after the Reformation, by failing to deliberately and repeatedly show their congregations the first use of the law, and the beauty of Christ's atoning work in the gospel, gradually crept back to the human default mode and preached good works as a condition of justification.

Preachers who confuse law and gospel, however scholarly, however zealous for holiness, will do the same. And all the while they will likely continue to give lip service to total depravity and man's utter inability to obey the law. Remember Satan's strategy has never been to attempt to destroy the gospel by frontal assault, rather "he taints its purity by introducing false and corrupt opinions."[9] And it is by confusing law and gospel that he does this most effectively.

Futile Treadmill

Then as now, when a congregation hears a law-keeping conditionality creep into the gospel, sincere listeners have either one of two reactions: If all is going well and they are not committing the big sins, they may be confirmed in their belief that they are externally keeping God's law, though they will never get down to dealing with the real heart issues of idolatry and self-love. If, however, all is not going well in their external behavior—let's say they've lied, or stolen, or committed adultery, or broken Lent, or forgotten to read their Bible, or skipped prayer meeting—they will find themselves glancing anxiously heavenward in despair.

As a result of this confusion in the pulpit, Christians then find themselves on a moral and spiritual treadmill. I want to please God; the first use of the law demands that I please him—but here is where we so subtly confuse the first use with the third use of the law—so in my sanctification I try by my efforts to keep God's favor, to verify my standing with him, by working hard to obey his law.

9. John Calvin, *Commentary on Galatians*, trans. and ed. John Owen (Grand Rapids: Eerdmans, 1974), 97.

However well meant, preaching that leaves the impression that I now must obey the law to gain or to keep my position with God has the practical effect of making my good behavior a condition of my position. However intellectual the protest to the contrary, and however repeated are the affirmations of orthodoxy, what has been communicated to the minds of hearers is no longer the pure doctrine of the gospel.

God's Faithfulness

The good news recognizes the perfection of God's holiness, the heinous nature of my sin, and the glorious, unearned deliverance Christ has accomplished for me in the gospel. Undershepherds who get the gospel right when preaching the imperatives of obedience labor never to give redeemed sinners the soul-damning impression that their position in Christ is somehow conditioned upon their faithfulness to obey God's law. Christians given that impression from their pastors will be very anxious about the blessing and cursing promised in the law, and they will cast about futilely looking to their efforts, their strength, their faithfulness to prove their acceptance with God. Though they may think they still adhere, in some vague way, to justification by faith alone, they unwittingly deny the doctrine by looking to their performance to verify God's acceptance of them. Instead of looking to the wonderful mercy of God in Christ who alone is the Christian's righteousness, we reduce sanctification to hand-wringing obedience to the moral code, and love and gratitude are eclipsed by fear and obligation.

An approach to ministry that does this will confuse and create anxious Christians, or it will confuse and create self-righteous ones. Either way, it will always erode the pure doctrine of the gospel and lead to the decline and decay of the church.

Getting It Right

In the Netherlands, or Geneva, or Scotland, or New England, it was never the moral code, the social ethic, the outward practice of the Christian religion that was first eroded. Historians often refer to the borrowed capital from the Christian past—social justice, education, art, or just cleanliness—qualities seen to some degree in these places yet today. But we must get the implication of this. The jury is long in; the external morality and ethics of Christianity will far outlive true proclamation of and belief in the gospel. Corrupt the gospel and decadence will follow, but it may take a few centuries. For this reason, the Enemy wants us to contend more for Christian morality than for the pure doctrine of the Christian gospel.

One of the ways he does this is by encouraging us—slowly, incrementally—to blur the distinction between law and gospel. This works so well for him because it will always lead us away from the truth about ourselves and about Christ and into self-righteous moralism, or into the soul-numbing bleakness of despair. I doubt that the Devil cares which it is; either one destroys the gospel and reduces Christianity to the self-salvation enterprise of every other religion.

The great champion of justification by faith alone, Martin Luther, understood just how essential getting the distinction between law and gospel is: "Whoever knows well this art of distinguishing between Law and Gospel, him place at the head and call a doctor of Holy Scripture."[10]

Why did Luther have such extravagant praise for preachers who don't make a mingle-mangle of law and gospel? I think it's because he understood the enormous damage done to the gospel by law-creep, when men allow the slightest degree of law-keeping conditionality to creep into the message of the gospel.

10. Martin Luther, *Dr. Martin Luther's* Sämmtliche Schriften (St. Louis: Concordia Publishing House, n.d.), 9:802.

Having a high view of inerrancy is little help if there is not the clear understanding that the Word of God is divided "into two principal parts or kinds," as Calvin's successor, Theodore Beza, put it. "The one is called the 'Law,' the other the 'Gospel.' Ignorance of this distinction between Law and Gospel is one of the principal sources of the abuses which corrupt Christianity."[11]

Nevertheless, there are well-meaning men in pulpits today who encourage their congregations to tear out the page between the Old and New Testaments in their Bibles. Zealous to avoid the error of the dispensationalists, these men plant their flag and make the continuity of the covenants the all-engrossing foundation of their preaching. But I wonder if it is a foundation that is able to support the scandal of the gospel.

If we care about the distinction between law and gospel— and if we care about the gospel, we must care about this distinction—then we will train our ears for those who don't seem to want us to keep the distinction between the old and new covenants. Their adamant insistence on the "continuity of the covenants" may prove to be a code phrase for making a whirling mess of law and gospel, the doctrine "on which men so readily and so fatally go astray,"[12] as John Knox put it. History unflinchingly bears out that when there is a merging of old and new covenants, it will never be law diminished by the gospel. It will always be the gospel fatally diminished by the law.

For Discussion

1. Discuss why Satan avoids frontal assaults on the gospel. What are ways he employs his subtle strategy for parents raising children in the church? For teens? For singles?

11. Theodore Beza, *The Christian Faith*, trans. James Clark (Lewes, England: Focus Christian Ministries Trust, 1992), 40–41.
12. John Knox, cited in Alexander Smellie, *The Reformation in Its Literature* (London: Andrew Melrose, 1925), 240.

2. Read Romans 10:3–4 in its context, then discuss Satan's strategy and just what it is he wants to keep us ignorant of and attempting to do.

For, being ignorant of the righteousness of God, and seeking to establish their own, they did not submit to God's righteousness. For Christ is the end of the law for righteousness to everyone who believes.

3. Review the three uses of the law from this chapter. Read Belgic Confession, article 24, and discuss the role of good works and the most common way(s) we misuse the law.

Therefore we do good works, but not to merit by them (for what can we merit?); nay, we are indebted to God for the good works we do, and not He to us, since it is He who worketh in us both to will and to work, for his good pleasure. Let us therefore attend to what is written: When ye shall have done all the things that are commanded you, say, We are unprofitable servants; we have done that which it was our duty to do.

Pray today for your pastor, for his ability to discern Satan's strategy and to proclaim faithfully the supremacy of Christ's righteousness and the sufficiency of the cross and resurrection power.

10

One Way of Salvation—
Not Two

THE REFORMERS, who got their theology from the apostle
Paul, understood that if they were going to get the gospel
right it was absolutely essential that they understand the distinction between two covenants. Charles Spurgeon traced the
church's error and defection back to confusion at precisely
this point: "He who well understands the distinction between
the covenant of works and the covenant of grace, is a master
of divinity. I am persuaded that most of the mistakes which
men make concerning the doctrines of Scripture, are based
upon fundamental errors with regard to the covenant of law
and of grace."[1]

On the one hand, one of the mistakes men make concerning
the distinction between two covenants is to think that there
are two ways of getting saved, an Old Testament way and a
New Testament way. This is a grave error, one that has its own
way of eroding grace in the covenant of grace.

Let's get something very clear: there is only one way of
salvation, and that is believing in the merits of Christ, his
atoning sacrifice and perfect righteousness for my sins. This
one way of salvation is the same whether we are reading in the

1. Charles H. Spurgeon, *New Park Street Pulpit* (Grand Rapids: Zondervan, 1963),
1:285.

Old Testament or in the New. Since the prototype proclamation of the gospel promised in Genesis 3:15, our sin problem has always been too great for us to solve. Salvation has always been of free, unmerited grace. Before or after Christ's incarnation, men have only been saved by an alien righteousness.

We'd like to think that, though the other guys may not be, we are good enough to be saved by our works. Knowing this, Moses warned obstinate Israelites not to say in their hearts, "It is because of my righteousness that the LORD has brought me in to possess this land" (Deut. 9:4). It is a serious error that says there are two kinds of salvation: Israel by keeping the law and Gentiles by the grace of the gospel. Israel in the Old Testament was saved one way, by believing in the promise of God to save them by the righteousness of the coming Messiah.

On the other hand, there are those who, in their zeal to maintain this single way of salvation, begin to make the fundamental error Spurgeon warned against: confusing and conflating a covenant of works into the covenant of grace. Luther knew the fundamental error of failing to observe the distinction; he knew that making law keeping part of the gospel forced him "to abandon Christ and His gospel boon." He personified the law when it does this as "a housebreaker": "You want to climb in where you do not belong, causing me to lose what has been given me. I would rather not know you at all than abandon my gift."[2]

The Ministry of Death

Where do we turn to keep works from climbing in where they do not belong? We go where Luther went, to *sola Scriptura*, to the Bible. But I've noticed something while reading my Bible over the years. When describing the gospel, and

2. Martin Luther, cited in C. F. W. Walther, *The Proper Distinction between Law and Gospel: Thirty-nine Evening Lectures* (St. Louis: Concordia Publishing House, 1928), 46–47.

especially the difference between the old and new covenants, Paul often uses language some of us intentionally avoid using. We're tempted to think that Paul has gone too far and has overstated the differences between covenants. We think his words need our careful handling.

For example, when he writes that God has made him and all gospel pastors "ministers of a new covenant" (2 Cor. 3:6), Paul uses language that some preachers are uncomfortable using; fearful of upsetting the oneness of the continuity of the covenants, they would never, without careful amendment, refer to themselves as Paul does. Though there is continuity in the whole of the Bible and thus in the old and new covenants, Paul seems much less concerned about this than we often are.

He never amends his words, never lessens their potency. He writes that his new covenant ministry is "not of the letter but of the Spirit. For the letter kills, but the Spirit gives life" (3:6). A minister groping for greater continuity and growing uneasy about being called a "minister of the new covenant" will hasten to amend Paul's words and tell us what he was really trying to say—explanations that sometimes sound more like a flip-flop of the words the apostle used.

As the uneasiness grows, some of us really get frantic when Paul terms the old covenant, "the ministry of death, carved in letters on stone" (3:7); and then when he repeats three times that this "ministry of condemnation" (3:9), was "brought to an end" (3:7, 11, 13), we begin to feel like Paul is not trying in the slightest to find indiscriminate continuity between the covenants. Sounding so unsophisticated and out of touch with the latest theological scholarship, Paul seems to be laboring to show us precisely the contrast between law and gospel.

Paul continues in his carefully crafted and divinely inspired argument to contrast the "ministry of death"—"the old covenant" (3:14)—with the "ministry of righteousness" (3:9), the new covenant. Misreading the Old Testament and not recognizing the difference between old and new covenants is not a new problem. "When they read the old covenant," Paul says, "that same veil remains unlifted, because only through Christ is it taken away" (3:14).

Paul is relentless. In his letter to the Romans he argues that in our union with Christ (Rom. 6:5), sin's dominion over the Christian is destroyed, "since [we] are not under law but under grace" (6:14). To be sure, in the very next verse he clarifies that freedom from the law does not give us a license to sin. But as he clarifies that Christians, united with Christ and "slaves of righteousness" (6:18), have been set free from the bondage to sin and now bear the fruit of sanctification (6:22), he never once amends his way of contrasting the old covenant and the new covenant.

In fact, Paul returns to the same kind of scandalous verbiage. After stating that we "have died to the law through the body of Christ" (7:4), Paul goes on to say an astonishing thing: "We are released from the law, having died to that which held us captive" (7:6). Anyone worried about antinomianism and moral laxity in the church, or anyone determined to find only continuity in the covenants, cringes and shudders at Paul's wording here. Doesn't he realize whom he's writing to?

Paul, writing to those loose-living Gentiles, ought to have known better and been more prudent; his words could be so easily misconstrued by antinomian pagans. But Paul just keeps using this kind of extravagant wording to describe grace and the gospel. He concludes this segment of his argument with one last indiscreet salvo: "so that we serve in the new way of the Spirit and not in the old way of the written code" (7:6).

There are many more examples of the kind of wording Paul employs when he writes about law and gospel. But when he says things like, "The law is not of faith" (Gal. 3:12), I find it difficult to conclude that finding continuity in the covenants is the hill to die on for Paul. I suspect that if our theology makes us afraid to use the Bible's inspired language, or if we find ourselves feeling the urge to explain what Paul really meant, we had better abandon our ideas and, like the Reformers, submit our thinking and speaking to Paul's biblical and gospel perspective—or brace ourselves for a corrupted gospel.

Faith, Not Faithfulness

I'm haunted by that young woman's words, "So we're justified by faith and by works?" I don't doubt the sincerity of the minister who led her to this bewildering conclusion. Intentional or otherwise, however, any preacher, in his zeal to teach his congregation faithfulness to the moral law, who preaches a distorted message that leads to this kind of confusion, has struck at the vital organ of the gospel.

How does any minister, while still claiming to believe in justification by faith alone, arrive at communicating a message that so mingles faith with works of faithfulness? How does any pastor, as Knox put it, "so fatally go astray"? By refusing to observe the difference between the old covenant and the new covenant.

The law will become a housebreaker and climb in where it does not belong, and preachers will go astray and lead their flocks astray when we fail to observe the distinction. We do violence to the gospel by not keeping the vast difference between the error of a righteousness earned by keeping the law and the scandalous freedom of an alien righteousness accomplished and applied to unworthy sinners entirely by Jesus Christ. Hence, whatever a preacher may intend to communicate to his flock, they will hear a gospel diminished by law-creep, a message that confuses the first and third use of the law. As such a message has done down through the centuries, it will inevitably lead congregations back into the wilderness.

Whether they are preachers long ago in the Netherlands, Switzerland, Scotland, New England, or in your church or mine today, men go fatally astray when they fail to "observe that in the contrast between the righteousness of the law and of the gospel," as Calvin put it, ". . . all works are excluded, whatever title may grace them (Galatians 3:11, 12). For Paul teaches that the righteousness of the law consists in obtaining salvation by doing what the law requires, but the righteousness of faith consists in believing that Christ died and rose again (Romans 10:5–9)."[3]

Calvin demonstrates that since "we derive from Christ" both the "blessings of sanctification and justification . . . Hence it follows, that not even spiritual works are taken into account when the power of justifying is ascribed to faith."[4]

Unlike ministers who lead their congregations to the conclusion that "those who obey [God's] commandments and those only will gain God's blessing and favor," observe closely how Calvin labors to accomplish the exact opposite, declaring that "all works are excluded." He wants to make certain that there is no law-creep in our understanding of justification. Calvin knew how fatal it is to the pure doctrine of the gospel if we get things out of order and mingle even a tiny amount of law keeping with the once-for-all-time justifying work of Jesus in the gospel.

For Discussion

1. Review the biblical citations from the apostle Paul in this chapter. What are the words and images Paul uses to describe the reality of the old covenant? The new covenant?
2. Read Hebrews 8:6 and discuss the implications of the "better promises." Why is Christ's role in the new covenant a more excellent one? More excellent than what?

3. John Calvin, *Institutes of the Christian Religion*, ed. John T. McNeil, trans. Ford Lewis Battles (Philadelphia: Westminster Press, 1960), 3.11.14.
4. Ibid.

But as it is, Christ has obtained a ministry that is as much more excellent than the old as the covenant he mediates is better, since it is enacted on better promises.

3. Read Westminster Larger Catechism 30 and discuss why the new covenant is called the "covenant of grace."

   Q. Does God leave all mankind to perish in the estate of sin and misery?

   A. God does not leave all men to perish in the estate of sin and misery, into which they fell by the breach of the first covenant, commonly called the covenant of works; but of his mere love and mercy delivers his elect out of it, and brings them into an estate of salvation by the second covenant, commonly called the covenant of grace.

4. If we are made free in the gospel, how is it we are called "slaves of righteousness" in Romans 6:18? Look also at Galatians 5:22–23.

Pray today for the body of Christ to see and understand the glorious differences between the old covenant and the new. Rejoice and give thanks to the Father for calling you to live under his Son's more excellent ministry of grace.

11

Getting the Cart before the Horse

STOPPING BY FOR A CHAT after school, one of my fresh, new English students shared an idea he had for a poem. "How about if I write couplets organized around what we do and then what God does?" I looked closely at him. Surely he had to be kidding. But there wasn't the slightest evidence that he was aware he had said anything out of order.

After thinking about it for a moment, I asked him if it wouldn't be more accurate to reverse the order. He frowned and said, "What I mean is, we are wise and then God rewards us."

One of the refreshing things about working with young people is that they often speak and write frankly about what they have been hearing. One thing was clear. However well intentioned the spiritual influences in this young man's life were, what he had been hearing was that he needed to do something and then God would reward him for doing it. Whatever the good intentions of his parents and his minister, the message this young man had heard had fatally inverted the order of things.

"But if we are wise," I asked him, "how did we get that way?" I explained further to him that there was only one way I could see that he could keep the order of our works and God's rewards in his couplets. His poem could feature what we do: our sins of thought, word, and deed; even the splendid sins of our good works—all that could form the first part. And the second part could then feature what Jesus has done once for all time in the gospel: united us with himself in redemption, justification, and imputed righteousness, forgiving us all our sins by taking our guilt and punishment on himself on the cross. That would make a grand poem, a hymn of glory to God for his amazing grace, and it would be so because it kept the order of salvation in its biblical order.

After growing up in a Christian home and attending church and youth group throughout his entire life, nevertheless, this fifteen-year-old young man was caught in a classic theological blunder, one entirely destructive to the gospel. He had confused what theologians term the *ordo salutis*, or the order of the different components of salvation. By inverting the order, by getting the cart before the horse, he had unwittingly done violence to the gospel.

Order Is Everything

Just as in making an omelet, the order is everything. Cook the eggs before you break them and you have boiled eggs but not an omelet. Attempt to whip them before cracking them and you have an inedible mess. Wait until the eggs hatch into chicks and go to work on them—and you have roadkill. Ridiculous as this sounds, many of us do the same thing in our thinking about the *ordo salutis*, the order of salvation.

Theologians since the Reformation have described the order of the components of salvation in this way: predestination, calling, regeneration, faith, repentance, justification, sanctification, and glorification. But let's be honest: most of us don't naturally think of the order in this God-initiated way. We are more inclined to give the order from our finite human vantage point. After all, that's the way we experienced things.

Hence, we prefer to think that our faith and believing come before regeneration, for example, and our own persevering in obedience comes before, and is a contingency of, glorification. Put more simply, we tend to think that salvation has to be something to which we contribute something—as my student was thinking.

Faith Out of Order

One of the more common ways justification by faith alone gets out of order is when we misunderstand faith to be man's part in salvation. In answer to Paul's question, "Who makes you different from anyone else?" (1 Cor. 4:7 NIV), many evangelicals today without hesitation would say their faith makes them different from unbelievers. I posed this question to a fellow who showed up at a community group meeting in our home one evening. "My faith," he said, as if it were obvious. "What makes me different from an unbeliever is my choice to believe. I heard the message. It made sense to me, and I chose to believe it." I attempted to help him see that this meant he was the final arbiter of his salvation. His will and choice were the things that set him apart from the unbeliever, not God's will and choice. He confidently reaffirmed that it was his will and choice.

When talking about God saving sinners, something seems rather out of order when the final thing that makes the difference in that salvation is something the sinner does. It is precisely what Paul is disabusing the Corinthians from thinking about themselves. "For who makes you different from anyone else? What do you have that you did not receive?" he asked them. "And if you did receive it, why do you boast as though you did not?" (1 Cor. 4:7 NIV).

The question itself reveals its own answer: everything we are and have comes as a gift from God; how much more is our eternal salvation from first to last a gift of God. Any doctrine of salvation that points us away from the will and purpose of God, the finished work of Christ, the effectual regenerating work of the Spirit, is just another self-salvation endeavor that says, "Do this and live"—the same message that every other religion presses upon its adherents.

What is happening here is another way we get things out of order. When we give sinners credit for exercising saving faith as an act of their free will, we are making the philosophical blunder of drawing ultimate conclusions from only what is immediately verifiable to our limited sight. We observe sinners as they hear the gospel, fall on their knees, and ask Jesus to save them, and Jesus does save them.

From our immediate observation, we leap to the conclusion—against mountains of biblical evidence—that there was a cause and effect being acted out before us. What we could observe was the sinner's repentance and faith, and we draw the conclusion that God passively waited to save him until he decided of his own free will to believe in God. What we could not observe, however, was the divine perspective, the saving operation of the Father, the Son, and the Holy Spirit.

Faith in Order

If we turn faith into a condition of salvation that man must on his own hook fulfill, there's no other way to slice it than that our faith is functioning in the role of our doing something. Protest all we want, faith understood this way is equal to merit. If God chose you because he passively foresaw that you would believe, your believing is what makes you different from the unbeliever, and it would make sense for you to boast in your faith.

When the Reformers preached justification by faith alone, they did not mean what many evangelicals mean by faith alone: salvation is a responsible partnership between God and man, and faith is man's part in salvation. God does his part, and it's up to the sinner to come up with enough faith to close the deal.

They used to get this right in Amsterdam, Geneva, Edinburgh, and Boston, and in all these places they either produced or adhered to carefully crafted confessions of faith in which they precisely defined the language of the gospel, including the meaning of the word *faith* itself. One of the finest of those statements we find in the Westminster Larger Catechism.

> Question 73: How doth faith justify a sinner in the sight of God?
>
> Answer: Faith justifies a sinner in the sight of God, not because of those other graces which do always accompany it, or of good works that are the fruits of it, nor as if the grace of faith, or any act thereof, were imputed to him for his justification; but only as it is an instrument by which he receiveth and applieth Christ and his righteousness.

Why were the Westminster divines so careful with their language here? They knew that error in our understanding of what faith is would corrupt the gospel. They wanted to make absolutely certain that everyone understood that faith is the instrument of receiving and applying Christ's righteousness, but what "always accompany it"—that is, the good works that flow from faith—are not a part of justification. They chose their words carefully here and throughout the confessional standards, precisely to avoid the error of including what faith produces (the fruit of good works) with faith alone in the imputed righteousness of Jesus alone.

Screwtape to Narnia

All the Protestant confessions make it crystal clear that faith is not something man must drum up, the deal-closing merit we must contribute, by an act of our free will, to finish our conversion. In short, there is no equivocation about the order of faith and regeneration in the confessions of the Reformation.

But our understanding of these things is often a process. I find it illuminating to trace the progression of C. S. Lewis' thinking on the *ordo salutis*, and on faith and man's free will. In 1942, when he had been a Christian for eleven years, Lewis wrote, "The Irresistible and the Indisputable are the two weapons which the very nature of [God's] scheme forbids Him to use. Merely to override a human will would be for Him useless. He cannot ravish. He can only woo. He is prepared to do a little overriding at the beginning."[1] In fairness, we must remember that Lewis wrote this in the persona of his infernal demon Screwtape, who, Lewis warns in his preface, does not always get things right. Nevertheless, Lewis here and elsewhere makes philosophical arguments in favor of man being capable of making salvific choices from his free will. He wrote that God "leaves the creature to stand up on its own legs—to carry out from the will alone duties which have lost all relish."[2]

When we look closely we can begin to observe that writers are sometimes at their best when writing poetry or imaginative fiction—and still more at their best when they have matured in their understanding of the depth of human depravity and the wonder of the sovereign, electing love that alone is capable of rescuing dead sinners. In a book published in 1953, fully eleven years later, Lewis seems to have developed in his understanding of the doctrine theologians term the *effectual calling*. In *The Silver Chair*, when Aslan tells Jill that he called her out of her world, Jill disagrees. "Nobody called me and Scrubb, you know. It was we who asked to come here. Scrubb said we were to call . . . And we did, and then we found the door open." Jill,

---

1. C. S. Lewis, *The Screwtape Letters* (New York: Macmillan, 1982), 38.
2. Ibid., 39.

like most, mistakenly thought that she was calling by her own free will and that it was her calling that had opened the door. A now wiser Lewis has his Christ figure, Aslan, reply, "You would not have called to me unless I had been calling to you."[3] Written twenty-two years after his conversion, Lewis here wonderfully illustrates the *ordo salutis*: that God sovereignly and effectually calls and awakens dead sinners first, and then, and only then, they call on him to save them.

Similarly, in *The Magician's Nephew* (1950), Lewis has Aslan utter "a long single note; not very loud, but full of power. Polly's heart jumped in her body when she heard it. She felt sure that it was a call, and that anyone who heard that call would want to obey it and (what's more) would be able to obey it, however many worlds and ages lay between."[4]

Here Lewis gives an imaginative and incremental explanation of the order of salvation: God's call comes first and is heard only by some, but those who hear his voice calling them, not only want to obey his call, "(what's more)" they are enabled by the grace of God alone to heed his call.

In his spiritual autobiography Lewis attempted to sort out what was happening when "God closed in on me,"[5] as he called it. Reflecting back on his conversion and newfound freedom in Christ, Lewis does not describe what happened in the terms he has Screwtape use—God never uses "the Irresistible or the Indisputable." He marvels at the divine mercy that compelled him to come in, and concludes, "God's compulsion is our liberation,"[6] which sounds much closer to a man who believes it was the sovereign power and authority of God that liberated him from his sins and gave him freedom in Christ.

But, at the end of the day, does any of this matter, really?

3. C. S. Lewis, *The Silver Chair* (New York: Harper Collins, 1994), 24.
4. C. S. Lewis, *The Magician's Nephew* (New York: Collier Books, 1970), 137.
5. C. S. Lewis, *Surprised by Joy: The Shape of My Early Life* (New York: Harcourt, Brace, Jovanovich, 1987), 123.
6. Ibid., 125.

For Discussion

1. Read Romans 6:7–11 and describe the order of Christ's finished work for us. What theological terms define these truths? Why is keeping them in order critical to the purity of the gospel and the life of faith?

   For one who has died has been set free from sin. Now if we have died with Christ, we believe that we will also live with him. We know that Christ, being raised from the dead, will never die again; death no longer has dominion over him. For the death he died he died to sin, once for all, but the life he lives he lives to God. So you also must consider yourselves dead to sin and alive to God in Christ Jesus.

2. Read Belgic Confession, article 24, and discuss the role of the Holy Spirit in producing a "new man." What is new about the "new life"?

   We believe that this true faith, being wrought in man by the hearing of the Word of God and the operation of the Holy Spirit, sanctifies him and makes him a new man, causing him to live a new life, and freeing him from the bondage of sin.

3. According to the author, what happens to the message of the gospel when we draw ultimate conclusions from our finite vantage point?

Pray today for a prominent Christian speaker you know; pray that he will keep things in their biblical order as he speaks.

12

The Order Really Matters

SOME GUFFAW AND SAY that the order of salvation is just theological wrangling, a divisive smoke screen. None of this really matters. Since doctrine divides, let's just set doctrine aside and get along. Theological wrangling often can be all about pride and being right and the other guy being an idiot for being wrong. There's no question that doctrine does divide. At its best, however, doctrinal debate helps us divide gospel truth from error. Hence, the order of the components of the gospel matters because error doesn't lead people to heaven; it leads people to hell.

All this is of cosmic importance because how we order the components of salvation in our minds and hearts will lead us either to a man-centered religion or a God-centered salvation that actually saves, that really works. If we cast into the shade the sovereignty of God's gracious initiative in the gospel and teach and believe a distorted gospel that weds faith and obedience, the church will again produce generations of people—young and old—who really do believe that the gospel is about their doing things and God rewarding them for doing them. Put bluntly, all this matters because getting things out of order castrates the gospel.

Geneva Debate

Calvin in his debate with a man with the unfortunate name of Albertus Pighius relentlessly posed Paul's question, "Who makes you different from anyone else?" (1 Cor. 4:7 NIV). Or, put another way, why does one man believe and another man reject the gospel? Pighius argued that the difference between a believer and an unbeliever was left up to man's free will to decide. Calvin replied, "Faith from its beginning to its perfection is the gift of God,"[1] which is straightforward commentary on what Paul wrote in Ephesians, "By grace you have been saved through faith. And this is not your own doing; it is the gift of God" (2:8).

We err by inverting the order when we make faith our autonomous contribution that completes our justification. Faith is the instrumental means whereby the sinner abandons hope in himself and lays hold of the merits of Christ alone. "With respect to justification," continued Calvin, "faith is a thing merely passive, bringing nothing of our own to conciliate the favor of God."[2]

Next Calvin demonstrated that the best early church fathers believed faith was a gift of God. "Augustine testifies that men are not chosen because they believe, but, on the contrary, are chosen that they might believe."[3] Calvin concludes that in our sinful hearts "faith could not possibly have existed except that God had then appointed it for us by the free grace of his adoption of us."[4]

For Calvin, understanding what faith is and where it comes from was critical to getting the order of salvation right. While some continue to stop their ears and insist that none of this matters, the apostle John seems to think the order matters a great deal.

In the opening paragraphs of John's gospel he lays down foundational understanding, critical to getting everything that follows in his account of the gospel right. "But to all

1. John Calvin, cited in David Otis Fuller, ed., *A Treasury of Evangelical Writings* (Grand Rapids: Kregel, 1961), 183.
2. John Calvin, *Institutes of the Christian Religion*, ed. John T. McNeil, trans. Ford Lewis Battles (Philadelphia: Westminster Press, 1960), 3.13.5.
3. Calvin, cited in Fuller, *Treasury of Evangelical Writings*, 184.
4. Ibid., 185.

who did receive him, who believed in his name, he gave the right to become children of God, who were born, not of blood nor of the will of the flesh nor of the will of man, but of God" (1:12–13). When we fail at the most primal level of conversion to acknowledge that we are born again not "of the will of the flesh nor of the will of man," we rob God. It matters deeply that we give God the glory for giving us the gift of faith in our salvation. This is no mere theoretical nit-picking.

There are two options here: God gets all the glory for his saving work, or we take some of it from him; that is, we rob him of his blood-bought right. It profoundly matters whether we take credit for something for which God alone deserves credit. It matters a great deal.

Failure to believe that regeneration is not left to our free will but to God's free will, fundamentally goes back to a failure to keep things in order: God's will and purpose graciously working salvation in us, and we the unworthy recipients of all his glorious benefits in the gospel. Call it by whatever theological name we choose, taking the minutest credit for any part of our salvation ultimately will erode the gospel.

No Big Deal

I have read Roman Catholics who insist that they believe in justification by faith, that the whole Reformation and the deal with Luther was all a big misunderstanding. But there was a reason why the Reformers insisted on the five *solas*: the Word of God alone is our authority (*sola Scriptura*), and in the Word we learn that salvation is by grace alone (*sola gratia*), through faith alone (*sola fide*), in Christ alone (*solus Christus*), all to the glory of God alone (*soli Deo gloria*). The medieval errors about justification had added a big dose of man's initiative and effort into the stages of salvation, thus forcing the Reformers doggedly to employ the word *alone*. Rome had done more than invert the order of the components of the gospel of salvation.

113

The medieval church taught that one must have faith in God and produce works of faithfulness, and that by a faith that produced sufficient works one would be justified. Of course you needed grace and Christ, and of course it was by your faith. But they taught that saving faith was never alone, and so faith and enough works of faithfulness, aided by Christ and his grace, eventually produced justification.

Notice that the same words are being used, and it sounds pretty good. But rearranging the order, even slightly, destroys the freedom of the gospel. The operative word is *alone*, and nudging the keystone of that word out of place brings down the entire structure. For Luther the doctrine of justification by faith alone was "the issue upon which the church stands or falls."[5] R.C. Sproul warns that there is a "full-scale assault" launched within Protestant evangelicalism against the doctrine of justification by faith alone. Without this doctrine, "the gospel is not merely compromised, it is lost altogether."[6]

Anathema

I have a neighbor who is a serious Roman Catholic, who attends church regularly, prays often, is intensely pro-life, is concerned that her nine children grow up in the faith, and who will as she passes by our home on her way to the coffee shop ask us to pray for concerns she has and assures us that she is praying for us. I do not pretend to know her heart, but she certainly is open and up front about being a Catholic Christian—more forthright than many Protestants, who too often and inexplicably blush and mumble when it comes to talking about the good news.

Though I cannot see into the condition of our neighbor's soul, I do know something about the confessional stance of her church,

---

5. Martin Luther, cited in R.C. Sproul, "Making Molehills out of Mountains," *Tabletalk*, May 1, 2010, http://www.ligonier.org/learn/articles/making-molehills-out-mountains/.

6. Sproul, "Molehills out of Mountains," *Tabletalk*.

which declares anathema anyone who claims that sinners are justified by faith alone. There has been no official repudiation by the Catholic Church today of the conclusions of the Counter-Reformation agreed upon at the Council of Trent 450 years ago. Note how the medieval theologians at Trent borrowed phrases like "justification by faith alone" from the Reformed confessions of faith to pronounce condemnation on the Protestant understanding of the sovereign work of God in the order of the salvation of a sinner. It's as if Trent is a counter-confession; hold the Belgic, or London, or Scots Confessions up to the mirror and you get the opposite theology in Trent. Moreover, lest we miss the full weight of what is being declared, the word *anathema*, referred to in the following text from Trent, means "assigned to damnation."

> If any one saith, that by faith alone the impious is justified . . . let him be anathema. . . .
>
> . . . If any one saith, that men are justified, either by the sole imputation of the justice of Christ, or by the sole remission of sins . . . let him be anathema. . . .
>
> . . . If any one saith, that the justice received is not preserved and also increased before God through good works; but that said works are merely the fruits and signs of Justification obtained, but not a cause of the increase thereof; let him be anathema. . . .
>
> . . . If any one saith, that the good works of one that is justified are in such manner the gifts of God, as that they are not also the good merits of him that is justified . . . let him be anathema.[7]

Let me make it clear that just as no one is justified by works, so no one is justified by getting her church affiliation correct. We are justified entirely by faith alone in the merits of Jesus' blood and righteousness alone. Nevertheless, I sincerely want to believe

---

7. *The Canons and Degrees of the Sacred and Oecumenical Council of Trent*, trans. J. Waterworth (London: Dolman, 1848), 45–48, *Hanover Historical Texts Collection*, accessed January 20, 2014, http://history.hanover.edu/texts/trent/ct06.html.

that my Catholic neighbor is a true Christian, but if she is so, it will be entirely by the Spirit's gracious application of the very gospel truths declared to be anathema by her church.

That's Them, Not Us

The crisis today, however, is not, for the most part, Catholics disagreeing with Protestants. The crisis is within the gates. It's within churches that claim to be Bible-believing and evangelical; it's within churches that claim to be confessional and Reformed, and in the seminaries of both. Increasingly ministerial candidates are taking exceptions with the wording of doctrines that were considered nonnegotiable, Theology 101 for their denominations.

One young man, fresh from completing his European PhD, while being examined by a committee of the church in which he hoped to minister, took exception to his denomination's confessional teaching on justification by faith alone; he felt there needed to be more language about works in the definition.

Without equivocation, the great Protestant confessions of faith are unanimous in their way of articulating this centrally important doctrine: "Justification is an act of God's free grace, wherein he pardoneth all our sins, and accepteth us as righteous in his sight, only for the righteousness of Christ imputed to us, and received by faith alone" (Westminster Shorter Catechism 33). For five centuries theologians have very precisely not included the language of works in the definition of justification by faith alone, yet this new ministerial candidate was certain it was time to add in works.

After deliberating over the young man's problems with justification by faith alone, the committee proceeded to ordain him to the ministry in his denomination. I doubt that Luther and the Reformers would have blessed the ministry of a man taking this exception. For them, justification by faith alone—*alone*, excluding works—was "the issue upon which the church stands or falls."[8]

8. Martin Luther, cited in Sproul, "Molehills out of Mountains," *Tabletalk*.

For Discussion

1. Explain how rearranging the order of salvation's components destroys the freedom found in the gospel. In what ways can we rob God?

2. Read Romans 6:5–11 and discuss why it is essential that we be united with Christ in his death and also in his resurrection.

   If we have been united with him in a death like his, we shall certainly be united with him in a resurrection like his. We know that our old self was crucified with him in order that the body of sin might be brought to nothing, so that we would no longer be enslaved to sin. (Rom. 6:5–6)

3. Discuss what faith is and how we get it:

   Q 86. What is faith in Jesus Christ?

   A. Faith in Jesus Christ is a saving grace, whereby we receive and rest upon him alone for salvation, as he is offered to us in the gospel. (WSC)

   . . . requiring faith as the condition to interest them in him, promises and gives his Holy Spirit to all his elect, to work in them that faith, with all other saving graces. (Westminster Longer Catechism 32)

Pray today for missionaries who are bringing the gospel to unreached peoples; pray they would be able to accurately translate these concepts of being united with Christ in death, united with Christ in resurrection, and filled with his Spirit.

13

The Dungeon Flamed
with Light

JUST AS THEOLOGICAL ERROR leads us over the cliff, it also doesn't sing well. While some theologians find themselves drawn to sophisticated innovations that seem to set them on a trajectory away from God's glory alone in salvation, generally speaking, the church's hymn writers have fared far better.

Retaining and appreciating the best hymns of the past can be one of the surest ways to correct our tendency to return to our default mode: giving ourselves a bit of credit in the salvation proposition. When we rise and sing the praises of our Redeemer in worship, we're forced to lay aside theoretical errors in our theology, errors that simply do not sing well.

A wonderful example of how this works is seen in eighteenth-century hymn writer Joseph Hart's hymn "Come Ye Sinners, Poor and Wretched." It is an evangelistic hymn, appealing to lost sinners to come to the Savior. We might expect and be inclined to forgive the writer of an evangelistic hymn for abandoning the order of salvation, but Joseph Hart doesn't do so. Notice how he points even the unregenerate sinner to the God-glorifying order of salvation.

> Let not conscience make you linger,
> Nor of fitness fondly dream;

All the fitness he requireth
Is to feel your need of him;
This he gives you;
'Tis the Spirit's rising beam.[1]

Hart understood that there was little to sing about if God requires some fitness of us; he knew that all the fitness God requires for salvation is to know our lost condition and desperate need. The hymn writer then thrills us with the glorious thought, "This he gives you." This, even this, the knowledge of our ruin and great need, God gives us by the effectual working of his gracious Holy Spirit. Hart has here observed the *ordo salutis*—and the result? Not stale theology, not head-nodding affirmation of orthodoxy, not arrogant argumentation, clubbing our opponent with a bundle of tulips. What results is worship—humble reverence and adoration. Violate the order, however, and there's not much left worth singing about.

Wesleyan Wesley

Joseph Hart, though converted under the preaching of a Wesleyan preacher, eventually aligned himself with reformational theology. Nevertheless, hymn writers—regardless of their declared theology—are often the church's best practical theologians. Something about setting down lines of poetry to be sung in praise and adoration of the glorious work of God in the gospel corrects our man-centered theological tendencies. There are few better examples of hymns that demonstrate getting and keeping the order in order than Charles Wesley's "And Can It Be." Written on the anniversary of his conversion, Wesley perhaps inadvertently demonstrates how we often sing our theology better than we theoretically articulate it:

1. Joseph Hart, "Come, Ye Sinners, Poor and Wretched," from William Walker, *Baptist Harmony*, p. 249, *Christian Classics Ethereal Library*, accessed April 23, 2014, http://www.ccel.org/ccel/walker/harmony/files/hymn/Invitation.html.

Long my imprisoned spirit lay,
Fast bound in sin and nature's night;
Thine eye diffused a quickening ray—
I woke, the dungeon flamed with light;
My chains fell off, my heart was free,
I rose, went forth, and followed Thee.[2]

Though on paper Wesley claimed to believe that man's free will makes the decisive difference in our conversion; nevertheless, notice how clear and incremental Wesley's order is here. The condition of the sinner before conversion is as of a man lying hopelessly chained in prison, "fast bound in sin and nature's night." Paul described the lost man as "dead in the trespasses and sins" (Eph. 2:1), totally depraved and unable to do anything to effect his release from the prison of death in which he lies. Wesley then credits God with the decisive and causative action. "Thine eye diffused a quickening ray"; that is, God by his Spirit makes the sinner alive.

As God breathed into Adam the breath of life in the first creation, so by the regenerating power of the Spirit, God makes us new creations by the new birth. Only after God has made the dead sinner alive, does the sinner then become aware of his chains, and that they are falling off by the gracious, regenerating activity of God himself.

Next in order, Wesley declares, "My heart was free." Notice that he is not saying it was his human freedom that caused or initiated his regeneration. It is not man's free will that breaks the chains or gives new life. "Man does not obtain grace by freedom," wrote Augustine—that is, by his free will. "Man obtains freedom by grace."[3]

---

2. Charles Wesley, "And Can It Be That I Should Gain?" 1738, *The Cyber Hymnal*, accessed April 23, 2014, http://www.cyberhymnal.org/htm/a/c/acanitbe.htm.

3. Augustine, cited in John Calvin, *Institutes of the Christian Religion*, ed. John T. McNeil, trans. Ford Lewis Battles (Philadelphia: Westminster Press, 1960), 2.3.14.

Grace, in the order of salvation, always and ever comes before freedom. And Wesley, at his best when writing a hymn of praise and adoration of Christ in the gospel, acknowledged in these words that freedom is the result not the cause of his regeneration. He concludes the stanza, moving from justification and regeneration to the always and inevitable consequence, "I rose, went forth, and followed Thee."

An anonymous hymn written in 1878 must have been penned by a man or woman particularly intent on getting the cause-and-effect order of events in salvation correct:

> I sought the Lord, and afterward I knew
> He moved my soul to seek him, seeking me;
> It was not I that found, O Savior true;
> No, I was found, was found of thee.[4]

I wish the aspiring-hymn-writer English student of mine had come wanting to write this kind of poem, a hymn adoring the Savior who moved the soul of the hymn writer in order first, and only then did he seek the Lord. The order is everything: God seeks us by regeneration and the new birth, and then, and only then, we seek him in repentance and faith. "The children of the Reformation," wrote Michael Horton, "though differing on specifics, join voices in the biblical affirmation that 'salvation is of the Lord' (Jonah 2:9) and that even our new birth is the result of grace alone, not of human cooperation with grace."[5]

Tempest in a Teapot

When Christians who have historically believed and taught that salvation is of the Lord, however, begin to get

---

4. "I Sought the Lord," *Trinity Hymnal*, (Atlanta: Great Commission, 1990), 466.
5. Michael Horton, "Final Thoughts," *Modern Reformation* 21, no. 2 (March/April 2012): 44.

things out of order, we should have serious concerns. When we minimize the central doctrine of justification by faith alone, and men in our pulpits have "pages of exceptions" with the historic confessions of faith they vowed that they believed when ordained—it is no exaggeration to say we have a crisis on our hands. "The crisis regarding the doctrine of justification," wrote R.C. Sproul,

> that provoked the Protestant Reformation in the sixteenth century has not yet been resolved. Thus, the Reformation is by no means over. The dispute over justification that split the church back then threatens to fracture contemporary, evangelical Christianity. At issue during the Reformation was the relationship of justification to sanctification. It was a question of the order of salvation. The difference is not a tempest in a teapot; it's one by which salvation itself is defined.[6]

The relationship of justification to sanctification, once again, is where Satan has leveled his guns. Flip things around and make sanctification a condition of justification—and we do violence to the gospel. And doing violence to the gospel is anathema.

For Discussion

1. The author writes, "Only after God has made the dead sinner alive, does the sinner then become aware of his chains, and that they are falling off by the gracious, regenerating activity of God himself." How does the Bible's imagery of a dead person being made alive, a slave being made a son, and a prisoner being made a free man help us understand God's saving work on our

6. R.C. Sproul, "Making Molehills out of Mountains," *Tabletalk*, May 1, 2010, http://www.ligonier.org/learn/articles/making-molehills-out-mountains/.

behalf? How does an understanding that "Man does not obtain grace by freedom. . . . Man obtains freedom by grace" aid us in overcoming sin?

2. Read Galatians 4:4–7 and discuss how God's timing and means, causes us to respond in awe and gratitude, not as prisoners but as sons.

> But when the fullness of time had come, God sent forth his Son, born of woman, born under the law, to redeem those who were under the law, so that we might receive adoption as sons. And because you are sons, God has sent the Spirit of his Son into our hearts, crying, "Abba! Father!" So you are no longer a slave, but a son, and if a son, then an heir through God.

3. According to Westminster Larger Catechism 39, what is accomplished for us by our Mediator becoming a man?

> It was requisite that the Mediator should be man, that he might advance our nature, perform obedience to the law, suffer and make intercession for us in our nature, have a fellow feeling of our infirmities; that we might receive the adoption of sons, and have comfort and access with boldness unto the throne of grace.

4. How is corporate singing in worship a declaration of the church's theology—a proclamation of what we believe Scripture says about God and about us?

Pray today for those writing hymns and spiritual songs for today's church to sing corporately. Pray for their attention to be arrested by God's mighty acts of power over sin and death, of rescue and adoption, and for their music to reflect his triumph.

PART 4

Adding Contingencies
to Justification:
*Ways We Erode the Gospel
with Good Intentions*

14

Corrupting Sanctification

"I DON'T THINK I'M HOLY enough to be a pastor," said a discouraged seminarian. The young man had sought out the counsel of the aging Edmund Clowney, long-time president of Westminster Theological Seminary, and in his retirement, professor emeritus at Westminster Seminary California. "It's not about you," replied the venerable theologian and preacher. "It's about Jesus."[1]

Like the discouraged seminarian, we too often look to our own fitness, our own performance, our sanctification, our holiness, to verify our worth and standing with God. "Let us know, therefore, that it is dangerous to look for that from ourselves," wrote Puritan Richard Sibbes,

> which we must have from Christ. . . . We are but subordinate agents, moving as we are moved, and working as we are first wrought upon, free in so far as we are freed, no wiser nor stronger than he makes us to be for the present in anything we undertake. It is his Spirit who actuates and enlivens, and applies that knowledge and strength we have, or else it fails and lies useless in us. We work when we

1. Presbyterian Church in America (PCA) teaching elder David Scott's account of his private conversation with Edmund Clowney while studying at Westminster Seminary California (Escondido, CA) in 1999.

work from a present strength; therefore dependent spirits are wisest and the ablest.[2]

As it appears Sibbes would have done, Dr. Clowney directed this young pastor in training away from his navel contemplation. He wisely understood that if this young man was to be useful as an undershepherd of the flock that Jesus purchased with his own blood, he needed to turn away from his assessment of his own personal holiness "to gaze upon the beauty of the LORD" (Ps. 27:4). He knew that the surest and only way to personal holiness is to keep our eyes fixed on the Holy One.

Backdoor Assault

Since the Devil generally avoids pitched battles, I wonder if he doesn't scheme behind the lines to corrupt the gospel by shifting things to another more "plausible-sounding" argument. His strategy seems to go something like this: If I can't get them to out-and-out deny justification by faith alone, I will get them to affirm true things, but true things that serve to blur the line between justification and sanctification. If I play my cards well, they will say true things like, "Faith that saves is never alone," until pretty soon that's the main thing they like to say about faith. Ever-perceptive Shakespeare seemed to understand this about the Devil and his strategy:

> And oftentimes, to win us to our harm,
> The instruments of darkness tell us truths,
> Win us with honest trifles, to betray's
> In deepest consequence.[3]

Christians in the pew must anticipate that it is of central importance to "the instruments of darkness" to insinuate

---

2. Richard Sibbes, *The Bruised Reed, Monergism*, accessed January 20, 2014, http://www.monergism.com/thethreshold/sdg/bruisedreed.html.

3. William Shakespeare, *Macbeth*, I.iii.125–28.

themselves into the church's discourse about justification and sanctification. The Devil may put it in these terms: If I can get them using words like *truncated* when they talk about the gospel of grace—it's such a fun word to say. And if I play my hand carefully, I can get them to mean that a gospel that's free and without conditions is a "truncated" gospel; I can get them thinking that a gospel that doesn't require them to do something is missing something. How immensely entertaining it will be to watch their distraction as they run around trying to sanctify themselves with the fire hose of their good works, dousing out the fire of God's free grace (so the Devil imagines).

Another venerable saint, Jerry Bridges, commenting on his best-selling book *The Pursuit of Holiness*, candidly said, "But I soon realized that a pursuit of holiness that is not founded on grace and the gospel can lead to a performance mentality." Knowing how destructive this mentality is to a biblical understanding of both justification and the pursuit of holiness, Bridges added, "That's when I began to emphasize grace and the gospel as foundational to the pursuit of holiness." He concluded that in our sanctification, "we are absolutely dependent on the Holy Spirit to enable us."[4]

This is where we can fatally go astray. "Satan knows that nothing can prevail against Christ, or those that rely upon his power," wrote Richard Sibbes. "Therefore his study is how to keep us in ourselves."[5] One of his favorite ways to do this is to choose his battles. He's okay with our thinking that faith may be, in theory, a gift in our justification, but in our sanctification and personal holiness the Enemy insinuates that it's up to us to step up to the moral plate, to cooperate with faith, to do our part by doing good works. Since this accords with our natural inclination to look to ourselves, to our performance, we easily believe the Deceiver's lie.

4. "The Pursuit of Holiness: An Interview with Jerry Bridges," *Tabletalk*, January 2012, 78.
5. Sibbes, *Bruised Reed*.

But believing the Enemy is always fatal. It will inevitably disconnect good works from faith, faith working through love. Once he has reordered our thinking, we return to where he wants us, to slavery, to a sanctification motivated in part by fear[6] and obligation. What he doesn't want us to realize is that no matter how splendid the good works, if they are not motivated by love and gratitude, they are "splendid sins," creative expressions of our self-love, elaborate charades of our self-righteousness. His goal is for us to think that when the Bible tells us we ought to do something, that we have a salvific obligation to do it, and we'd better—like it or not—get going and do it, or else. And before we know what has happened, to the Enemy's delight, he has us thinking that our standing with God depends on fulfilling our obligation rather than on God's grace promised in gospel sanctification.

Satan has his allies to accomplish this: we parents with our children, and preachers unwittingly or otherwise act as his agents when they shift their flock from looking to, believing in, and finding rest in what Christ has already fully accomplished for their salvation. Pretty soon we're looking to our good works to keep the favor of God; and then for all practical purposes, we have come to believe that we're justified to some degree by our sanctification. Thinking this way will always corrupt the gospel.

Hydra-headed Monster

Like the monster in Greek mythology whose heads grew back double every time one was hewn off, so the error of making sanctification, in some form or another, a condition of justification rears its gospel-crushing head every genera-

---

6. We are absolutely to pursue holiness in the fear of God, out of reverence and awe of his perfections. Here, I refer to fear as in slavish uncertainty, doubt about the completeness of our position in Christ, of the Spirit's gracious application of the saving benefits of the gospel, in defiance of our imperfections.

tion. Lop them off as we will, it has had as many different arguments as proponents to support it through the centuries.

We're not surprised to hear the medieval church argue that righteousness is "preserved and . . . increased before God through good works," and that the sinner's good works are not merely the "fruits and signs of justification," but are "the cause of the increase." It makes sense to hear the Church of Rome flatly deny that "the good works of the one justified are gifts of God." Troubling as it is, we expect to hear Rome declare anathema on someone who ascribes sanctification to the gracious work of the Holy Spirit alone in the redeemed sinner's heart and deeds.[7]

But what are we to think when a man who called himself a Protestant says virtually the same thing? Charles Finney, celebrated revivalist preacher, among other serious theological problems, argued against justification by faith alone—"the Antinomian view," as he termed it. Inevitably, his hostility toward a reformational view of justification led to or resulted from his antagonism toward gospel sanctification. "Perseverance in obedience to the end of life," he insisted, "is also a condition of justification." He put it still more bluntly, "present sanctification is another condition of justification." Decrying what he considered to be the "erroneous view," he wrote, "Some theologians have made justification a condition of sanctification, instead of making sanctification a condition of justification. But this we shall see is an erroneous view of the subject."[8]

At least Finney didn't try to beat around the bush about his departure from biblical and historic theology. Perseverance and sanctification, in his view, are not enabled by the gracious operation of the Spirit; far from it; they are conditions we must and had better supply—or else.

7. Michael S. Horton with Christian Smith, "Exit Stage West," *Modern Reformation* 21, no. 2 (March/April 2012): 12.

8. Charles G. Finney, *Systematic Theology* (Minneapolis, MN: Bethany, 1976), 326–27.

Nudged by the Enemy, we're tempted to dismiss the relevance of this. Don't be ridiculous, we say. That was Finney and that was way back in the nineteenth century. Surely no real Protestant evangelical ministers would teach this way today. Let's see.

For Discussion

1. The author quoted Richard Sibbes in this chapter: "Let us know, therefore, that it is dangerous to look for that from ourselves, which we must have from Christ . . . We work when we work from a present strength . . . wisest and the ablest." Discuss this in light of Psalm 37:5 and Hebrews 2:2.

2. Paul says in Galatians 2:21, "I do not nullify the grace of God, for if righteousness were through the law, then Christ died for no purpose." Compare this with Belgic Confession, article 22, and discuss Christ's works and holy merits and the role of faith:

   But Jesus Christ, imputing to us all His merits, and so many holy works which He has done for us and in our stead, is our righteousness. And faith is an instrument that keeps us in communion with Him in all His benefits.

3. If Satan knows that nothing can prevail against those who rely on Christ's power, what does he labor to make us rely on, and how does this work alongside our natural tendencies? How can good works be "splendid sins" in the life of an adult, a teen, a child?

Pray today for those you know studying at seminary and new pastors entering the ministry; pray that they will not be discouraged by their own inadequacies but look to Christ. Pray for God to raise up Christ-centered young men for the ministry in your church.

15

Mingling Works with Grace

THOUGH FINNEY IS LONG DEAD, the perennial strategy of the Enemy to corrupt the gospel lives on. In recent decades the Enemy's strategy has shifted to blurring the distinction between faith and faithfulness. The difference two syllables can make in an English word has never been more damning.

Justification by faith alone keeps the justified sinner's eyes on the One who justifies: Jesus Christ. Justification by faithfulness, however, shifts the source of justification back to the individual. However one slices it, faithfulness is simply another way of saying obedience, and justification by obedience is simply another way of saying justification by my efforts, my performance, my works. Substitute even a tiny bit of faithfulness for faith alone in justification, and we have another gospel.

Though we're quick to say, surely no one in our circles, our churches, our seminaries would do this, a leading theologian while teaching at a conservative seminary said precisely this. "We must not set faith and faithfulness over against each other as antithetical and mutually exclusive principles of gospel and law when it comes to the justification of a sinner before almighty God."[1] This man and all whom he influenced for

1. Norman Shepherd, cited in P. Andrew Sandlin, ed., *A Faith that Is Never Alone: A Response to Westminster Seminary in California* (La Grange, CA: Kerygma Press, 2007), 72.

decades may affirm orthodoxy until they burst their clerical collars; nevertheless, when a preacher makes faithfulness a principle of the gospel in justification, he is preaching another gospel—a fatally corrupted one.

After tracing the unfaithfulness of Peter, including his betrayal, my pastor said, "It's not salvation by faithfulness. It's not spiritual Darwinianism, a survival of the fittest."[2] And it's not just Peter; the profound unfaithfulness of every hero in the Bible proves this. Yet the Enemy persists in helping us think that salvation is only for those who are fit enough to pull off sufficient faithfulness. He seems to favor shrouding this error in eloquence, but he'll do anything to make us believe that the opposite of the gospel is the gospel.

Though a justification by faithfulness stands in defiance of the biblical doctrine of grace and salvation rediscovered in the Protestant Reformation and agreed on by every credible theologian produced by that great movement, it is ironically within the very ranks of reformational preaching and teaching today where the attacks against those doctrines are being mounted. The Enemy must find ironic twists more entertaining. Be sure of this, if churches birthed in the Reformation, many of whose champions died at the stake for the pure doctrine of the gospel, if these churches can corrupt the doctrine of grace, the attack can happen in any of our churches.

Obedience and Rewards

Vigilance against corruptions of the gospel would be so much easier if we could simply tar a denomination, or seminary, or individual minister as the culprit. The Dutch church probably thought it was the Swiss, and the Americans probably thought it was the Scots. The Enemy wants us to think precisely this way: not in my church; my church is exempt.

2. David Scott in a sermon preached at Resurrection Presbyterian Church (PCA), Tacoma, WA, January 2013.

The Devil is all about corrupting the gospel, and he has no scruples. He will insinuate himself into any pulpit, any denomination, any seminary, and he works unstintingly to accomplish this in every generation. All who love the gospel will be on guard for him. The Enemy sometimes works alongside even ministers with the best of intentions; when he does, they may begin insisting that the only faithful reading of a passage from the Bible

> is that reading which leads you to stop doing what you know is displeasing to the Lord. It is that reading that compels you to begin to live your life in new ways because you know that faith, true faith in God requires it. It is that reading that leads you to want to know all of the commandments of your God and the regulations of his word that makes you determined then to obey them all and confident that in obeying them you will have your reward both now and forever. That and that only is a faithful reading of the book of Numbers.

We wonder how any preacher who cares about the purity of the gospel message would ever say any portion of the Bible leads to these conclusions. Surely this is a straw-man caricature of real preaching; no minister who claims to be biblical and orthodox would say this. But this is precisely the all-encompassing summation one minister, zealous for holiness, wanted his flock to hear.

The Enemy, however, is never satisfied when only one minister says these kinds of things. He wants an elite cadre of faith-and-faithfulness preachers within conservative Christianity teaching that the faithful may be "confident that in obeying [all of the commandments of your God] you will have your reward both now and forever."

Even Charles Wesley doesn't put it this way. When Wesley declared in his hymn, "With confidence I now draw nigh,"[3] the

3. Charles Wesley, "Arise, My Soul, Arise," *Trinity Hymnal* (Atlanta: Great Commission, 1990), 305.

bedrock of his confidence was based not on how well he had obeyed the law, but on the five bleeding wounds of Christ his Surety who had reconciled him to his Abba Father. This was Wesley's confidence both now and forever.

How different from a wrong-headed sermon that sends us for confidence in our reward to our obedience. When we hear a message that does this, it acts as a catalyst; there's no other option. It jolts us into the futile process of inspecting the quality and quantity of our obedience. Am I measuring up? Am I holy enough? Have I obeyed enough? Hurled back on the treadmill of inspecting our own performance, we inevitably stop looking with confidence to Christ's performance for us.

How drastically different will a faith-and-faithfulness preacher's words sound from those of Clowney, Bridges, and Sibbes—how different from the preaching of everyone, dead or alive, faithful to the gospel through the centuries. "Only where our piety forgets about ourselves," said Sinclair Ferguson, "and focuses on Jesus Christ will our piety be nourished by the ongoing resources the Spirit brings to us from the source of all true piety, our Lord Jesus Christ."[4]

Tragically an increasing number of Christians are hearing preaching so unlike what Christ and his apostles modeled for us. When hearers are compelled to look to their obedience to all God's commandments and by their faithfulness to keep all of them, thereby to secure for themselves the favor and reward of God, they will have little time to look to the finished work of the Savior. In this kind of preaching, Christ will inevitably be muted.

What Faith Requires

It's chilling when the closest faith-*and*-works preaching gets to referencing true faith comes in the form of a coer-

---

4. Sinclair Ferguson, "Union with Christ" (sermon), confirmed in an e-mail conversation between Dr. Ferguson and the author, June 2012.

cive statement calling the congregation to obey the moral law "because you know that faith, true faith in God requires it." Eager for morally upright behavior among Christians—especially our children—we can easily get wooed into thinking this kind of teaching can't be all that bad; it might even help keep the kids in line.

This way of thinking, however, may betray our distrust of the gospel; we may be trying to improve on grace, adding in just a bit of additional obligation to faith. But if faith has any requirement added to it, then justification can no longer be by faith *alone*. Any requirement is antithetical to the absolute exclusivity of its being alone. After hearing a message like this, few things could be more certain: the sheep will think their final justification will be decided based on their faith *and* on how well they manage to fulfill what faith requires.

Confusion like this destroys gospel confidence and is wholly unnecessary. The classic Protestant statement on justification declares that God imputed the perfect righteousness of his Son to sinners, "requiring nothing of them for their justification but faith, which also is his gift, their justification is to them of free grace" (Westminster Larger Catechism 71).

The gospel rediscovered in the sixteenth century has always taught that true faith in God is contrary to works (Gal. 3:12), is the gift of God, and doesn't require anything. The best Christian hymnody has celebrated this truth:

> All the fitness he requireth
> is to feel your need of him.

All the fitness required in justification, even "this he gives you."[5]

"In the matter of justification," wrote Genevan Reformer Francis Turretin, "faith and works are opposed as opposites and

---

5. Joseph Hart, "Come, Ye Sinners, Poor and Wretched," from William Walker, *Baptist Harmony*, p. 249, *Christian Classics Ethereal Library*, accessed April 23, 2014, http://www .ccel.org/ccel/walker/harmony/files/hymn/Invitation.html.

contraries."[6] And when faithfulness is held out as a requirement of saving faith, a condition of saving reward, and as the source of our confidence in our salvation, however well intentioned, all that remains is a fatally flawed corruption of the gospel.

Never One without the Other

Just as the medieval church subsumed justification within sanctification, so that the latter became a condition of the former, so do men today who proclaim a conditional justification, one that is dependent on you "keeping all the commandments of your God." The flock will be confused and discouraged by this message.

However sincerely motivated, ministers refashioning the message will find themselves in a quandary. Suspicious of an unconditional justification, some ministers will feel the need to show the superiority of their new ideas, while at the same time they also feel the need to normalize the distortions they're teaching. Even as they criticize their own confessional standards, some will claim all the commentators agree with them or that they're in the mainstream of orthodoxy. The vigilant Berean will recognize the doublespeak and be on guard.

Constant vigilance requires us to test the teaching we hear about justification and sanctification. How does their message measure up with what the best gospel and Christ-centered pastors preach in the present and in the past? "Although we may distinguish [justification and sanctification]," wrote Calvin, "Christ contains both of them inseparably in himself. He bestows both of them at the same time, the one never without the other."[7] There's no room for wrenching sanctification from the grace of Christ and turning it into a contingency of jus-

6. Francis Turretin, *Institutes of Elenctic Theology*, ed. James T. Dennison Jr., trans. George Musgrave Giger, vol. 2 (Phillipsburg, NJ: P&R Publishing, 1994), 582.
7. John Calvin, *Institutes of the Christian Religion*, ed. John T. McNeil, trans. Ford Lewis Battles (Philadelphia: Westminster Press, 1960), 3.16.1.

tification. All the great preachers—Calvin, Clowney, Bridges, Sibbes, Ferguson, and many more—point us for both justification and sanctification to the all-sufficiency of Jesus.

This must be the test. Any preaching that does not point you to Jesus for your sanctification is pointing you away from the gospel. But Satan knows that "the safest road to hell is the gradual one—the gentle slope, soft underfoot, without sudden turnings, without milestones, without signposts."[8] It is the supreme objective of the Enemy to separate us from the all-sufficiency of Jesus. But he'll do so very gradually, a little here, a little there. He'll do it with "honest trifles," but we can be certain he will "betray [us] in deepest consequence."[9] We must beware.

Confessional Bulwark

Therefore, the more familiar the flock becomes with the confessional summaries of the gospel, the better equipped will we be to hear the gospel-corrupting deviations. Your gospel red flags will unfurl and snap passionately in the wind of doctrine that says you must obey all the commandments and regulations of the law and "confident that in obeying them you will have your reward both now and forever." This ought to unhorse us like a theological thunderclap.

Like the vanguard preachers before them, the godly pastors that assembled in Westminster Abbey in 1642 knew the gospel, and they knew how critical it was to the pure doctrine of the gospel to maintain that both justification and sanctification are entirely works of God's free grace, and the danger to the gospel when we make a mingle-mangle of the two. They posed the question, "Wherein do justification and sanctification differ?" and their answer makes imminently clear both the truth and the danger when we miss the truth:

8. C. S. Lewis, *The Screwtape Letters* (New York: Macmillan, 1982), 56.
9. William Shakespeare, *Macbeth*, I.iii.127–28.

> Although sanctification be inseparably joined with justification, yet they differ, in that God in justification imputeth the righteousness of Christ; in sanctification his Spirit infuseth grace, and enableth to the exercise thereof; in the former, sin is pardoned; in the other, it is subdued: the one doth equally free all believers from the revenging wrath of God, and that perfectly in this life, that they never fall into condemnation; the other is neither equal in all, nor in this life perfect in any, but growing up to perfection. (WLC 77)

Notice first how "inseparably joined" these wise, old Puritans want you to understand justification and sanctification to be, and notice how this agrees with what Calvin said, "[Christ] bestows both of them at the same time, the one never without the other."[10] In both it is God at work, Christ's righteousness imputed in justification, and the Spirit infusing grace and enabling holy obedience in sanctification. How different this sounds from obeying the law to gain favor and reward from God—how diametrically opposed it sounds.

Justification, as an act of God's free grace (WSC 33), frees us from the wrath of God perfectly in this life and without any fear of condemnation. While sanctification is never perfect in this life, we are, nevertheless, being brought along by the Spirit of grace toward the perfection we will finally enjoy in heaven. But what the Westminster divines want us to have clearly in our minds is that there is no conditionality in either justification or sanctification: "Christ contains both of them inseparably in himself."[11]

For Discussion

1. Discuss and compare Hebrews 10:14, "For by a single offering he has perfected for all time those who are being sanctified," with Westminster Larger Catechism 75:

10. John Calvin, *Institutes*, 3.16.1.
11. Ibid.

Sanctification is a work of God's grace, whereby they whom God has, before the foundation of the world, chosen to be holy, are in time, through the powerful operation of his Spirit applying the death and resurrection of Christ unto them, renewed in their whole man after the image of God; having the seeds of repentance unto life, and all other saving graces, put into their hearts, and those graces so stirred up, increased, and strengthened, as that they more and more die unto sin, and rise unto newness of life.

2. Discuss from this chapter how the distinct yet inseparable nature of justification and sanctification keeps us from soul-killing gospel error.
3. What are ways we betray our lack of trust in the power of the gospel? How is trusting in the gospel different from trusting the quality and quantity of our obedience?

Pray for your pastor as he counsels members of your church and talks to others in your community; pray that the Spirit enables him to speak words that cause people to trust in God's saving grace alone.

16

Inseparability of Faith and Works

"IT IS JUST AS IMPOSSIBLE to separate faith and works," wrote Martin Luther, "as it is to separate heat and light from fire!" He called all those who don't believe and teach this "the greatest of fools"![1] The instant we begin to separate them, we inevitably make works a requirement, a condition, of faith. Hence, Satan's strategy is by all means to get us to separate faith and works—and to preen ourselves for the wisdom of our new discovery—but he never wants us to realize that we've become the greatest of fools.

In his commentary on Paul's reference to "faith working through love" (Gal. 5:6), Puritan Matthew Poole speaks with equal clarity:

> There is but one way of justification, one of salvation, for them both; and that is, by believing in Christ Jesus; which faith is not an idle, inactive, inoperative faith, but such a faith as worketh by love, both towards God and towards man, in an obedience to all the commandments of God: yet is not the

1. Martin Luther, "An Introduction to St. Paul's Letter to the Romans," in *Luther's German Bible of 1522*, trans. Robert E. Smith (Erlangen, Germany: Heyder and Zimmer, 1854), 125, accessed May 1, 2014, http://www.iclnet.org/pub/resources /text/wittenberg/luther/luther-faith.txt.

soul justified, nor shall it stand righteous before God, in and for this obedience, which neither is faith, nor goeth before it, but followeth it, as the true, proper, and necessary effect of it.[2]

Poole takes pains to make absolutely certain that no one thinks their obedience has anything to do with gaining God's favor or rewards.

While errant preaching in every generation will point us to our obedience as the condition of God's reward and eternal blessing, Poole labors to make the opposite clear: obedience follows justifying faith and is "the true, proper, and necessary effect of [faith]." All the requirements and conditions of salvation, wrote the wise, old Puritan, are fulfilled in the completeness of Jesus' saving work on our behalf.

Getting this wrong is a great tragedy, but the Enemy enjoys tragedy and wants to see it acted out on the stage of once-gospel-centered churches in every generation—no doubt as it was in Amsterdam, Geneva, Edinburgh, and Northampton in former days.

No place or time or church should think itself exempt. "To hear some men preach today," said Bryan Chapell, "one would think that sanctification was a condition of justification."[3] Since this error plays out in every generation, "we must," as Calvin has it, "exercise the utmost caution lest we allow any counterfeit to be substituted for the pure doctrine of the gospel."[4]

Gospel Sanctification

"You can't confuse what the gospel produces," said Voddie Baucham, "with what the gospel requires. Obedience is what

2. Matthew Poole, "Commentary on Galatians 5," *Matthew Poole's English Annotations on the Holy Bible*. 1685, *StudyLight*, accessed January 14, 2014, http://www.studylight.org/com/mpc/view.cgi?bk=47&ch=5.

3. Bryan Chapell, "Union with Christ" (sermon, Faith Presbyterian Church, Tacoma, WA, April 24, 2011).

4. John Calvin, *Commentary on Galatians*, trans. and ed. John Owen (Grand Rapids: Eerdmans, 1974), 97.

the gospel produces, not what the gospel requires."[5] The pure doctrine of the gospel will always produce a growing holiness, a joyful and heartfelt obedience. But the gospel is neutered when faithfulness is conjoined with faith and made a requirement of the gospel. When we do this, we supplant the good news with crushingly bad news.

"The gospel has to be the foundation and motivation for the pursuit of holiness," said Jerry Bridges. "Believers need the gospel to remind them that our standing with God is not based on our own obedience but on the perfect, imputed righteousness of Christ. Otherwise, the pursuit of holiness can be performance driven: that is, 'If I'm good, God will bless me.'" Bridges argues that the only way to correct this performance-driven error is for Christians "to embrace the gospel every day." We "seek to pursue holiness out of gratitude for what God has done for us in Christ." He concludes that the more we see the magnitude of the forgiveness of sins that we have in Christ, the more our "'ought to' mentality [will be] replaced with a 'want to' attitude."[6]

Grace-Enabled Holiness

We often hear that in the first part of Paul's epistles he gives us the doctrinal indicatives and in the second part he gives us the practical imperatives. This distinction is helpful only insofar as we do what Paul actually does in his epistles: keep the imperatives rooted in their doctrinal indicatives. Notice, for example, how he concludes his first letter to the Thessalonians:

> Now may the God of peace himself sanctify you completely, and may your whole spirit and soul and body be kept blameless

5. Voddie Baucham, sermon on gospel nurture of children from Deuteronomy 6:7, (sermon, Teach Them Diligently Conference, Spartanburg, SC, March 15–17, 2012).
6. "The Pursuit of Holiness: An Interview with Jerry Bridges" *Tabletalk*, January 2012, 78.

at the coming of our Lord Jesus Christ. He who calls you is faithful; he will surely do it. (5:23–24)

Hearing some preachers, we can walk away with the impression that Paul concluded the practical imperatives of his letter with the words, "You must surely do it." But he does not say that. Paul declares that "[Christ] will surely do it." We might expect Paul to point them to doing good works and to confidence in their obedience and confidence in their faithfulness. But he does the opposite: "He who calls you is faithful; he will surely do it." Though the transforming grace of the gospel makes totally depraved sinners into new creations in Christ, Paul points once-pagan Greeks away from their vacillating and partial faithfulness to the perfect faithfulness of Christ.

Consider further how Paul addresses the pagan, fornicating Corinthians. He tells them that Jesus Christ "will sustain you to the end, guiltless in the day of our Lord Jesus Christ" (1 Cor. 1:8). "Guiltless"? What an astonishing thing to say to loose-living Corinthians! We're inclined to think that Paul is being indiscreet—again. But it's Paul who is getting the gospel right. He understands that both justification and sanctification are rooted in the imputed righteousness of our substitute, Jesus Christ—the first a one-time act, the second an ongoing work, but both of God's free grace.

"The apostle does not say that [Christ] was sent to help us attain righteousness," wrote Calvin, "but himself to be our righteousness."[7] It's not as if Christ's work is to assist us in becoming righteous, that his redemptive work was merely a starting nudge and we must step up and complete the process with our obedience, with our performance, our efforts. Christ is himself our righteousness. That's justification. And Christ by his Spirit is our sanctification as well. Christ will sustain us guiltless to the end.

7. John Calvin, *Institutes of the Christian Religion*, ed. John T. McNeil, trans. Ford Lewis Battles (Philadelphia: Westminster Press, 1960), 3.15.5.

Christ is the One who will surely do it, who will himself complete our sanctification, as promised—no conditions, no recalls.

The Reformers, the Puritans, the best men preaching the gospel today all agree on this: justification and sanctification both have their source and cause solely in the free, unmerited mercy of God, his decree, his power and purpose, through the merit and mediation of Christ alone.

"The gospel speaks of Christ and his benefits," wrote Puritan William Perkins, "and of faith being fruitful in good works."[8] And therein lies all the difference. We ought never to approach encouragement to holiness by holding up the fruit of holiness; we encourage righteous living by placarding the root of holiness, by holding high the source, cause, and object, Jesus Christ the Righteous One. Grace is the cause, the source, the catalyst to all true obedience, obedience enabled by grace, motivated by love and gratitude, and flowing from transformed hearts, so dazzled by Christ and his gospel they will and must—and are enabled—to obey. Get this out of order even slightly and we do violence to the gospel. Grace alone produces saving faith, faith that overflows in good works, which is "faith working through love" (Gal. 5:6).

> I find, I walk, I love; but, oh, the whole
> Of love is but my answer, Lord, to thee!
> For thou wert long beforehand with my soul;
> Always, thou lovedst me.[9]

The hymn writer understands that love must motivate his walking, love must and will be the engine that drives the sanctified life. He understands what we so easily forget, "love is but my answer, Lord, to thee!"

8. William Perkins, *The Art of Prophesying* (1592; repr. Edinburgh: Banner of Truth Trust, 1996), 54–55.
9. "I Sought the Lord, and Afterward I Knew," *Trinity Hymnal* (Atlanta: Great Commission, 1990), 466.

For Discussion

1. Read Jesus' words in John 15:4–5 and discuss the connection between union with Christ and bearing fruit.

   As the branch cannot bear fruit by itself, unless it abides in the vine, neither can you, unless you abide in me. I am the vine; you are the branches. Whoever abides in me and I in him, he it is that bears much fruit, for apart from me you can do nothing.

2. Read Westminster Larger Catechism 55 and discuss how Christ's intercession for us enables us to abide in the vine.

   Christ makes intercession, by his appearing in our nature continually before the Father in heaven, in the merit of his obedience and sacrifice on earth, declaring his will to have it applied to all believers; answering all accusations against them, and procuring for them quiet of conscience, notwithstanding daily failings, access with boldness to the throne of grace, and acceptance of their persons and services.

3. What are ways we distort the gospel by turning what the gospel produces into a condition the gospel requires?

4. What happens when we attempt to motivate ourselves and others to holy living by holding up the fruit of holiness instead of pursuing the Holy One?

Pray today for your elders as they assist your pastor in shepherding; pray that as they meet with families and speak to individuals, they will encourage members to take comfort in the power of abiding in Christ the Vine and his ongoing intercession for them.

17

Holiness by Grace Alone

TROTSKY WAS RIGHT: war is definitely interested in us. But it would be so much easier if it was a medieval pitched battle: knights and horses lined up in tidy rows, in broad daylight, banners unfurled, heraldic allegiances clearly displayed, no espionage, no counterintelligence. That is most definitely not this kind of engagement. The war on the pure doctrine of the gospel is guerrilla warfare, devoid of scruples, engaged behind the lines. The generation that fails to ready its children to wage that war, to contend earnestly against covert black ops attacks on the gospel, must ready itself for the gospel counterfeits that will be the inevitable result.

Paul, who knew about this warfare, warns first-century Christians to guard against attacks that happen from within the church, "that no one may delude you with plausible arguments" (Col. 2:4). Now as then, the Enemy deludes the visible church with recurring plausible-sounding arguments to sabotage the gospel.

When we become a casualty of this stealth attack, though we will continue the obligatory gospel affirmations, listeners in the pew will think that their salvation is based at least in part on some conditionality in them. Before long, this error morphs the gospel into yet another self-salvation enterprise, another enslaving spin on bad-news religion.

The Enemy's Strategy

As he did in Amsterdam and Geneva, the Enemy's strategy seems to be to recruit intellectual and theological innovators as his advance guard in this war. Winning them with the "honest trifle" that the confessions were written by mere men and are not inspired, he encourages them to level their guns at the church's historic confessions of faith. Pretty soon his intellectual recruits sound very much like Charles Finney, who ranked the Westminster Confession on a par with the modern equivalent of a steamy romance novel.

How do we ready ourselves and the next generation to defend against such an attack and the recurring confusion about faith and faithfulness in sanctification? It begins by resisting the temptation to become critics of the collective theological wisdom of the past. Instead, we need to rediscover the wealth of biblical clarity that lies in those confessions:

> Faith justifies a sinner in the sight of God, not because of those other graces which do always accompany it, or of good works that are the fruits of it, nor as if the grace of faith, or any act thereof, were imputed to him for his justification; but only as it is an instrument by which he receiveth and applieth Christ and his righteousness. (WLC 73)

Why would it be so important to the Westminster divines to speak of faith justifying sinners by using the qualifying language "not because of those other graces which do always accompany it, or of good works that are the fruits of it"? They understood the bombardment to the gospel that results when the fruit of faith is infused into faith itself. Hence, the crafters of the best confessions of faith anticipated the Enemy's strategy and the mortal wound it would inflict on the message of the gospel, so they chose their words with the greatest of care.

150

God "giveth his Holy Spirit to all his elect, to work in them that faith, with all other saving graces; and to enable them unto all holy obedience, as the evidence of the truth of their faith and thankfulness to God" (WLC 32). Nothing could be clearer: God gives his Holy Spirit to work faith in the elect and thereby to enable them to holy obedience. But when our obedience back-washes into God's work alone in our salvation, we add a rival to the gracious work of the Spirit in the elect. Such a not-so-good news will always turn us from the completeness of Christ's work back to the soul-killing futility of taking a dipstick to our holiness: am I on full, a quart low, or worse than that?

A Holy Life

We're not left to our own devices to hold off the slings and arrows of the Enemy's attacks. The old adage, "What goes around, comes around," applies in spades to attacks on biblical theology. We'll see faithfulness-creep before it gets its fangs into our generation far more readily if we feed on the teaching of the best preachers and theologians throughout church history. "God neither chose them nor called them because they were holy," wrote C. H. Spurgeon,

> but he called them that they might be holy, and holiness is the beauty produced by His workmanship in them. The excellencies which we see in a believer are as much the work of God as the atonement itself. . . . Salvation must be of grace, because the Lord is the author of it: and what motive but grace could move him to save the guilty? Salvation must be of grace, because the Lord works in such a manner that our righteousness is forever excluded. Such is the believer's privilege—*a present salvation*; such is the evidence that he is called to it—*a holy life*.[1]

1. Charles Haddon Spurgeon, "Evening, June 12," *Morning and Evening: Daily Readings, Christian Classics Ethereal Library*, accessed January 14, 2014, http://www.ccel.org/ccel/spurgeon/morneve.html.

Excluding any of our righteousness, Spurgeon relentlessly drives us back to the grace of God in Christ alone. Where does the holy life come from? "Holiness is the beauty produced by His workmanship in them."

Where did Spurgeon get this? Paul declares that the Father has "blessed us in Christ with every spiritual blessing in the heavenly places, even as he chose us in him before the foundation of the world, that we should be holy and blameless before him" (Eph. 1:3–4).

We will never be more justified, more "holy and blameless" before God, than we are in Christ right now. Though our sanctification is a process, a growing in holiness, in glory we will be completely sanctified, at last made experientially "holy and blameless" as we were chosen by God one day to be. But in the present we stand "holy and blameless" in the perfect righteousness of Jesus alone.

"The Christian is perfectly saved *in God's purpose*," wrote Spurgeon; "God has ordained him unto salvation, and that purpose is complete."[2] Knowing this, when we hear preaching that motivates us to pursue holiness and sanctification and obedience as a way of winning or keeping the favor and blessing of God—we put our fingers in our ears and flee to the cross.

When we are directed to look to anything in us for confidence in God's favor, we are hearing a different gospel, a message that says: "It wasn't completely finished." Or "There may very well be condemnation for those who are in Christ Jesus." Or "Work out your salvation with fear and trembling, because if you don't you may forfeit justification." Or "We aren't actually his workmanship created in Christ Jesus for good works; we need to do good works to become his workmanship and keep the favor of God." What a horrendously bad-news gospel this would be! But the Enemy is ever so discreet. He'll never make it this obvious.

2. Ibid.

Tearing Jesus in Pieces

After telling us we are saved by grace through faith, faith which is a gift of God, Paul sums up sanctification to the Ephesians this way, "For we are his workmanship, created in Christ Jesus for good works, which God prepared beforehand, that we should walk in them" (Eph. 2:10). How different Paul sounds from preaching that tears Christ from his saving benefits and attempts to give us confidence because we have kept "all the commandments of our God."

Calvin, as if facing similar faithfulness-creep in his day, wrote, "Just as one cannot tear Jesus Christ into pieces, so also these two [justification and sanctification] are inseparable since we receive them together and conjointly in him."[3] Satan lacks imagination; he recycles the same errors generation after generation, and he does so because they work so well. He knows our proclivities. And he also knows how much better his strategy works if he can convince us that we're better theologians than those ancient roughs wearing the funky robes and headgear. His scheme works still better when he gets us preening ourselves at the cleverness of our latest theological ideas, when he gets us to stop taking the theological wisdom of the past seriously.

Satan is the great divider, and he knows how easily we default to disconnecting Christ from his saving and from his sanctifying benefits. It just takes a nudge here, an insinuation there. Knowing how vulnerable we are to the Enemy's scheme, Sinclair Ferguson offers a guiding principle for all preachers of the gospel: "We must never separate the benefits (regeneration, justification, sanctification) from the Benefactor (Jesus Christ)."[4] We need to hear this over and over again,

3. John Calvin, *Institutes of the Christian Religion* , ed. John T. McNeil, trans. Ford Lewis Battles (Philadelphia: Westminster Press, 1960), 3.11.6.
4. Sinclair Ferguson, "Union with Christ" (sermon), confirmed in an e-mail conversation between Dr. Ferguson and the author, June 2012.

because we persist in falling prey to the Enemy's strategy and, hence, passing on to the next generation a gospel subverted by faithfulness-creep.

Insubvertible Security

I have listened to a number of young people over the years tell me of their fears that they may have forfeited grace by their sins, that they may have had justification by walking down an aisle and praying the sinner's prayer, but they wonder if it was real. Some have been taught that in their infant baptism they have had election, union with Christ, regeneration, adoption, forgiveness of sins—everything, but that by their lack of faith *and* faithfulness they may no longer have these.

One works-centered preacher told his congregation that the unforgiving servant experienced genuine saving forgiveness of his debt, but "failed to live up to the grace shown to him, and so the privilege of that forgiveness was revoked." And another such minister insists that loyalty to what the Bible says about "justification and the other saving benefits of Christ's redemption," makes it obvious that "forgiveness may be temporary, even the love of God temporary."

The best preachers and theologians have always understood how destructive preaching temporary forgiveness is to the gospel. If you could have it but it could be revoked, "we would always be in doubt, tossed back and forth without any certainty," as martyr Guido de Bres put it in the Belgic Confession, "and our poor consciences would be continually vexed if they relied not on the merits of the suffering and death of our Savior" (article 24).

Goaded on by the Enemy, there is a persistent error that reasserts itself, and it seems to do so without discriminating between denominations or theological systems. Call it what you will, the error tells people that they can forfeit salvation. They can have it, but unless they try harder, unless they work more faithfully, unless they obey all God's commandments, they will lose their reward. This kind of teaching will start subtly; it will sound like such a plausible argument, and it may never be clearly owned and stated, but the effect on the flock and on the purity of the gospel will be no less devastating. The tragedy of this new message is that it necessarily turns people back on their performance and away from what God has fully accomplished in his Son, the Lord Jesus, for our salvation. It fixes our eyes on ourselves and our efforts to live up to grace, and away from resting in "the merits of the suffering and death of our Savior."

I tossed and turned and sweated on my pillow as a youth, fretting over whether I was really converted. Had I been sincere enough when I professed faith in Christ? Had I sinned too much since my conversion to have any real hope of salvation? Some theological systems intentionally set about to keep people in a sweat of uncertainty; I suppose, thereby, to motivate greater white-knuckle resolve to work harder.

How does anyone irrefutably know if his soul is secure for eternity? Is it possible to say with the certainty of the apostle Paul, "I am sure" (Phil. 1:6) about my salvation? If we are directed to look at our obedience or faithfulness for confidence and security, our poor consciences would, indeed, be in torment. Despair, not security, is all we could hope for.

But Calvin argues that in the pure doctrine of the gospel insubvertible security is available to the Christian. Listen to his thrilling doxological summary of the biblical foundation of the Christian's security:

> Hence, therefore, arises the impregnable and insubvertible security of the saints. The Father, Who gave us to the Son as His peculiar treasure, is stronger than all who oppose us; and He will not suffer us to be plucked out of His hand. What a cause for humility then in the saints of God when they see such a difference of condition made in those who are, by

nature, all alike! Wherever the sons of God turn their eyes, they behold such wonderful instances of blindness, ignorance and insensibility, as fill them with horror; while they, in the midst of such darkness, have received divine illumination, and know it, and feel it, to be so.[5]

Contrary to our default setting, Calvin directs us to look away from ourselves for security. We don't look to our sanctification, our holiness, to gain confidence in our salvation. Doing so leads only to torment and doubt. But when we look to the eternal purposes of God himself, who gave us as the "peculiar treasure" to his Son, Jesus, from whose pierced hand no one can pluck us, we can say with Paul, "I am sure of this, that he who began a good work in [me] will bring it to completion at the day of Jesus Christ" (Phil. 1:6).

We are told that not only can we know with "impregnable and insubvertible" certainty, we can also feel it to be so. But this feeling is not unfounded and insubstantial. We can be assured of salvation and feel that assurance aright only as we keep our eyes off ourselves and our performance and fix our gaze on Jesus, the Author and Perfecter of true saving and sanctifying faith.

His Faithfulness, Not Ours

Today, as in ancient Israel's day, the problem for sinners is intractable. "There is no faithfulness or steadfast love, and no knowledge of God in the land" (Hos. 4:1). If any component of our salvation depended in the tiniest degree on our faithfulness, none of us would have any ground for security. But when our salvation depends entirely on the faithfulness of God to accomplish by his steadfast love and mercy all that he has promised in our justification and in our sanctification, we find rest. "I will betroth you to me forever. I will betroth you

5. John Calvin, cited in David Otis Fuller, ed., *A Treasury of Evangelical Writings* (Grand Rapids: Kregel, 1961), 181.

to me in righteousness and in justice, in steadfast love and in mercy. I will betroth you to me in faithfulness. And you shall know the LORD" (Hos. 2:19–20). The gospel according to Hosea could not be more certain.

Hence, the apostle Paul could pose the rhetorical question, "Who shall separate us from the love of Christ?" (Rom. 8:35). Children's author Sally Lloyd-Jones gives Paul's own answer in her paraphrase: "Nothing can ever, no, not ever! separate us from the Never Stopping, Never Giving Up, Unbreaking, Always and Forever Love of God he showed us in Jesus!"[6] Where did she come up with this logorrhea of modifiers? From the Bible alone.

Indelible Grace

Hymn writer Augustus Toplady—like Sally Lloyd-Jones, like Calvin, like everyone who has ever understood the scandalous grace of God in the gospel—understood that no one justified by God could ever forfeit the grace of God secured for all time by the Son of God.

> A debtor to mercy alone,
> Of covenant mercy I sing;
> Nor fear, with Thy righteousness on,
> My person and off'ring to bring.
> The terrors of law and of God
> With me can have nothing to do;
> My Savior's obedience and blood
> Hide all my transgressions from view.
>
> The work which His goodness began,
> The arm of His strength will complete;
> His promise is Yea and Amen,
> And never was forfeited yet.

6. Sally Lloyd-Jones, *The Jesus Storybook Bible: Every Story Whispers His Name* (Grand Rapids: Zondervan, 2007), 340.

Things future, nor things that are now,
Nor all things below or above,
Can make Him His purpose forgo,
Or sever my soul from His love.

My name from the palms of His hands
Eternity will not erase;
Impressed on His heart it remains,
In marks of indelible grace.
Yes, I to the end shall endure,
As sure as the earnest is giv'n;
More happy, but not more secure,
The glorified spirits in heav'n.[7]

Toplady sounds like ancient apostle turned English poet. "The work which His goodness began, the arm of His strength will complete." The hymn writer then looks unafraid at all the forces of the universe that are impotent to sever his soul from the saving love of God in Christ Jesus his righteousness.

If our justification is contingent, however, on the faithfulness of our sanctification, Toplady's poetry wouldn't sound anything like it does. If we could have all the saving benefits of the gospel by our identity with the visible church and then forfeit these by our lack of faithfulness, or if we could have the saving love of God and the forgiveness of our sins but only temporarily, as the Enemy wants us to believe, then Toplady's words would be a mockingly cruel ditty. Toplady was writing about a grace that actually does work; it does do in us what God says it will do, and that means the Christian can say confidently with Toplady, "I to the end shall endure."

We may be certain that any teaching that shifts us away from the promise and purpose of God applying his "indelible grace" to our souls for all eternity is another subversion of the

---

7. Augustus Toplady, *Diary and Selection of Hymns* (Leicester, England: Gospel Standard Baptist Trust, 1969), 177–78.

gospel. We can be equally assured that it will turn our church into another casualty of the Enemy.

For Discussion

1. Discuss Romans 6:4 and how we stand holy and blameless now, even though our sanctification is an ongoing process.

   We were buried therefore with him by baptism into death, in order that, just as Christ was raised from the dead by the glory of the Father, we too might walk in newness of life.

2. How does Heidelberg Catechism 43 help us understand Christ's power working in us and prevent us from separating the benefits from the Benefactor?

   Q. What further benefit do we receive from the sacrifice and death of Christ on the cross?

   A. That by virtue thereof, our old man is crucified, dead and buried with him; that so the corrupt inclinations of the flesh may no more reign in us; but that we may offer ourselves unto him a sacrifice of thanksgiving.

3. Define "indelible grace." Why should this kind of grace daily thrill our soul afresh?

Pray for the administration and leadership in seminaries; pray that as they provide for the training of new ministers, they will resist the temptation to be critics of the collective theological wisdom of the past and seek to rediscover the wealth of biblical clarity that exists from our forebears in the faith.

PART 5

How to Interpret the Bible:
And Ways We Misinterpret It

18

What the Bible Is All About

DAVID MATHIS, one-time executive pastoral assistant to John Piper, describes an experience he had listening to a tenured professor with a designer PhD, teaching at a conservative, Bible-believing seminary. As he listened to the professor's concentration on the old covenant, Mathis says he began to realize that the man was "subtly muting the uniqueness and centrality of the new covenant." The learned professor admitted that "Jesus has a role to play," but "it's all about kingdom and covenant." Mathis expressed his gratitude that at least the man was explicit about it. "It would have been more dangerous if the Jesus-minimizing effect of his system stayed implicit, left unnamed to ever so subtly influence the students to be centered on kingdom while diminishing the King, or be captivated by covenant while muting the Mediator."[1]

Grand Vision

I had a similar experience while writing this book. In a written dialogue with a young teaching elder with an MDiv from one of those confessional seminaries, I began to wonder if he had sat under the same professor—but with a sadly different outcome than for Mathis. Taking umbrage

1. David Mathis, "Keep Both Eyes Peeled for Jesus," March 20, 2012, *Desiring God*, http://www.desiringgod.org/blog/posts/keep-both-eyes-peeled-for-jesus.

with many leading theologians' interpretation of Luke 24:27 ("And beginning with Moses and all the Prophets, [Jesus] interpreted to them in all the Scriptures the things concerning himself"), this young seminary graduate attempted to argue that Jesus' teaching in this verse "doesn't mean that Jesus taught them that everything in Scripture was about him." After making his point that only some parts of the Bible are about Jesus, and that it's kind of naïve to think it would all be about him, he proceeded to explain that he thinks the whole Bible is about the restoration of the Kingdom of God. "That means that without Jesus it doesn't work. But it also means that without you, it doesn't work. The kingdom needs both a king and subjects to be a kingdom." Sounding very much like the Jesus-minimizing of Mathis's seminary professor, he declared, "We need a more grand vision to be sustained, one that takes into account all of life and beyond."

I confess that his words knocked the gospel wind out of me. I was not conversing with a liberal, a man trained in the unbelieving, dime-a-dozen seminaries around the country and abroad. He was trained in one of our seminaries, preaching in one of our pulpits, a man who claims to be theologically confessional and conservative.

When I could breathe again, I managed to reply. " 'A more grand vision'? Explain to me how Jesus is somehow not the Alpha and Omega of that 'more grand vision' you describe. More grand than what? The gospel of Jesus Christ is absolutely about 'all of life and beyond.' "

Christ Preeminent

Jesus' words in Luke 24:27 are far from the only thing Scripture says about Jesus being the center of the Bible and of everything in it. Paul declares "that in everything [Christ] might be preeminent" (Col. 1:18). It is a mystery to me how the preeminence Paul says Christ is to have in everything does not, for some, extend to the pulpit, to hermeneutics (how we interpret the Bible), and to theology. When Paul wrote, "Whatever you do, in word or deed, do everything in the name of the Lord Jesus, giving thanks to God the Father through him" (Col. 3:17), surely the "everything" includes expounding the whole Bible, expository preaching of its sacred words. Paul is making an all-encompassing statement of the most stupendous vision, that all of life and beyond is about Jesus. It frankly baffles me that any true Christian would want to attempt a contrary argument here. Yet arguments that insist that the Bible is not all about Jesus are being delivered with great passion, alas, even from pulpits that claim to be confessional and Bible believing.

We ought to expect the Enemy to stir up—in every generation, within the ranks of conservative Christianity—an elite insurgency hell-bent on diminishing Christ. But a message that is no longer all about Jesus, in word and deed, regardless of how learned-sounding, is no longer the good news of what Jesus came and fully accomplished for us in the gospel.

I'm left to speculate on why some ministers would not want the Bible and their handling of it to be about Jesus. I fear that this is yet another expression of our suspicion of the good news. Deep down where it counts, we are afraid of too much grace, too much gospel, and, hence, too much Jesus. But think just how bland the gospel would be if it was merely about kingdom and covenant. What good is a kingdom without a King? What good is a new covenant without a Mediator of that new covenant? The Bible is no more kingdom and covenant centered than it is unleavened bread and circumcision centered. What the Bible is, is King and Mediator centered, and so must we be—in our homes, churches, schools, and in our seminaries. "A sermon without Christ as its beginning, middle, and end," said Spurgeon, called the Prince of Preachers, "is a mistake in conception and a crime in execution."[2]

We shouldn't be overly surprised that the Enemy levels his cannon at this kind of corruption. Deflect preachers away from Christ in the pulpit, and his job is so much easier. We must be on guard for those who will dismiss all the talk about Christ-centered preaching as a new thing, a fad. The Enemy wants us to hear that readers of their Bibles and preachers who look for Christ on every page of sacred Scripture have an axe to grind. He doesn't want us to know and believe that it's not an axe; it's a banner, and it's one that preachers who love the Savior will always be waving.

The Sum of the Whole Bible

Sophisticated detractors of the redemptive-historical method of interpreting the Bible will always claim that such an interpretive method is simplistic, out of touch with the latest scholarship, and lacking in vision. When the allure of those arguments has begun to draw me in, I've found that turning to the best preachers of the Bible, throughout the ages, dispels my doubts.

"Christ is the true subject-matter of Scripture," wrote J. I. Packer. "All was written to bear witness to him. 'He is the sum of the whole Bible, prophesied, typified, prefigured, exhibited, demonstrated, to be found in every leaf, almost in every line, the Scriptures being but as it were the swaddling bands of the child Jesus.'"[3] Packer is quoting from Thomas Adams (called the Shakespeare of the Puritans); both men are completely consistent with the hermeneutic of the great Reformers on whose shoulders they are standing.

2. C. H. Spurgeon, *The Metropolitan Tabernacle Pulpit: Sermons Preached and Revised by C. H. Spurgeon during the Year 1881*, The Metropolitan Tabernacle Pulpit, vol. 27 (London, England: Passmore & Alabaster, 1882), 598.

3. J. I. Packer, *A Quest for Godliness: The Puritan Vision of the Christian Life* (Wheaton: Crossway, 1990), 103.

"We ought to read *the Scriptures*," wrote John Calvin, "with the express design of finding Christ in them. Whoever shall turn aside from this object, though he may weary himself throughout his whole life in learning, will never attain the knowledge of the truth."[4] Calvin implies that men who don't read and preach the Word to see Jesus on every page are likely wearying themselves in learning; so enamored with sophisticated interpretations, they may be erecting idols out of their own scholarship. Be sure of it, any interpretation that obscures or diminishes Jesus, nudging him to the sidelines for a more grand vision, will always corrupt the gospel.

None but Jesus

People read the Bible for many different reasons. But the pure doctrine of the gospel will not endure in its purity when we read the Bible for moral advice, for advice on how to have better relationships, better marriages, better behaved kids; when we read it to verify our preconceived notions about what it says or means; when we use it to find a rationale for male headship or home church, or homeschooling, or Christian schooling, or public schooling, or political action; even when we use it as a club against competing worldviews. Clearly the Bible has instruction with implications that instruct us about many of these things, but that's not what we ought to go hunting for when we read it. We look for Christ in every phrase.

We read the Bible, all of it—law, history, wisdom literature, prophecy—with eagerness and expectancy to "see the Lord of the Word in the Word of the Lord," as Edmund Clowney put it.[5] In his introduction to his landmark work, *The Unfolding Mystery: Discovering Christ in the Old Testament*, Clowney described

---

4. John Calvin, *Commentary on John*, vol. 1, *Christian Classics Ethereal Library*, accessed January 16, 2014, http://www.ccel.org/ccel/calvin/calcom34.xi.viii.html.

5. Edmund Clowney, *The Unfolding Mystery*, 2nd ed. (Phillipsburg, NJ: P&R Publishing, 2013), 17.

the neglect of Christ-centered hermeneutic and preaching: "The Bible is the greatest storybook, not just because it is full of wonderful stories but because it tells one *great* story, the story of Jesus."[6] Nevertheless, we must ready ourselves for the critics who line up to disparage what they consider to be the naiveté and inadequacy of Christ-centered preaching.

Preach Christ Crucified

Perhaps one of the most valuable instructions that preacher and poet Augustus Toplady left for Christian ministers today is his record of a visit to Exeter and the succinct instruction he received from "that excellent Christian, Mr. Brewer, the old ambassador of Christ." The venerable minister recounted to young Toplady the charge he had given to another young minister in his installation service.

1. Preach Christ crucified, and dwell chiefly on the blessings resulting from his righteousness, atonement, and intercession.

2. Avoid all needless controversies in the pulpit; except it be when your subject necessarily requires it, or when the truths of God are likely to suffer by your silence.

3. When you ascend the pulpit, leave your learning behind you: endeavor to preach more to the hearts of your people than to their heads.

4. Do not affect too much oratory. Seek rather to profit than to be admired.[7]

Toplady, who hereafter preached Christ crucified, seems to have been much impressed and affected by this wise minister's

6. Ibid., 11.
7. Augustus Toplady, *Diary and Selection of Hymns* (Leicester, England: Gospel Standard Baptist Trust, 1969), 54.

advice, and embraced the admonition as his own. What would happen if every generation of new preachers heeded these four straightforward guidelines as Toplady did?

The apostle Paul knew the danger that lurks for preachers to impress their congregation with their learning and oratory. "For Christ did not send me to baptize but to preach the gospel, and not with words of eloquent wisdom, lest the cross of Christ be emptied of its power" (1 Cor. 1:17). And he knew that preacher-centered preaching always ends up in Christ-minimizing.

One fresh-out-of-seminary pastor, in his efforts to prove that the Bible isn't all about Jesus, used this red herring: "There's only four miles between Jerusalem and Emmaus. Do you really think that if the entire Old Testament is about Jesus he would have had time to show all that in only four miles?" By diverting the argument from theology to topography, he not only made Jesus' interpretive model sound ridiculous, he aligned himself with those who labor to minimize—rather than magnify—Jesus Christ.

We do well to ask ourselves how our way of interpreting the Bible would work as a hymn. "When I read my Bible, I want a more grand vision than Jesus," doesn't sing so well. Toplady's fellow hymn writer, Joseph Hart, beautifully captured why Christ must be preeminent in preaching all the Scriptures, why nothing must be allowed to intrude on Christ's preeminence:

> Lo! th'incarnate God, ascended,
> Pleads the merit of his blood;
> Venture on him, venture wholly,
> Let no other trust intrude:
> None but Jesus, none but Jesus, none but Jesus
> Can do helpless sinners good.[8]

8. Joseph Hart, "Come, Ye Sinners, Poor and Wretched," from William Walker, *Baptist Harmony*, p. 249, *Christian Classics Ethereal Library*, accessed April 23, 2014, http://www.ccel.org/ccel/walker/harmony/files/hymn/Invitation.html.

For Discussion

1. Read Colossians 1:13–14. Discuss ways we can encourage one another to have renewed wonder at the greatest story ever told, the story of King Jesus' redeeming love for his children.

   He has delivered us from the domain of darkness and transferred us to the kingdom of his beloved Son, in whom we have redemption, the forgiveness of sins.

2. Read Westminster Larger Catechism 45 and discuss why it matters that we believe and proclaim a King- and Mediator-centered gospel rather than a kingdom-and-covenant-centered message.

   Christ executes the office of a king, in calling out of the world a people to himself, and giving them officers, laws, and censures, by which he visibly governs them; in bestowing saving grace upon his elect, rewarding their obedience, and correcting them for their sins, preserving and supporting them under all their temptations and sufferings, restraining and overcoming all their enemies, and powerfully ordering all things for his own glory, and their good; and also in taking vengeance on the rest, who know not God, and obey not the gospel.

3. Discuss the effects of being afraid of too much grace, too much gospel, too much Jesus. Share examples of those you've heard who have no fear in this area.

Pray that your pastor will grow daily more enchanted by the one great story, and that God will continually reveal the magnificence of Jesus Christ to him.

19

Same Text, Different Message

VISITING DIFFERENT CHURCHES on summer vacation can be both a healthy rebuke and a rich blessing. When we encounter joyful reverence in worship and a Christ-centered ministry where we did not expect it, the monster of our pride is confronted; we're not the only ones who get it right after all. Getting out of our cave and enjoying fellowship with God's people in a different community, in a different denomination, can help correct our tendency to think that we are members of an exclusive club, that we alone rank as initiates.

My family and I had an uncanny experience while on a recent summer vacation. Two consecutive weeks we visited two different churches, many miles apart and neither from the same denomination. Two very different preachers (neither knew the other), with different gifts, different levels of public speaking skill—and here is the uncanny part—both preaching from the exact same text of Scripture!

Unbeknown to either preacher, that experience was a remarkable demonstration of how the Bible can be disastrously mishandled. These two men represented in flesh and blood the two kinds of preachers: one zealous for finding and elucidating what we must do; the other zealous for discovering and adoring Christ for what he has already done and continues to do in us by the free grace of the gospel.

Same Text, Opposite Sermon

Hearing those two sermons back-to-back cemented the problem in my mind. Consider with me briefly 2 Peter 1:1–11, the biblical text from which both preachers preached two very different sermons:

> Simeon Peter, a servant and apostle of Jesus Christ,
>
> To those who have obtained a faith of equal standing with ours by the righteousness of our God and Savior Jesus Christ:
>
> May grace and peace be multiplied to you in the knowledge of God and of Jesus our Lord.
>
> His divine power has granted to us all things that pertain to life and godliness, through the knowledge of him who called us to his own glory and excellence, by which he has granted to us his precious and very great promises, so that through them you may become partakers of the divine nature, having escaped from the corruption that is in the world because of sinful desire. For this very reason, make every effort ... (1:1–5)

An engaging speaker, the preacher of the first sermon on this text was witty, relational, a fellow who clearly wanted to connect with his flock.

What We Do

The first preacher read out the text and then spent two or three minutes hastily summarizing the opening four verses, as if Peter were just giving perfunctory, introductory chatter, "Hi, folks, how's it going?" sort of material. We heard nothing about Christ's righteousness (1:1) being the means of obtaining faith, nothing about grace being multiplied to us (1:2), or God's "divine power" granting to us "all things that pertain to life and godliness" (1:3), nothing about God "call[ing] us to his own glory and excellence" (1:3). And nothing about God granting us in Christ "his precious and very great promises, so that through them" we are being made holy like Christ and so we will escape the corruptions of sinful desire (1:4). It is no exaggeration to say that this misguided pastor spent virtually no time at all expounding the meaning of these magisterial proclamations.

Eager to get on to the word *effort* (1:5), he settled into the important part of his sermon, where Peter was saying what we must do. It was as if Peter had not grounded what followed in verses 5–11 in the phrase, "For this very reason" (1:5), thereby rooting everything that follows in the doctrinal indicatives that the preacher just skipped over.

The sermon that followed fell somewhere between the relational and therapeutic, often on the menu of the broad evangelical pulpit, and the covenant moralism gaining steam in some reformational pulpits. This well-intentioned preacher did what so many preachers do when they open their Bibles. They latch onto what they can urge their congregations to be up and doing. But he neglected the glorious foundation: what God has already done in Christ. It was tragic but, alas, all too common.

Godliness Grounded in Christ

One week later, many miles away, we listened as the second preacher invited us to turn to 2 Peter 1:1–11, the exact same text as the week before. I passed the word to my wife and children for us all to sit up and pay particular attention. Clearly God our Father in his kind providence wanted us to learn something particular from this passage of his Holy Word.

> Simeon Peter, a servant and apostle of Jesus Christ,
> To those who have obtained a faith of equal standing with ours by the righteousness of our God and Savior Jesus Christ:
> May grace and peace be multiplied to you in the knowledge of God and of Jesus our Lord. (1:1–2)

173

There was nothing perfunctory about what followed. To this preacher Peter's opening words were not to be skimmed over lightly. They were the foundation on which not only the next paragraphs were built, but also the remainder of the epistle. He took pains to root the coming imperatives in the gift of faith and the "righteousness of our God and Savior Jesus Christ" (1:1). He proceeded to unpack the riches of this phrase, just how glorious the righteousness of Jesus actually is, to thrill us with the wonder of imputed righteousness. And then he developed what Peter was getting at when he addressed his readers with those words, "May grace and peace be multiplied to you in the knowledge of God and of Jesus our Lord" (1:2). With wonder at saving mercy, he further rooted what followed in grace, given and overflowing in the saving knowledge of Christ secured and promised in the gospel.

By this time in the sermon we had heard the previous week, the minister all about works was elucidating what self-control looked like in marriage, in parenting, in the workplace, in politics, in cultural engagement. And then he really warmed to his address when he launched into the need to diligently "confirm [our] calling and election" (1:10), because it's all contingent on us fulfilling our part and doing all that Peter is warning us we'd better be up and doing—or else. Listeners to this kind of preaching are left bewildered: election must just be a broad-sweeping covenantal thing for the group, but as far as the individual is concerned, it's so uncertain that we'd better try harder or we may in the end forfeit the whole enchilada.

Meanwhile, in the second sermon, the one rooted in the imputed righteousness of Christ and the grace of the gospel, we were hearing that "his divine power has granted to us all things that pertain to life and godliness, through the knowledge of him who called us to his own glory and excellence, by which he has granted to us his precious and very great promises, so that through them you may become partakers of the divine nature" (1:3–4).

In other words, the pastor who cared about grace was actually expounding the text, taking Peter's inspired words seriously and thereby rooting sanctification in what the divine power of God has already accomplished in the gospel. As he rounded up on his conclusion, he pointed to the larger context of Peter's letter; the apostle would end the book as he began it, in an inclusio of grace, "Grow in the grace and knowledge of our Lord and Savior Jesus Christ. To him be the glory both now and to the day of eternity" (3:18).

Some are hasty to claim that preachers who care so much about grace will go light on holiness and sanctification. But a faithful preacher of grace knows that his flock will never be able to fulfill the imperative commands of the Bible without enabling grace. Precisely *because* he's so committed to the sanctification of his flock, he will never, never want his congregation to hear imperatives disconnected from their doctrinal foundation in the power of God by the grace of Christ in the gospel.

The best theologians and preachers always get this right. They are careful to be like the apostles, never diminishing the power of God and the grace of God when they preach holiness and sanctification. In a sermon, Sinclair Ferguson put it better and more succinctly than most:

> We must never separate the benefits (regeneration, justification, sanctification) from the Benefactor (Jesus Christ). The Christians who are most focused on their own spirituality may give the impression of being the most spiritual . . . but from the New Testament's point of view, those who have almost forgotten about their own spirituality because their focus is so exclusively on their union with Jesus Christ and what He has accomplished are those who are growing and exhibiting fruitfulness.[1]

1. Sinclair Ferguson, "Union with Christ" (sermon), confirmed in an e-mail conversation between Dr. Ferguson and the author, June 2012.

I am confident that the first preacher, the one who skipped over the Benefactor to get to the benefits, had the best of intentions. He probably wanted to see more holiness, more piety in his congregation, perhaps especially among the young people. And so he exhorted with zeal their need to grow in self-control, in virtue. But he skipped over the foundation; he failed to dazzle his congregation with Jesus the Benefactor, the source of self-control, virtue, and the rest. Ironically, inverting the priority never produces the desired result: godliness.

> Historically speaking, whenever the piety of a particular group is focused on our spirituality that piety will eventually exhaust itself on its own resources. Only where our piety forgets about ourselves and focuses on Jesus Christ will our piety be nourished by the ongoing resources the Spirit brings to us from the source of all true piety, our Lord Jesus Christ.[2]

That unexpected episode in our summer vacation demonstrates the two kinds of preachers: one hones in on what we must do (the benefits of grace), while the other grounds the benefits and motivates his congregation to godliness by placarding Jesus Christ the Benefactor.

Which one of these men is your pastor? Which one of these men do you resemble when counseling the wayward, when disciplining your children, when engaging culture, when nurturing loved ones in the Word of God? When confronting sin in your own heart?

For Discussion

1. Read 2 Corinthians 5:17–21 and discuss what happens when we are focused on our own spirituality. What is the antidote?

2. Ibid.

Therefore, if anyone is in Christ, he is a new creation. The old has passed away; behold, the new has come. All this is from God, who through Christ reconciled us to himself and gave us the ministry of reconciliation; that is, in Christ God was reconciling the world to himself, not counting their trespasses against them, and entrusting to us the message of reconciliation. . . . For our sake he made him to be sin who knew no sin, so that in him we might become the righteousness of God.

2. Read Heidelberg Catechism 34 and discuss what precautions and steps we can take to "root sanctification in what the divine power of God has already accomplished in the gospel."

Q. Wherefore callest thou him "our Lord"?

A. Because he hath redeemed us, both soul and body, from all our sins, not with silver or gold, but with his precious blood, and has delivered us from all the power of the devil; and thus has made us his own property.

3. Reread 2 Peter 1:1–5 and compare it with other salutations in other epistles. Discuss how these greetings are intended to be theological foundations for what follows.

Pray today for your pastor as he reads the Word; pray that seemingly insignificant introductions and greetings will take on richer significance in holding forth aspects of the gospel to his flock.

20

More Ways We Diminish Jesus

"PROVERBS IS NOT THE GOSPEL." So began a sermon series on the book of Proverbs, the preacher conveying this thesis with absolute certainty. Statements like this make me anxious. When someone says any portion of the Bible has nothing to do with the gospel, though he may not intend to, he's also just told us that Proverbs is not about Jesus Christ.

When I hear things like this from pulpits, I'm tempted to wonder if I am getting things wrong. When I hear that "God's covenant and the Law of Moses are the foundation upon which a life of wisdom is to be built," it seems to me that something significant is missing. Maybe I'm looking for the wrong thing, building on the wrong foundation. Maybe the foundation of Proverbs and the Wisdom Literature in the Bible isn't Jesus the Cornerstone and his good news. Maybe vast portions of the Bible have nothing to do with Jesus and the gospel after all, and I'm the one misinterpreting the text by superimposing the Savior onto the sacred pages.

My hermeneutical doubts, however, are swept away when I go back and listen to what centuries of Bible interpreters say Proverbs is about. "Jesus Christ is the Alpha and Omega of the Bible," wrote Charles Spurgeon. "He is the constant theme of its sacred pages; from first to last they testify of him." After describing the types and shadows of the law, he finds "the Redeemer abundantly foreshadowed. Prophets and kings, priests and preachers, all look one way—they all stand as the cherubs did over the ark, desiring to look within, and to read the mystery of God's great propitiation."[1]

How different this sounds from hearing that the old covenant and the law of Moses are Proverbs' foundations and that there's no gospel of Jesus in Proverbs. From first to last, Proverbs testifies of Jesus! Breathing in that air somehow refreshes me, gives me perspective, helps me—when I open Proverbs, or any other book of the Bible—to look with eager expectation in one single direction.

Certainly Proverbs is primarily concerned with showing us how God's world works. It is akin to the Renaissance painter attempting to portray things in the ideal. Read it as a book of imperatives and promises, however, and you will be profoundly disappointed. If you read it thinking that you can be righteous and wise as an act of your free will, by teeth-champing resolve, by self-discipline, or that you earn a reward by being wise enough to follow its advice, you have reverted to the soul-killing error of the self-righteous Pharisee. And you will utterly fail.

What Is Wisdom?

The key to understanding the Bible's wisdom literature and the Proverbs begins by rightly defining wisdom. Just what is wisdom?

Some tell us that wisdom is "the skill, the expertise in living a good, responsible, holy, faithful, successful, fruitful, happy life. . . . Mastery of one's circumstances, that is biblical wisdom." One thing I agree with about this definition: it does

---

1. Charles Haddon Spurgeon, "Evening, June 10," *Morning and Evening: Daily Readings, Christian Classics Ethereal Library*, accessed January 14, 2014, http://www.ccel.org/ccel/spurgeon/morneve.html. He is commenting on John 5:39, "They are they which testify of me" (KJV).

sound very much lacking in the gospel. Frankly, it sounds much closer to the way devotees of the prosperity gospel might define wisdom and distort the gospel.

Presbyterian Church in America (PCA) minister Paul Tripp says that wisdom is "not a book. . . . Wisdom is a Person."[2] Notice how diametrically opposite this is to saying there's no gospel in Proverbs and that its foundation is the law of Moses. Where does Dr. Tripp get the idea that Jesus himself is the wisdom everyone of us lacks? He gets it from an entirely different way of reading and understanding his Bible. Whereas men like the first preacher isolate Proverbs from its fulfillment in the new covenant—read it in the dark, as it were—Tripp and the best interpreters read Proverbs in light of its fulfillment in the new covenant, like all the great preachers for centuries before him. The first looks through the wrong end of the telescope, which makes Christ and his gospel veiled and miniscule—or altogether missing. The second interpretation turns the telescope around and understands Proverbs in the magnified splendor of its fulfillment in "the wisdom that comes down from above" (James 3:15); that is, Jesus. Hence, "wisdom is a Person," the person of Jesus the Christ. And if that's true, then Proverbs is going to have a great deal to say about our fallen condition and prepare us for our only hope in the gospel of Jesus.

Wherever I'm reading in my Bible, Proverbs or elsewhere, I don't want to miss seeing Jesus, so I've common-placed several key passages on the opening margins of Proverbs. Christ himself is the wisdom from God (1 Cor. 1:30). Wisdom comes down from above as God's gracious gift (James 3:15–17). The Word of God (Jesus, according to John 1:1) is "able to make you wise for salvation" (2 Tim. 3:15). "In [Christ] are hidden all

2. Paul Tripp, "Psalm 51: Wisdom Is a Person," *Paul Tripp Ministries* (blog), June 20, 2007, http://paultrippministries.blogspot.com/2007/06/psalm-51-wisdom-is-person.html.

the treasures of wisdom and knowledge" (Col. 2:3). The "Spirit of wisdom" is a gift of God's grace in the gospel (Eph. 1:17). Jesus himself is the "manifold wisdom of God" made known "according to the eternal purpose that he has realized in Christ Jesus our Lord" (Eph. 3:10–11).

I review these texts often as I read and reread the book of Proverbs. Why? Because when I fail to keep Christ and his gospel at the center of my reading, I inevitably place myself and my white-knuckle determination at the center, and that never works.

Wicked Declared Righteous

If we read Proverbs primarily to find out how to be "good, responsible, holy, faithful, successful, fruitful, happy," what are we going to miss? If we have decided that "Proverbs is not the gospel," that Proverbs is not about the gospel of Jesus, what are we going to miss? The key to a sound interpretation of everything it contains.

In his preface to his exposition of Proverbs, venerable Charles Bridges wrote, "But with all care to preserve a soundly disciplined interpretation, we must not forget that the Book of Proverbs is a part of the volume entitled, 'The word of Christ' (Colossians 3:16)."[3] Arguing that we should read Proverbs with Christ much and frequently before our minds, "the true Key that opens the Divine Treasure house," Bridges insists, "If we do not see the golden thread through all the Bible marking out Christ, we read the Scriptures without the Key."[4]

Using the Key, let's unlock just a few examples from Proverbs.

"Whoever says to the wicked, 'You are in the right,' will be cursed by peoples, abhorred by nations" (Prov. 24:24). Certainly there's wisdom here that applies to civil justice

3. Charles Bridges, *An Exposition of Proverbs* (New York/Pittsburgh: R. Carter, National Foundation for Christian Education, 1846), ix.
4. Ibid.

and how we enforce our laws. But there's far more. This is precisely what God the Father says about the wicked in the gospel: to sinners whom he loved while they were yet enemies, he says, "You are in the right." How can this be? There's only one answer: through the gospel. This is the key to understanding everything. God declares us in the right, righteous through the substitution of his Son dying in our place on the cross.

In the world's eyes this is scandalous. No wonder people cursed and continue to curse Jesus. No wonder Christ the righteous one, who gave himself, the just for the unjust, is abhorred by the nations. No wonder we find it so natural a thing to doubt and turn from such a counterintuitive message. "How can these things be?" we ask, and then cast about for something we must do, some skill we can acquire, some fitness, something in ourselves that makes us somehow worthy of this indescribable gift.

This is no small thing. We can't afford to miss this in our reading of Proverbs. We can't afford to miss the Savior who is the constant theme of the sacred pages of the Bible—including the pages of Proverbs.

Guided by the new covenant texts that tell me that Jesus is the wisdom that comes down from above (James 3:15–17), I read on, using the Key and looking for wisdom. And then I alight on this verse in Proverbs that is supposed to have no gospel in it. "He who justifies the wicked and he who condemns the righteous are both alike an abomination to the LORD" (Prov. 17:15). In our civil government, when we do this we have overturned and ignored justice, an all-too-frequent commentary on human history. But when Jesus "justifies the wicked," as he did once for all time on the cross, "justice smiles and asks no more,"[5] as John Newton has it.

5. John Newton, "Let Us Love and Sing and Wonder," *Trinity Hymnal* (Atlanta: Great Commission, 1990), 127.

Jesus came to seek and to save, to justify, that which was lost—the wicked. "I came not to call the righteous, but sinners" (Mark 2:17). Jesus came to condemn the "righteous" (that is, the self-righteous), those who thought they could be holy on their own hook, those who denied God's perfect holiness and thus denied their utter inability to measure up to his perfect standard. But he did come to justify sinners, the wicked, his enemies. And he did so by substitution, by taking my place, by becoming sin for me. And when Jesus did this, when he laid down his life to justify the wicked, he became an abomination to his holy Father. "My God, my God, why have you forsaken me?" cried Jesus while dying on the cross (Matt. 27:46; Mark 15:34). Why had his Father forsaken him? Because Jesus was justifying the wicked by taking their place, becoming sin for us, and sin is an abomination to the holiness of the Father.

Pharisees were great readers of the Old Testament, and we can assume they too refused to use the Key; they too found no gospel in Proverbs. A good test of whether a preacher is interpreting an Old Testament passage aright is to ask ourselves if his message would be offensive to the Pharisees. Would a Jewish rabbi be offended by sermons preached from the book of Proverbs if those sermons had nothing to do with the gospel of Jesus Christ? Not likely. True Christians must reject sermons from Proverbs that a rabbi would not reject.

Disconnecting Doctrine from Doing

The tragic result of refusing to see the gospel in Proverbs and of muting the doctrinal indicatives in the Epistles will always be to disconnect the benefit, growth in holiness, from the Benefactor, Jesus the Holy One.

For some ministers attempting to do expository preaching, this can be a serious problem. As they work phrase by phrase through the biblical text—week after week, month after month, in some cases, year after year—they can lose touch with the context and grow weary of the doctrinal foundation that all the apostles begin with in their epistles. To be sure, Peter and Paul and the rest give us lots of imperatives in their epistles, call us to do holy things, to do good works. But the apostles always, always, ground the imperatives, "Be holy, be righteous," in the indicatives of grace and the finished work of Christ in the gospel. Yet as the weeks of preaching go on, the context rooted in the enabling grace of God easily fades, gets forgotten, left far behind, and eventually lost altogether.

Some ministers want to persuade us that they are merely being faithful to the biblical text to preach the moral imperatives that are in a particular paragraph of the text. Here's a place where we might want to consider earplugs. It is manifest unfaithfulness to the text when what we must do is not uncompromisingly rooted in our being freed by the power and grace of God to be able to do it. What results is weeks, even months, where the flock is given heaps of moral instruction, but it is made impotent by discontinuity: the fruit has lost its connection to the root.

What Our Kids Hear

A teaching elder soberly recounted a conversation he had with his teen daughter after she returned from a summer Bible camp. When he asked her what the speaker talked about, she replied, "The love of Jesus." She was quiet for a moment, then added, "We don't hear much about the love of Jesus at our church. Why is that?"

After absorbing the blow to his solar plexus, he was forced to agree that there was truth in his daughter's observation. Apparently, if her observation was correct, she and the other children and young people in her church had heard lots of law and moral instruction but not much about the love of Jesus. Her question was a good one. "Why is that?"

Some ministers are afraid of preaching the love of Jesus because they fear communicating a message of "easy-believism." They don't want their kids to hear what they call a truncated gospel, so they emphasize the moral imperatives of the law, the things good kids do and bad kids don't do. After all, they don't want their kids to be antinomians, to rebel, to live two parallel lives, to leave the church, to abandon the faith, as statistics keep telling us many kids raised in Christian homes are doing.

Notre Dame sociologist Christian Smith ended a four-year study of the spirituality of Protestant teenagers in America with this conclusion: to them, "being religious is about being good and it's not about forgiveness. It's unbelievable the proportion of conservative Protestant teens who do not seem to grasp elementary concepts of the gospel concerning grace and justification. It's across all traditions."[6]

It would be so much easier to deflect Smith's findings if he gathered them from liberal church kids, nominally religious ones. But his findings came from young people hailing from conservative Protestant homes and churches—from your church and mine.

The accumulative effect when our children grow up not hearing much about the love of Jesus, reading Proverbs but neutered of the gospel, will be devastating. When they are subjected to prolonged sermon series on passages they're told few other ministers preach on, but with little or no reference to how these Old Testament books are fulfilled in Christ, we should not be surprised at the result.

Our children will come away from these sermons not dazzled with Jesus Christ and all that he accomplished for sinners in the new covenant. They may come away impressed by scholarship, impressed by the cleverness and prowess of the preacher, but they won't be much impressed with Jesus. Some

6. Christian Smith, cited in Michael Horton, *Christless Christianity: The Alternative Gospel of the American Church* (Grand Rapids: Baker, 2008), 42.

ministers take great pains to fix their congregation's attention more on the covenant than on the Mediator of the new covenant, more on the kingdom than on the King of Kings. While straining every nerve to show their congregation just how complete is the continuity with Moses, this kind of preaching can leave us wondering what is the big deal about Jesus. If everything was so clear and complete in the old covenant, what's so special about the new covenant? What's so superior about the superiority of Christ?

A generation of listeners subjected to this kind of message cannot help being affected by it. And the effect is devastating to their view of Christ. If the old covenant was so complete, so great, the Mediator of a new covenant will seem less glorious. Sure he's there, but look at how much greater was the Jewish worship. Think how graphic all the sacrificial blood would have been to worshipers.

Preachers of these kinds of sermons will inevitably send their flocks backward into the elementary foundational teachings about Christ, "the word of the beginning of Christ," which obscures the fulfillment of these things in Christ. Commenting on Hebrews 6:1, John Piper warns preachers "that they should not occupy themselves so much with the pre-Christian foundational preparations for Christ that they neglect the glory of the gospel."[7] In other words, the elementary teachings about Christ that the writer of Hebrews calls us to leave (6:1) are all the types and shadows now gloriously fulfilled in the new covenant, in Christ alone. When the Galatian church reintroduced "the old shadows of the law that had been abolished by Christ's coming," as Calvin puts it, "the clarity of the gospel was obscured by those Jewish shadows."[8] Thanks be to God, in Christ, we no longer dwell in the shadows.

---

7. John Piper, "Let Us Press On to Maturity" (sermon, Bethlehem Baptist Church, Minneapolis, MN, October 6, 1996).

8. John Calvin, *Institutes of the Christian Religion*, ed. John T. McNeil, trans. Ford Lewis Battles (Philadelphia: Westminster Press, 1960), 1:835.

"Christ is the truth and substance of all the types and shadows," wrote Puritan Isaac Ambrose. "Under the Old Testament Christ is veiled, under the New Covenant revealed."[9] Retro preaching that stops the clock in the old covenant will result in a confused message that veils Jesus, the Mediator of the new covenant.

What Our Kids Need to Hear

At its root, retro preaching that diminishes Christ is a theological problem, but we must always remember the Enemy's strategy: he wants us to think it is some other church's problem, some other denomination, some other tradition, some other family, but not ours.

Senior managing editor of *Christianity Today*, Mark Galli, seems to think the theological problem of diminishing Christ is significantly alive and well, and it's everybody's problem. "Without a quick infusion of robust and realistic theology grounded in the work of Christ, I fear we will soon enough be gasping for air."[10] Let's be realistic; it will be our children who've been hearing less about the finished work of Christ who will give off the last gasp. It will be our children who have not heard much about the love of Jesus who will yawn at scandalous good news and turn to covenant moralism. Oh, they may retain some of the borrowed capital of the religious morality and formal traditions of Christianity, but there will be little of the pure doctrine of the gospel that remains.

"The Reformed witness to grace," wrote University of Chicago's Brian Gerrish, "may be even more needed than it was in the sixteenth century, since now Pelagianism seems com-

9. Isaac Ambrose, cited in J. I. Packer, *A Quest for Godliness: The Puritan Vision of the Christian Life* (Wheaton: Crossway, 1990), 103.

10. Mark Galli, "A Potentially Beautiful Day in the Neighborhood: Why Evangelicals Need the Young, Restless, and Reformed," *Modern Reformation* 21, no. 1 (January/February 2012): 49.

fortably at home in the Reformed churches."[11] The bottom line of the teaching of fourth-century British monk Pelagius was that he didn't think much of the free grace of the gospel. He insisted that though it is helpful to have Christ, man must be able of his own free will to obey what God commands in his Word. Pelagius was convinced that if man is unable on his own to obey, then God is being unjust to demand obedience.

Self-Help

You and I don't have to be experts in historical theology to sniff out problems with this kind of Groundhog Day theology. Here's the test. Any teaching, by whatever name, that rears its head to place man closer to the center of his own self-salvation proposition is false teaching. Any message that makes us think we are in need of less grace and less Christ is a theology that pairs nicely with the Enemy's stratagem: corrupting the pure doctrine of the gospel.

As we open the Word of God we must be vigilant to ground every command to obey in the indicatives of what Christ has already fully accomplished in the gospel. Short of this, we will foster a generation of our own church kids who think of Christianity more as a behavioral plan than as a rescue plan, more as a plan for self-improvement to win the favor of God than as the liberating good news of God's plan to accomplish by his grace and power the redemption of sinners.

This generational danger is rooted in our fallen nature. Satan so readily insinuates law-creep into the gospel because we're so ready to hear him; we're predisposed to think moralistically about religion, that it really is a responsible partnership between God and us. "Moralistic religion of self-salvation is our default setting as fallen creatures," wrote Michael Horton. "If we are not explicitly and regularly taught out of it, we will always

11. B. A. Gerrish, "Sovereign Grace: Is Reformed Theology Obsolete?" *Interpretation* 57, no. 1 (January 2003): 45; cited in Horton, *Christless Christianity*, 48.

turn the message of God's rescue operation into a message of self-help."[12] That distorted message may sound like the glitz of the celebrity pastor, the tinsel of the prosperity preacher, or it may sound like a learned minister who tells us and our children that there is no gospel in Proverbs, thereby cutting the flock off from "Christ the Sun of the whole Scripture system."[13]

Whichever it is, Satan's stratagem has worked again. As in Amsterdam and Geneva, the gospel has been corrupted and another generation has been left without the Key. Imagine the Enemy's euphoria!

For Discussion

1. Read Galatians 3:21–26 and discuss the purpose of the law and why Paul refers to the law holding us captive and imprisoning us.

   Is the law then contrary to the promises of God? Certainly not! For if a law had been given that could give life, then righteousness would indeed be by the law. But the Scripture imprisoned everything under sin, so that the promise by faith in Jesus Christ might be given to those who believe.

   Now before faith came, we were held captive under the law, imprisoned until the coming faith would be revealed. So then, the law was our guardian until Christ came, in order that we might be justified by faith. But now that faith has come, we are no longer under a guardian, for in Christ Jesus you are all sons of God, through faith.

2. Read Belgic Confession, article 24, and discuss how this understanding helps us to pursue good works and godly living, yet without diminishing Christ.

12. Horton, *Christless Christianity*, 48.
13. Charles Bridges, *An Exposition of Proverbs*, ix.

These works, as they proceed from the good root of faith, are good and acceptable in the sight of God, forasmuch as they are all sanctified by His grace. Nevertheless they are of no account towards our justification, for it is by faith in Christ that we are justified, even before we do good works; otherwise they could not be good works, any more than the fruit of a tree can be good before the tree itself is good.

3. Read a passage from Proverbs and discuss how believing that wisdom is not a thing but a Person changes the way you understand the passage.

Pray today that God would give you grace to know and believe that wisdom is a Person and to help others know Wisdom.

21

Comparing Scripture with Scripture

MARK TWAIN is often quoted as having said, "It ain't those parts of the Bible that I can't understand that bother me; it's the parts I do understand."[1] Though far from a theologian, Twain may have been giving us more than a mere witticism.

Critics of the Bible, bothered like Twain by its unified message, attempt to shape the argument in order to silence the plain-speaking parts of the Bible. They, on some level, do understand. But by insisting that the whole thing is so confusing, so open to individual interpretation, they hasten to the conclusion that it's impossible to claim that the Bible is saying anything clear about anything.

Inspired by the Holy Spirit, who reveals the Son on its sacred pages, the Bible is, in fact, intended to be clear and accessible to readers. There's grave danger on the horizon for any church where preaching and teaching erode the clarity and accessibility of the Bible's message. Sure, some pretty tough images hurtle before our eyes in Ezekiel and in Revelation, but the parts of the Bible that are hard to understand should never be used to muddy the crystal clarity of the gospel of Jesus

1. Mark Twain, cited in Lawrence Farley, "Evolution or Creation Science?" *Orthodox Church in America*, May 30, 2012, http://oca.org/reflections/fr.-lawrence-farley /evolution-or-creation-science.

Christ, the central and overarching message of all the Scriptures. Finally, it's the gospel message that bothers us. Hence, we set about recasting the gospel so that it stops bothering us. Goaded on by the Enemy, we often do this by distorting how we interpret the Bible.

Unity, Not Diversity

I've found that *Modern Reformation* magazine is a great read anytime, but it works especially well when I'm flying. While on a flight from Washington, DC, to Seattle, I read a perceptive article, "Interpreting Scripture by Scripture." In it Michael Horton addressed some critical hermeneutical understanding necessary to interpret Scripture aright. "The Westminster Confession properly reminds us that not everything in Scripture is equally plain or equally important." Next he says what we can no longer assume to be obvious in biblical interpretation. "We have to interpret the more difficult passages in the light of clearer ones. Scripture interprets Scripture, and we learn the whole meaning of Scripture by studying its parts and its parts by learning the whole."[2]

This unified approach to understanding what the Bible is saying—what precisely God is revealing about his will and way, his redemptive purpose in Christ—has been the standard of interpretation for centuries. The best Bible teachers and preachers have always taken great pains to get this bedrock rule of interpretation right.

The primary rule of hermeneutics was called "the analogy of faith." The analogy of faith is the rule that Scripture is to interpret Scripture: *Sacra Scriptura sui interpres* (Sacred Scripture is its own interpreter). This means, quite simply, that no part of Scripture can be interpreted in such a way as

2. Michael S. Horton, "Interpreting Scripture by Scripture," *Modern Reformation* 19, no. 4 (July/August 2010), http://www.modernreformation.org/default.php?page=articledisplay&var2=1150.

to render it in conflict with what is clearly taught elsewhere in Scripture.[3]

The rule goes hand in hand with *sola Scriptura*, the understanding that the Bible alone is the sole authority—not popes, councils, the magisterium (the collective teaching of the church), or the private individual's spin on what the Bible says. The Bible itself demonstrates by comparison what the Bible is saying. Therefore, any interpretation of a passage that conflicts with another explicit teaching of the Bible is an irresponsible interpretation and will lead to error.

Flat Earth Theology

"Implications drawn from Scripture," wrote R.C. Sproul, "must always be subordinate to the explicit teaching of Scripture. We must never, never, never reverse this."[4] Dr. Sproul is here summing up the infallible rule of interpreting Scripture, the rule that every faithful preacher of God's Word, dead or alive, has carefully observed.

But what happens when we reverse the rule, when we subordinate the explicit passages to the implicit ones? I like to think of what happens like this: reverse things and we become like the man standing on the seashore gazing at a seemingly flat horizon, and then drawing the ultimate conclusion, "I've seen it with my own eyes and the earth really is flat!"

The gospel will necessarily get eroded when ministers turn texts that tell us to "work out [our] own salvation with fear and trembling" (Phil. 2:12) or to "be holy, for I am holy" (Lev. 11:44, 45; 1 Peter 1:16) into proof texts supporting free will and human ability, or, worse yet, supporting a salvation based at least in part on my effort and merit. Confessional

3. R.C. Sproul, *Knowing Scripture*, rev. ed. (1977; repr., Downers Grove, IL: IVP Books, 2009), 51.
4. R.C. Sproul, *Chosen by God* (Carol Stream, IL: Tyndale House, 1986), 74.

preachers, however, "never, never, never" let these texts trump the Bible's explicit statements that clearly teach man's total inability to be holy ("For the mind that is set on the flesh is hostile to God, for it does not submit to God's law; indeed, it *cannot*" [Rom. 8:7]).

We rejoice as we see a sinner repent and confess his faith in Jesus. Few things ought to thrill as much as this. But the danger comes when we misinterpret the sinner's repentance and faith to be the cause of God's grace being applied savingly to his heart; the sinner by an act of his will is asking for salvation, and God, who has been wringing his hands waiting, responds by saving the sinner. This is like the man on the seashore concluding that because the horizon line looks flat from his finite perspective the earth must, in fact, be flat.

A similar thing happens when preachers silence the explicit teaching of the Bible with conclusions derived from implicit passages. It is a far more consequential error to draw ultimate theological conclusions based merely on the immediately observable.

Plenty of explicit passages make clear what is the cause of saving faith (God's sovereign grace) and what is the effect (repentance and faith brought about by the new birth). Consider John's statement: "To all who did receive him, who believed in his name, he gave the right to become children of God" (John 1:12). His words do make it sound as though man acts, then as a result God saves. Taken alone, this verse does imply that order (just as a flat horizon implies a flat earth), though the verse does not explicitly say this. But John doesn't even pause for breath; he continues the same sentence with, "who were born, not of blood nor of the will of the flesh nor of the will of man, but of God" (1:13). Now the explicit clarification makes plain the divine order of salvation: sinners are not born again as acts of their free will—"not of the will of man"—they receive the new birth by the will and power of God.

To be sure, there are other passages that seem to imply man's will as the cause of the new birth, ones that don't always have as immediate and explicit a clarification as John gives us. But no honest interpreter of the Bible is going to silence the clarity of the host of explicit passages from throughout the pages of the Bible that make plain that it is first-to-last God who saves sinners.

So when Scripture appeals to sinners "to believe on the Lord Jesus and be saved," some stop the car, plug their ears, and insist that this has to mean sinners are able to believe by their free will—end of discussion. Only those who really don't like John's explicit doctrinal teaching, and all the other concurring passages, will be satisfied with trumping the clear teaching with inferences extrapolated from implied passages.

At the end of the day, though it may be completely unintentional, sloppy interpretations that elevate the implied over the explicit will inevitably elevate man's will over God's will. When this happens—however sincere and well meaning the preacher—eventually Christ and his cross will be made subordinate to man's will. Hence, responsible interpreters of the Bible, ones who care about the pure doctrine of the gospel of Jesus, will always understand the implied passages in light of the explicit; that is to say, they will always respect the analogy of faith—always.

Nevertheless, we should not be aghast that rivals to this infallible rule of interpreting the Bible will rear their heads. Folks in the pew like us, moms and dads, children and young adults, must prepare ourselves for the various masks these new interpretive methods will wear.

For Discussion

1. Read the following verses and discuss what happens when we don't compare Scripture with Scripture and isolate verses we don't like. John 5:21: "For as the Father raises

197

the dead and gives them life, so also the Son gives life to whom he will." John 6:37: "All that the Father gives me will come to me, and whoever comes to me I will never cast out." John 6:44: "No one can come to me unless the Father who sent me draws him."

2. Westminster Larger Catechism 157 asks, "How is the Word of God to be read?" How does a right view of the reading of the Bible help us to hear what he has to teach us? How are any of us enabled to read the Word of God with understanding?

   The holy Scriptures are to be read with an high and reverent esteem of them; with a firm persuasion that they are the very Word of God, and that he only can enable us to understand them; with desire to know, believe, and obey the will of God revealed in them; with diligence, and attention to the matter and scope of them; with meditation, application, self-denial, and prayer.

3. When interpreting a passage of Scripture, according to Dr. R.C. Sproul, what order must we never, never, never reverse? Discuss examples that demonstrate what happens when we do.

Pray today for missionaries you know who are out in remote places proclaiming the gospel to unreached people groups. Pray for them to have the Spirit's presence as they make the truths of the gospel known to people who may never have heard of Jesus.

22

Preaching Opposite Poles

FEW WOULD DISPUTE that Karl Marx's dialectic materialism was the historical and economic theory responsible for producing the arch-murderer of all time, Joseph Stalin. The numbers are so large that it's impossible to have a fully accurate body count, but most historians agree that Stalin had the blood of more than forty million of his own people on his hands.

Stalin's application of the dialectic political theory[1] was deadly. But another troubling application of the dialectic has emerged, this one used for interpreting and preaching the Bible. A leading purveyor of the dialectic preaching method put it like this, "The dialectic is what you have to see if you are going to understand the Bible rightly. The Bible speaks to us in extremes. Truth lies in the poles." The preacher's task is to hold "the two poles of truth in tension that are always wanting to fly apart." Some of the advocates of this new hermeneutic

1. Dialectic materialism said the cause of conflict in society was the disproportion between the rich and the poor (rich and poor being the dialectic or two opposite poles). The theory argued that if the government was empowered to annex all private property to the state and redistribute wealth equitably there would be no more cause of the dialectic (private wealth) and so a utopian society would result. Dialectic interpretation of the Bible finds opposites (dialectics) in the Bible's teaching; advocates argue that the preacher is obligated to preach the opposites without recourse to cross-referencing from other texts, making this method of interpreting the polar opposite to the analogy of faith (comparing Scripture with Scripture) used by the Reformers.

will admit they discovered it in the works of Karl Barth, the Father of Neoorthodoxy.

Preaching Opposite Poles

Though the dialectic method is a recent innovation, a method no champion of the gospel of free grace whom I know of has ever employed, preachers using the dialectic method are convinced that it's the only way to preach the burden of the text. Which makes me nervous. Are we really supposed to believe that no preacher before Barth ever preached the burden of a single biblical text? And Barth did?

This may all sound a bit theoretical, so let's look at a few brief examples. Men using the dialectic preaching method will be likely to speak often about the divine side and the human side of the poles of salvation. They may say things like this: "In the entire Bible, it is the case that the divine side of salvation makes the human side no less significant or even unimportant or unnecessary." Though this may sound reasonable at first blush, a careful listener will begin to hear dialectic preachers consistently weighing in on the human side, the divine side assumed but ever-increasingly diminished.

Men using Barth's dialectic interpretation will continue to make the obligatory affirmations of confessional orthodoxy, but increasingly their dialectic method will make them feel free to teach things that are incompatible with confessional orthodoxy. This is built into the method. Though the Bible occasionally does jolt us with extremes, dialectic preaching as an interpretive method provides a playing field on which it is normal to affirm opposite doctrines. Thus, dialectic preachers will theoretically affirm the divine side of salvation, but then they will leave the pole of the divine side behind altogether and swing to the pole of the human side.

In practical terms, God's gracious purpose in the gospel will be affirmed, but it is not the thing that makes the real difference. Let me illustrate. We may begin to hear a message that says the *only difference* between the generation that died in the wilderness and the generation that entered the Promised Land is that one trusted and obeyed God's commandments and the other did not. Be prepared to hear a dialectic preacher assert that so much is this the "only difference that it is entirely faithful to say, entirely consistent with the language and teaching of Holy Scripture to say, that the generation that came out of Egypt failed to obtain the promised land *no matter their election, no matter their redemption, and no matter the Holy Spirit's work in and among them*" (emphasis mine).

Regardless of how virulent the affirmations of orthodoxy are, this is the gospel shanghaied by yet another men-centered self-salvation endeavor. And the dialectic interpretive method provided the getaway vehicle. The divine work of salvation in election, redemption, and regeneration—the saving work of the Trinity: Father, Son, and Holy Spirit—just got thrown under the dialectic bus. Whether intentionally or otherwise, this preacher has just told his congregation that the "only difference" between being saved and being lost is something we must do: trust *and obey*. The tragic practical effect of this kind of interpretation is that the flock has just heard that they are to keep their eyes on their will and work, on their trusting and on their obeying—and not on Jesus the Author and Perfecter of faith.

To invert Shakespeare, there's madness in the method. According to the dialectic interpretative method, the divine work of God in salvation is not what matters, is not what is actually profitable for salvation; what is profitable for man's salvation is man's will and obedience, "the only difference" between the saved and the lost. Though it may seem like protesting too much, this preacher claimed that the determining factor in salvation is what man wills and does and that this is "entirely consistent with the language and teaching of Holy

Scripture." If the sheep are Bereans, after they regain their senses from any message that sounds like this, they'll probably stampede.

What Is Profitable

Christians who care about the purity of the gospel will agree that preaching that places man at the center of salvation is missing the point, and we will be careful not to dismiss it as someone else's problem. By whatever name, corruptions that elevate man's action in salvation over God's are always with us.

Hundreds of years ago, Calvin understood the gospel-eroding danger lurking when preaching diminishes God's sovereign will and elevates man's will in salvation: "Whatever mixture men study to add from the power of free will to the grace of God is only a corruption of it; just as if one should dilute good wine with dirty water."[2] Regardless of our theological or denominational predispositions, we must tune our ears to hear the havoc being done to the gospel of free grace when man's will trumps God's will.

One important way to do this is to hear the clarity of God's work in salvation from the best preachers of the past. "Those who are saved are saved by election, by grace, by the will of God, not by their own," wrote Jacques Lefèvre d'Étaples, the Wycliffe of France. "Our own election, will, and work, are of no avail: the election of God alone is profitable. When we are converted it is not our conversion that makes us the elect of God, but the grace, will, and election of God which convert us."[3] While dialectic preachers invert things, making the will and obedience of sinners the tipping point of salvation, Lefèvre

2. John Calvin, *Institutes of the Christian Religion*, ed. John T. McNeil, trans. Ford Lewis Battles (Philadelphia: Westminster Press, 1960), 2.5.15.

3. Jacques Lefèvre d'Étaples, cited in J. H. Merle d'Aubigne, *History of the Reformation of the 16th Century*, trans. H. White (London: Religious Tract Society, 1846), 3:342.

carefully lays out the divine order: God's sovereign redeeming grace alone is profitable for converting sinners.

Yet, tragically, there are those who claim to be reformational Christian ministers who seem apologetic about the doctrines of redeeming grace, ignoring the very doctrines on which so many other gospel truths get their traction. Preachers growing suspicious of electing grace while still claiming to be getting at the burden of Paul's epistle to the Ephesians, the *locus classicus* of electing love (1:3–11), may gloss over the text with something like this, "Paul is merely introducing themes he will address later in the book." Preachers enthralled with grace never skip over Paul's euphoric declaration that God "chose us in [Christ] before the foundation of the world" (1:4), yet this was sadly the sum total of this minister's exposition of the text. Spurgeon knew the relentless impulse to diminish grace and urged us to resist that impulse:

> Those who doubt the doctrines of grace, or who cast them into the shade, miss the richest clusters [of grapes]; they lose the wines on the lees well refined, the fat things full of marrow.... When you have mounted as high as election, tarry on its sister mount, the covenant of grace. Covenant engagements are the munitions of stupendous rock behind which we lie entrenched; covenant engagements with the surety, Christ Jesus, are the quiet resting-places of trembling spirits.[4]

Preaching in Isolation

There are many other problems with dialectic preaching, but the root systemic problem is that it isolates vast portions of the Bible from their fulfillment in Christ. Preaching the poles,

4. Charles Haddon Spurgeon, "Morning, October 28," *Morning and Evening: Daily Readings, Christian Classics Ethereal Library*, accessed January 14, 2014, http://www.ccel.org/ccel/spurgeon/morneve.html. He is commenting on John 15:19, "I have chosen you out of the world."

the opposites, means that cross-referencing an Old Testament passage with its fulfillment in Jesus will be either off-limits or greatly downplayed. By whatever name, the latest interpretive method will be presented as the only way to get at the burden of the text, and the sheep will be assured that it is the hermeneutic based on the finest scholarship.

Those assurances notwithstanding, problems with dialectic preaching are coming more to the attention of the best theologians and preachers. The author of a recent *Christianity Today* Book of the Year recounts a conversation with an advocate of the dialectic preaching innovation. "A noted pastor once told me," wrote Michael Horton, "'When I'm preaching through the Sermon on the Mount, I sound like a legalist; when I'm preaching through Galatians, I sound like an antinomian.'"[5] Horton offers his critique of this man's method of preaching incompatible opposites:

> Although this sounds like fidelity to the text—wherever it leads us—it is problematic for at least two reasons. First, it's naive. No one comes to the Bible without presuppositions. We all have some doctrinal framework we have acquired. Second, this assumption undermines confidence in the unity of Scripture. Jesus did not teach legalism and Paul did not teach antinomianism. As an apostle commissioned with the authority of Jesus himself and writing under the Spirit's inspiration, Paul's message is Christ's message. If we interpret the Sermon on the Mount as something completely unrelated (much less, contradictory) to Galatians, then we haven't gotten either right.[6]

When a preacher teaches opposite things and then insists he is merely preaching the burden of the text, the gospel alert

5. Michael S. Horton, "Interpreting Scripture by Scripture," *Modern Reformation* 19, no. 2 (July/August 2010), http://www.modernreformation.org/default.php?page=articledisplay&var2=1150.

6. Ibid.

should go off in our heads and hearts. Our first impulse should be to drop to our knees and pray for our pastor. He may believe that his method and message are somehow still faithful, but claiming fidelity to the text is far from enough. Karl Barth claimed to be faithful to the text, and he may very well have believed he actually was faithful. But he wasn't.

The Enemy is a deceiver and the last thing he wants is for preachers drawn into the dialectic way of interpreting the Bible to realize they have gone badly off the rails. As he guides preachers on a trajectory that leads away from the pure doctrine of the gospel, Satan will take great pains to keep them from realizing they are on the journey.

This is nothing new. The teachers of the law in Jesus' day claimed the highest fidelity to the biblical text. And what did Jesus say to these self-acclaimed Bible experts? "Is this not the reason you are wrong, because you know neither the Scriptures nor the power of God?" (Mark 12:24).

Renouncing Underhanded Ways

Listeners impressed with learned preachers must especially beware of the fine print. Men confident in their dialectic method of interpretation will often lay on plausible-sounding arguments, sometimes using erudite shock and awe to intimidate hearers into mute acquiescence to the expert's conclusions. We must never be convinced by cunning arguments—not when they dissect the Word and diminish the glory of Christ.

Dialectic interpretation demands that implied passages be preached in isolation, making the explicit biblical texts that would shed gospel light on them off-limits. The tragic result is that Christ, by these interpreters, must share glory with man's will and work in salvation. Charmed by scholarly sounding dialectic preaching, unsuspecting listeners may be regularly hearing a message fudging the gospel, a gospel concocted of partly Jesus and partly me—but sadly may not realize it.

None of this ought to shock us. Satan is like the audio in a Chatty Cathy doll. Though he uses a variety of means, there's an endgame to his strategy: diminish Jesus. Nor should we think that flawed interpretive methods are merely a modern-world assault on the meaning of the Bible. The apostle Paul faced erroneous interpretations in his own day. What did he do? "We have renounced disgraceful, underhanded ways. We refuse to practice cunning or to tamper with God's word, but by the open statement of the truth we would commend ourselves to everyone's conscience in the sight of God" (2 Cor. 4:2). We must do the same.

Stalin's dialectic interpretation of history, politics, and economics resulted in an incalculable twentieth-century blood-bath. From our finite vantage point, tallying the violence done to the bodies and lives of people is far easier than measuring the effect on souls and hearts. God, by his unchangeable decree, has purposed to save sinners, and has given us his indelible promise:

> The soul that on Jesus hath leaned for repose,
> I will not, I will not desert to his foes;
> That soul, though all hell should endeavor to shake,
> I'll never, no never, no never forsake![7]

Nevertheless, since Christ-centered gospel preaching is the central means by which God brings in his sheep, we ought to expect that dialectic preaching must bear some responsibility for a sullied message that leads some to spiritual ruin.

Like Paul, we too must renounce any interpretive method—by whatever name—that does violence to the unity of Scripture, that makes the Bible say opposite things, and that facilitates a doctrinal framework that diminishes Christ and his saving faithfulness.

7. "How Firm a Foundation," *Trinity Hymnal* (Atlanta: Great Commission, 1990), 94.

For Discussion

1. Read Galatians 5:1 and discuss how we lose our "quiet resting-place," and submit again to a yoke of slavery when we add anything to the sovereign redeeming grace of the Trinity.

   For freedom Christ has set us free; stand firm therefore, and do not submit again to a yoke of slavery.

2. Read Belgic Confession, article 22, and discuss various ways we say Jesus is not all sufficient.

   Therefore, for any to assert that Christ is not sufficient, but that something more is required besides Him, would be too gross a blasphemy; for hence it would follow that Christ was but half a Savior.
   Therefore we justly say with Paul, that we are justified by faith alone, or by faith apart from works.

3. In this chapter the author wrote, "Dialectic preaching . . . provides a playing field on which it is normal to affirm opposite doctrines." Discuss why employing a methodology of preaching that does this is problematic in maintaining the purity of the gospel.

Pray for theologians and pastors to have a clear biblical view of how to talk about Scripture's mysteries. Pray that they will understand the parts (especially the less clear ones) in light of the whole and that they will lift high the sovereign, saving, finished work of the Trinity on behalf of God's people.

PART 6

How We Say One Thing but
Believe Another:
*How Departing from Confessions
of Faith Corrupts the Gospel*

23

Believing What We Confess

THERE IS SOMETHING invigorating about conversation with new Christians. It's thrilling to share in their fresh zeal, to be reignited by their passion for the gospel of grace, to be prodded by their enthusiasm for friends and neighbors to know Jesus and the liberating power of gospel truth.

I was reminded of this while talking over dinner with a successful businessman who had recently been converted to Christ. He told me he had been reading a book he'd found that was a compendium of historic confessions of faith: the Belgic Confession, the Scots Confession, the Westminster Confession, the London Confession, the Heidelberg Catechism.

"These are amazing documents!" he exclaimed. "Why doesn't the church still adhere to them?" I tried to explain that some churches actually do still believe them. "Maybe for now some do," he said, and then he began listing a number of denominations he had been reading about who used to subscribe to these confessions but who had incrementally departed from them. This baby Christian concluded with a remarkably perceptive statement. "If we just stuck with these old confessions, the church wouldn't constantly drift away from the gospel."

Our Distaste for Confessions

Whether it's because of the consumerism of popular culture, the allure of the latest scientific and medical discoveries, the newest technology, postmodernism's suspicion of words and forms, or intellectual hubris, we don't really like having documents drafted by old dead guys acting as regulators on our lives today. And it's not just secularists who resent this.

"There are powerful currents within modern life," wrote Carl Trueman, "that militate in various ways against the positive use of creeds and confessions in the church."[1] As much as we want to believe we are immune to them, these powerful currents have their influence on Christians. Many well-meaning Christians I know have come to the settled conclusion that confessions of faith are a danger to the church; they fear that confessions of faith will replace the sole authority of the Bible.

As proof, they may cite the many mainline denominations that are now liberal but that devolved from confessional Christian ranks. Some then leap to the conclusion that these churches somehow became liberal because they used to be confessional churches. While many churches have simply forgotten the historic confessions of faith, others have very intentionally distanced themselves from confessional Christianity. The latter are convinced that by leaving behind such archaic theological statements of belief they will be more likely to remain faithful to the Bible.

"No creed but Christ," went the rallying cry of fundamentalism. "No law but love." Though post-conservative churches have been scrambling like rats from a sinking ship to distance themselves from fundamentalism, our suspicion of confessions of faith seems to have remained firmly onboard. Nevertheless, to be a Christian means to confess that you believe essential truths about Jesus Christ. It's not possible to be a true Christian without making a confession of faith, without declaring that you actually believe something (Rom. 10:9).

Renowned church historian Philip Schaff states, "The Christian Church has never been without a creed." True Chris-

---

1. Carl Trueman, *The Creedal Imperative* (Wheaton: Crossway, 2012), 47.

tian confession is founded "not on any words of man but on the word of God; yet it is founded on Christ as confessed by men, and a creed is man's answer to Christ's question, man's acceptance and interpretation of God's word."[2]

Bible-Centered Confessions

Every Christian understands that something would be missing if someone confessed his faith by simply saying "I believe the Bible." Such a confession is too general, too broad and sweeping to mean anything in itself. Inevitably a true confession of faith must summarize and be specific, as with Peter's great confession, "You are the Christ, the Son of the living God" (Matt. 16:16). When Jesus asked his disciples, "Who do you say that I am?" (Matt. 16:15; Mark 8:29; Luke 9:20), it would have been inadequate for Peter simply to have said, "I believe the Bible."

It is a nonnegotiable of being a Christian to declare just what exactly we believe about the Bible's message. Far from being rival authorities to the Bible, the best confessions of faith clearly declare themselves to be subordinate to the Bible alone as the only infallible authority. Hence, "the value of creeds depends upon the measure of their agreement with the Scriptures."[3]

Therefore, if we actually care about the authority of the Bible and the purity of the gospel message that it is, we may have hoisted ourselves on our own petard by abandoning historic creeds and confessions of faith. "To claim to have no creed but the Bible is problematic," wrote Carl Trueman. "The Bible itself seems to demand that we have forms of sound words (2 Timothy 1:13), and that is what a creed is."[4] By thinking

2. Philip Schaff, *The History of Creeds: The Creeds of Christendom* (Grand Rapids: Baker, 1998), 1:5.

3. Ibid., 1:6.

4. Trueman, *Creedal Imperative*, 76.

that the best historic statements of faith are in opposition to the Bible, we have actually removed an essential organ for the church to remain true to the Bible's teaching and to be healthy and reproduce. "We remove the organ and demand the function," to borrow from C. S. Lewis; we've theologically castrated future generations of the church, yet we continue to "bid the geldings be fruitful,"[5] but without a confession of faith.

What detractors or neglecters of confessions fail to realize is that the opening chapter of every credible confession of faith roots and subordinates all that follows in the Word of God, the Bible. By discrediting historic confessions, the church has inadvertently dismantled the bulwark guarding Bible truth. When we ignore the best confessions of faith, we slay with our own hands our greatest ally in defining and defending the truth of the gospel.

There are several tragic ironies in this. One is the church's certainty that getting rid of confessional standards is a healthy thing. The second is perhaps still more problematic. The church actually does have and use confessions; it just prefers ones of recent invention to the centuries-old confessions crafted by some of the greatest theological minds of the Reformation era. We seem to say, "Those old ones are impositions that might lead us away from the Bible, but this new one, the one we just came up with after men's breakfast at the church planting meeting, ours will be immune to doing that." I wonder.

Every church website has a navigation button that says, in effect, "What we believe." Though created in the last milli-second of church history, and not subject to public scrutiny, all these, in principle, are confessions of faith. There is, however, an enormous danger in this. When a church can cook up a confession of faith and make it public on its website without the comprehensive collaboration of the greatest theological minds, we are intensely vulnerable. In such a momentary

5. C. S. Lewis, *Abolition of Man* (New York: Simon and Schuster, 1996), 37.

and fragmented confessional climate, generational vigilance against the Enemy's schemes to corrupt the pure doctrine of the gospel is almost destroyed. We institutionalize a single-generation Christianity—at best—and I suspect the Enemy gives us rousing applause for doing it.

Many church leaders who think they don't like confessions may know very little about them. If they did, they would likely react more like my new-believer friend, "If we just stuck with these old confessions, the church wouldn't constantly drift away from the gospel."

Amsterdam, Geneva, Edinburgh—none of these places once saturated with reformational revival in the sixteenth century departed *because* of their confessions of faith. They have become places of unbelief and open hostility to the gospel precisely because they abandoned their confessions of faith. Churches depart from the gospel as they depart from their confessions, as they take exceptions with and reinterpret the biblical summaries of what they used to believe about the gospel. All this is made easier by our general distrust of the past.

The New Is Always Better

When I first held a smartphone in my hand and tried to negotiate my way through the labyrinth of its technological intricacies, I felt poorly matched. Nagging at my mind was the thought that smartphones need smart guys to operate them, and it is no exaggeration to say that I am the arch-techno-moron. Anyone who knows me will heartily agree. The danger is that as we realize just how greatly telephones alone have been advanced in the last decades, it's fairly easy to sell the nonnegotiable idea that everything old is inferior and everything new is better.

What may be true in technology, however, is manifestly not so in the world of unchanging truths and realities. C. S. Lewis gives us a gritty, demonic perspective, humorous but poignant, into the way this works in the milieu of postmodern scholarship. Screwtape describes an intellectual climate in which "only the learned read old books, and we have now so dealt with the learned that they are of all men the least likely to gain wisdom by doing so."[6]

Lewis' Screwtape goes on to demonstrate how demons have made modern scholars so impressed by their own scholarship that they never read something from the past and ask if it is true. And it would be "unutterably simple-minded" to view the "ancient writer as a possible source of knowledge." It is essential to the demonic strategy "to cut every generation off from all others" so that the errors of the current generation won't be exposed and corrected by the truths understood in the past.[7]

When we lock step with the Enemy here, what results is generational bankruptcy for the church. When the church cuts itself off from the theological past by ignoring or replacing confessions of faith, we forbid the next generations from drinking deeply at the well of rich, spiritual wisdom from the past.

What Lewis observed about classic literature in general applies precisely to the attitude of many Christians toward confessions of faith. Enamored with what's new, they silence the wealth of spiritual insight and breadth of biblical understanding in the collective wisdom of the framers of the finest confessions of faith. By preferring the latest thing, they silence the vast theological consensus that alone will keep the church from being the theological yo-yo of the centuries.

Theological Romance

Charles Finney, regarded by well-meaning admirers as one of the great evangelists, was a nineteenth-century Presbyterian minister, but one who developed a great dislike for "the framers of the Westminster Confession of Faith," the confes-

6. C. S. Lewis, *The Screwtape Letters* (New York: Macmillan, 1982), 128.
7. Ibid., 129.

sional standard historically adhered to by Presbyterians. He didn't have anything against the framers of the confession personally, but he increasingly disliked their theology, calling the confession a "Paper Pope." Rejecting the confession's teachings about the imputed righteousness of Jesus to sinners, Finney wrote, "If this is not antinomianism, I know not what is."[8] Of the legal transfer of the sinner's punishment to Christ and of Christ's righteousness to the sinner, Finney concluded, "I regard these dogmas as fabulous, and better befitting a romance than a system of theology."[9]

Consider one specific example of the gospel richness Finney was rejecting with his increasing hostility toward the Bible's system of theology summarized in the Westminster Standards.

> Those whom God effectually calleth He also freely justifieth; not by infusing righteousness to them, but by pardoning their sins, and by accounting and accepting their persons as righteous: not for anything wrought in them, or done by them, but for Christ's sake alone: nor by imputing faith itself, the act of believing, or any other evangelical obedience, to them as their righteousness; but by imputing the obedience and satisfaction of Christ unto them, they receiving and resting on Him and His righteousness, by faith: which faith they have not of themselves; it is the gift of God. (Westminster Confession of Faith 11.1)

Notice how Pauline and biblical the confession is, how careful the framers were to extol the imputed righteousness of Christ alone for the sinner's justification, that salvation in all its parts includes nothing done by us; even the faith by which we lay hold of the merits of Christ is the gift of God.

8. Charles G. Finney, *Systematic Theology* (Minneapolis, MN: Bethany, 1976), 332.
9. Ibid., 333.

Fungus and New Theology

Depart from the clarity of confessional statements about the gospel of grace like this and we should not be surprised when our children drift. One man who had grown up in an evangelical church but later converted to Roman Catholicism made this observation, "Once Protestantism starts to move away from the confessional approach and a self-conscious embracing of history, then I think it's all over in the long run."[10] Nevertheless, many once-confessional churches tout their criticism of their confessional standards, some even advocating hoisting them over the rail in favor of a more up-to-date confession.

"The voracious appetites of all of us for the new and the novel," wrote Carl Trueman, drives all of us to reinvent products. This "intentional obsolescence,"[11] however, is not just about consumer goods. In a variety of ways, this "voracious appetite" infects the church and her attitude toward the past and toward her confessions of faith. Intellectually minded churches always think all this is some other church's problem; the hipster church runs to the new and the relevant but we, we would never do that.

Satan, however, employs this fascination with the latest thing with theologians and confessional churches as well. Here's how I imagine it works: After thorough investigation, we discover what we think is some problem in how the church understands some part of the Bible. Next, we have an intellectual epiphany and light upon a new reading of a passage of the Bible. What follows works like a fungus in a damp, warm room: our new reading expands. Gradually, our discovery begins to overwhelm other passages and doctrines.

10. Christian Smith in an interview with Michael Horton, "Exit Stage West," *Modern Reformation* 21, no. 2 (March/April 2012): 11.

11. Carl R. Trueman, "How Consumer Culture Fuels Change," *Tabletalk*, April 2010, 15.

Next, with a little nudge from the Enemy, we begin to think a bit too highly of our latest theological discovery, though he will be careful not to let us realize this. He may flatter us and get us to write an article or a book about it. Proportionate to how enamored we are at our new discovery, we begin to have increasing criticism of the church's past. Pretty soon we will shake our heads in wonder at the naiveté of bygone generations: How could those ancient roughs have missed what I have discovered? How could they have been such theological want-wits?

While some churches expend energy in reinventing the church in the image of popular culture and what is hip, or metro, or emergent, or whatever else lurks around the next theological or liturgical corner, the more cerebral theologian preachers will increasingly set themselves up as critics of the confessional wisdom of the past. They prefer the so-called wisdom of current scholarship, the latest research, the best thinkers alive today. I suspect that for some ministers and preachers a good deal of this fascination with the latest thing may be fueled largely by intellectual hubris, by pride. After all, confessional standards are so restrictive to intellectual innovation and freedom.

Preachers fueled by the desire to gain intellectual respect-ability for the church and for their ministerial profession may prove to do more long-term damage to the gospel than they are sure the tattooed and pierced hipster church is doing. We all have our ways of expressing "the myth that every generation likes to believe about itself—that this time, here and now, is unique and special, and the rules of yesteryear can no longer be applied with any credibility."[12]

One thing we can be sure of, this attitude will sooner or later erode the message of the unchanging truths of the gospel.

12. Ibid.

For Discussion

1. Read Westminster Shorter Catechism 1 and discuss how this outlook stands in contrast to our natural understanding of our purpose in life.

   Q. What is the chief end of man?

   A. Man's chief end is to glorify God, and to enjoy him forever.

2. Over the next weeks, read through the Westminster Shorter Catechism, the Heidelberg Catechism, and the Belgic Confession. Discuss how these documents support *sola Scriptura* rather than stand as rivals to the authority of the Bible.

3. Drawing from evidence cited in this chapter, discuss why sound bites like "No creed but Christ" and "No law but love" actually serve to dismantle bulwarks guarding biblical truth.

Pray for those in your church and others who organize programs for youth and children. Pray that they will be drawn again and again to the enchanting truths of Scripture; pray that they will discover the catechisms as great allies in defending the truths of the gospel.

24

Beware the Fine Print

SINCE THE ENEMY KNOWS how corrosive to the gospel it is for Christians to distance themselves from historic confessions of faith, he likely is a big fan of the trend. He must be ecstatic when we do away with or replace historic confessions of faith.

In some denominations, ministerial candidates are ranked more highly when they take a mounting number of exceptions with confessional standards (an exception is a point of disagreement with the teaching of the confessional standards). Some see these new candidates as better thinkers: the more criticisms of the confessional standards, the more theologically astute they are.

It would make us so smug if we could dismiss this as only happening to the other guys, the ones in liberal churches. I'm sure the Enemy would prefer us to think this way, as he helped folks begin thinking in Amsterdam and Geneva, Edinburgh and Northampton. Liberal churches were once upon a time confessionally orthodox churches. It happened to them. I suspect the church will be vigilant in exact proportion to how real we believe the threat is, not in someone else's church, but in *our* church.

Amend It or Replace It

I read a disturbing statement in an article written for the newsletter of a conservative Presbyterian church. "It is high time for those standards," wrote the minister (referring to the Westminster Confession of Faith), "either to be amended or replaced." This ought to halt us in our theological tracks. Amended or replaced? With what? A new confession of faith? We're compelled to wonder whose new theological ideas will replace the old confession.

In various ways ministers who have become critics of the confessional standards of their churches may begin to let it out that they now have pages of exceptions with the confessional standards of their church. Like a mushroom culture, their exceptions to the rigorously tried-and-true theological standard of their church may swell to "fifty and counting."

Yet it will be important for ministers on a trajectory away from confessional standards to normalize their new ideas. Some men may be very sincere about it; they really believe they've discovered the truth. And so they will insist that their new theology fits within the banks of the confessional stream. All the while, they will maintain that they still believe in reformational doctrines such as justification by faith alone and the rest.

Vigilant Bereans will hear the obvious fallacy. If it were true that a minister agrees with reformational truths about the gospel, why then would he be calling for the amendment or replacement of the very confessional standards that have, for more than four hundred years, defined that reformational theology? Fallacies like this one remind me of what advertisers and politicians sometimes do: they tell us one thing really loudly, but there's something else in the fine print—the old bait and switch. Careful shoppers and voters always read the fine print, because the fine print is the deal breaker. It's what really matters.

Large Print, Small Print

"The large print giveth, and the small print taketh away,"[1] croaks experimental songwriter Tom Waits. Just as we feel

---

1. Tom Waits, "Step Right Up" (Fifth Floor Music, 1976), accessed May 1, 2014, http://www.tomwaitsfan.com/tom%20waits%20library/www.tomwaitslibrary.com

cheated when someone who wants to sell us something uses the large-print, fine-print deception, all the more so ought we to feel cheated when we hear less-than-open statements from the pulpit. Paul warned against the problem long ago. "We have renounced disgraceful, underhanded ways. We refuse to practice cunning or to tamper with God's word" (2 Cor. 4:2). If Paul faced it in the first century, we too must know the danger and renounce "disgraceful, underhanded ways" that tamper with the meaning of God's Word.

Satan would not want folks in the pew to hear open statements of the truth. He would not want us to sit up and realize that the Bible's theology of salvation is not defined by the new ideas of any individual in one generation, no matter how often and loudly someone repeats those ideas. The Enemy is hell-bent on keeping us from the Bible's teaching; what better way than by keeping us from actually believing that the centuries-old confession of faith accurately encapsulates biblical theology.

Vigilance for the gospel demands that we get this straight. A preacher can't go on record as having pages of exceptions with the confessional standards he once vowed he believed and still insist that he believes the reformational gospel defined and summarized by those standards. Confessions of faith were designed precisely to protect the church from individual ministers defining their own terms and creating their own new theologies. They were designed to be a theological standard outside and above one individual's opinion, a standard that transcends the vicissitudes and changing priorities of any given moment in history.

/lyrics/smallchange/steprightup.html. Many attribute the phrase to a statement made by Archbishop Fulton J. Sheen in 1957; it was later used by singer-songwriter Tom Waits in a 1976 song. The statement has appeared in print as early as 1941 and may have been coined as a result of the fine print in insurance contracts. The radio program Amos 'n' Andy (1928–55) may have been the original source. What is certain is that it is a derivation of Job 1:21, "The LORD gave, and the LORD hath taken away" (KJV).

Guerrilla Warfare

Urging preachers of the gospel to submit to confessional standards, Carl Trueman paraphrased Charles Hodge, "Ministers take vows to honor the rule of the church's assemblies; when those assemblies make a decision, one must actively support, passively submit or peaceably withdraw." In an age of intellectual individualism, many are unwilling to choose any of these options. "One does not have the option," Trueman continued, "of simply ignoring the ruling and carrying on regardless; nor does one have the option of mounting a kind of perpetual guerrilla warfare within the church."[2]

The church must beware of men who define themselves by what they disagree with in the confessional standards of the church, and in their place hold up their preferred new ideas, and in subtle ways solicit the support and loyalty of their congregations to those new ideas.

This is no new problem; it's a perennial problem, one that doesn't just happen in somebody else's church. In a letter to Philipp Melanchthon, Calvin cautioned against the danger when the church elevates the opinions of one man over the collective wisdom of the church and her confessions. "In the church we must always be upon our guard, lest we pay too great a deference to men. For it is all over with her when a single individual, be he whosoever you please, has more authority than all the rest."[3]

Calvin could have been addressing this letter to men in ministries today. Tragically, there seems to be an inevitable downfall awaiting men who are in prominent ministries, often ones that have emerged to fill a cultural or theological niche. However noble the original *raison d'etre* of the ministry—Christian manhood and the family, relevance of the gospel to pop culture, overcoming

---

2. Carl R. Trueman, "How Consumer Culture Fuels Change," *Tabletalk*, April 2010, 15.

3. John Calvin, *Letters of John Calvin*, ed. Jules Bonnet (Philadelphia: Presbyterian Board of Publication, 1858), 1:467.

basic youth conflicts, rediscovering sacraments and liturgy, covenant succession in parenting, you name it—a day of reckoning looms. If recent decades of church scandals tell us anything, it's that celebrity church leaders who set themselves above confessional standards or other ministries and denominations, who think they have discovered the one thing everybody else has been missing, seem to have set themselves up to topple in a pathetic heap when their own glass house shatters and their hubris at last catches up with them. Knowing my own sinful heart, I write these words with trepidation—and clinging to grace.

New Creed

When biblical orthodoxy is measured by an individual preacher's or theologian's standard, however sophisticated seeming, the net result will be an individualistic creed that at its core is more like this, "No creed but my scholarship, no theological standard but my amendment or replacement of the old passé confession." I fear there may be something sinister afoot when preachers set themselves up as critics of the confession of the gospel they vowed in their ordination to uphold. We should not be surprised at the result.

When men superimpose their new priorities over the confession, it sets us on a course that will eventually undermine the pure doctrine of the gospel, grounded on the unshakeable truths encapsulated in the five *solas* codified in reformational confessions of faith. We must be absolutely clear: The large print affirmations of orthodoxy are not what matter. What we actually believe is always in the fine print. "The large print giveth, and the small print taketh away." We must train our ears. When the fine print differs from the large print, what it takes away will, sooner or later, be essential to gospel truth.

My new-convert friend was right. "If we just stuck with these old confessions, the church wouldn't constantly drift away from the gospel."

For Discussion

1. Read Hebrews 6:17–19a and discuss how the unchangeable nature of God and his counsel gives us confidence to confess the sound words of the apostles' doctrine in Scripture.

   So when God desired to show more convincingly to the heirs of the promise the unchangeable character of his purpose, he guaranteed it with an oath, so that by two unchangeable things, in which it is impossible for God to lie, we who have fled for refuge might have strong encouragement to hold fast to the hope set before us. We have this as a sure and steadfast anchor of the soul.

2. Read Heidelberg Catechism 26 and discuss the reasons given why we can have unshakeable confidence in God our Father.

   Q. What believest thou when thou sayest, "I believe in God the Father, Almighty, Maker of heaven and earth"?

   A. That the eternal Father of our Lord Jesus Christ (who of nothing made heaven and earth, with all that is in them; who likewise upholds and governs the same by his eternal counsel and providence) is for the sake of Christ his Son, my God and my Father; on whom I rely so entirely, that I have no doubt, but he will provide me with all things necessary for soul and body and further, that he will make whatever evils he sends upon me, in this valley of tears turn out to my advantage; for he is able to do it, being Almighty God, and willing, being a faithful Father.

3. How does awe and wonder at God's fatherly provision and created order enable us to trust the ancient paths more

readily than the "vicissitudes and changing priorities of any given moment in history"?

4. How does intellectual individualism undermine confidence in the foundations of our creeds and confessions of faith built on the unchanging Word of God?

Pray for seminary professors who face strong temptations to innovate and stay in step with the latest scholarship. Pray today that they refuse to superimpose individual priorities and accomplishments over the unshakeable truths of the Bible codified in the best confessions of faith.

25

Teaching Our Children
What We Confess

JOHN WITHERSPOON was an oddball. Princeton divine
and signer of the Declaration of Independence, Witherspoon
was a theologian and preacher of confessional integrity. He
was a Bible Christian who knew what he believed and why he
believed it, and he was confident that the confession of faith
he had ascribed to was a consistent and accurate summation
of what his Bible taught. But he was an oddball because a
growing number of ministers in eighteenth-century Scotland
and North America emphatically did not agree.

Witherspoon was surrounded by men who had taken confessional ordination vows but who, under the influence of the
Enlightenment, were careful "never to speak of the Confession
of Faith but with a sneer."[1] Frustrated by this mounting attack
on the confession, he wrote a witty satire exposing the intellectual arrogance of his day, a day when a rational minister
would "give sly hints, that he does not thoroughly believe it,"
and had nothing but "contempt and reproach"[2] for such an
antiquated theological standard.

1. John Witherspoon, *The Selected Writings of John Witherspoon*, ed. Thomas Miller
(Carbondale: Board of Trustees, Southern Illinois University, 1990), 69.
2. Ibid.

Witherspoon knew his contemporaries' arguments; per-haps, as an academic, he had felt the intellectual tug of them himself. He knew that subscribing to a confession that was more than one hundred years old in his day was a "disagree-able necessity" to men living in an age of reason. He knew that it was intellectual suicide to speak well of the confession when his fellow ministers had nothing but "utter abhorrence at the vile hedge of distinction." He knew that "rigid adher-ence" to the confession was deemed "narrow-minded, big-oted, uncharitable," and that "the admirers of this antiquated composition, who pin their faith on other men's sleeves," who refuse to apply the confession "differently with the change of the times," could expect nothing but scorn from the more enlightened clergy of his day.[3]

Alas, not much has changed. Pastors with confessional integrity such as Witherspoon had are once again becoming theological and intellectual oddballs.

Erudite Shock and Awe

Since it is Satan's stratagem to insinuate corrupting ideas into the purity of the gospel message, what better way than to prompt the scholar-theologian-minister to plant his flag as a superior to the confessional standards of his denomination? What better way than when a learned preacher becomes a critic where the Lord and his confessional vows require him to be a pupil?[4]

Learned preachers who arrogate their individual interpre-tations over the confessional ones they vowed they believed and would uphold remind me of Chaucer's satirical portrayal of the know-it-all theology student at Oxford depicted in his general prologue to *The Canterbury Tales*. With his gown and his books, the student appeared to be scholarly but, like indi-

3. Ibid.
4. C. S. Lewis, *The Screwtape Letters* (New York: Macmillan, 1982), 73.

vidualist minister critics today, his own "scholarship was what he truly heeded."[5]

Unlike some pastor scholars enamored with new ideas and modern commentators, Charles Hodge, faithful defender of Reformed orthodoxy, made no apologies that during his life and ministry the *Princeton Journal* had never declared "an original idea."[6] While academia urges, even requires, men to innovate in their research for advanced degrees, a healthy dose of Hodge's hold-the-line humility, anachronistic though it sounds to some sophisticated scholar theologians, would do every preacher good.

While some of my living heroes hold terminal degrees from the finest European universities, they are proportionately some of the humblest men I know. One such theologian I know is one of the most brilliant minds I have ever read, heard, or spoken with; the only things that outstrip his learning and scholarship are his humility and commitment to confessional standards.

But it seems he is the exception, not the rule. There is a special problem for American ministers who aspire to scholarship. We Americans are still afraid that others think of us as frontiersmen with coonskin caps, colonial blockheads, intellectually deficient roughs. I wonder if some ministers don't care far too much about this caricature. Men wanting to bring intellectual credibility to the ministry can be desperate to prove to the world and to their fellow Americans that they can be just as learned, be just as smart, hold just as many degrees from the right institutions as the other guys.

"All of this is simply deadly to Christian faith," wrote Christian scholar David Wells in an interview. He describes

5. Geoffrey Chaucer, cited in Albert C. Baugh, *Chaucer's Major Poetry* (New York: Appleton-Century-Crofts, 1963), 244.

6. Charles Hodge, cited in D. G. Hart, "Princeton and the Law: Enlightened and Reformed," *The Law Is Not of Faith: Essays on Works and Grace in the Mosaic Covenant*, ed. Bryan D. Estelle, J. V. Fesko, and David VanDrunen (Phillipsburg, NJ: P&R Publishing, 2008), 44.

the corrosive demands of professional academia on Christian scholars and "how easy it is to compromise," to replace their sense of their "place in God's world as His servants, and as His witnesses to Christ's gospel,"[7] with the careerist demands of secular scholarship.

A yet more corrosive problem arises when a minister wants to prove to the church that his scholarship supersedes the confessional standards. Men who want to amend or replace the confession may use the clout of their new intellectual status to engage in a preaching ministry that depends in part on intimidation, on a sort of cerebral bullying. Such men, by the use of erudite shock and awe, bring their congregations and leadership into a servile passivity, a slavish acquiescence to their superior theological acumen. If all goes well, the impressive scholar preacher will seem to his congregation so much more sophisticated than a confession of faith written by stodgy old dead guys wearing Elizabethan tights.

Forgotten Doctrine

Pressure is mounting in some denominations for ministers to acquire advanced doctoral degrees, better still if earned from prestigious European universities—that is, if they want to have real clout. Meanwhile, the church and her children generally are becoming more ignorant of the Bible and its teachings, and this across denominational lines.[8]

The disparity between an increasingly more learned clergy and mounting ignorance of the Bible among the laity ought to trouble us. If we care about guarding the purity of the gospel, we will care deeply about this widening gap. But why, if our ministers are becoming more educated and adding more

7. "The Soul-shaping Reality of the Gospel: An Interview with David Wells," *Tabletalk*, January 1, 2011, 78.

8. Many studies have concluded that Bible literacy is in decline, not only in the general culture but in the church. For example: Rodger Crooks, *The Evangelical Magazine*, May 12, 2012, http://www.emw.org.uk/magazine/2012/05/biblical-literacy/.

advanced degrees to their names, why do major studies keep demonstrating that the flock is becoming less so?

One leading scholar offers the reason for this. "I think our doctrine has been forgotten, assumed, ignored, and even misshaped and distorted by the habits and rituals of daily life in a narcissistic culture."[9] Michael Horton finds the cause of this largely in "the disparity between what churches say they believe and what they are actually communicating week in and week out."[10] This sounds like another example of giving with the large print, but taking away with the fine print, and it ought to trouble us deeply.

Bible Literacy for All

Presbyterians and other denominations have had a long history of expecting and requiring an educated clergy, and rightly so. But what can be easily overlooked is of equal importance: having an educated laity. A highly educated clergy without a theologically informed and vigilant congregation is a formula for disaster. We should not be surprised when it produces a one-generation orthodoxy.

Keenly aware of this more than four hundred years ago, John Knox wanted everyone in Scotland to be able to read and understand the Geneva Bible. "Seeing that God hath determined that his church here on earth shall be taught not by angels but by men, it is necessary to be most careful for the virtuous education and godly upbringing of the youth of the realm."[11]

Implicit in Knox's words is the certain knowledge of the fallibility of ministers. They're not angels; they're men, and as men they are prone to error. Hence, a healthy church and

9. Michael Horton, *Christless Christianity: The Alternative Gospel of the American Church* (Grand Rapids: Baker, 2008), 42.

10. Ibid.

11. John Knox, cited in Alexander Smellie, *The Reformation in Its Literature* (London: Andrew Melrose, 1925), 16.

ministry will know the importance of having people in the pew who can read and understand their Bibles, who have their ears and hearts tuned to hear the pure doctrine of the gospel, and so to hear when it is being tampered with. This is why Knox was instrumental in establishing the first national education system in the Western world. He wanted everyone—rich and poor, boys and girls—yes, to have well-trained preachers, *and* he wanted the laity to have their Bibles open on their laps. Knox wanted this so the congregation was equipped to guard the pure doctrine of the gospel lest a rogue preacher—wittingly or unwittingly—use his scholarship to lead them astray.

Would that more preachers today not only welcomed the careful and vigilant listening of their people but intentionally equipped their flocks to help keep their pastor riveted on the pure gospel of Jesus Christ. Without this vigilance the gospel will be corrupted from within the gates, sometimes by the distortion of the very sacraments ordained to be means of signposting the grace of the gospel.

Means of Grace

"The early church placed central importance," said the minister, as he bounced the infant in his arms, "on baptism. They spoke of baptism as synonymous with justification, union with Christ, regeneration, forgiveness of sins." He then paused, scanning the congregation. "Of course they understood that all of these could be forfeited without faith and obedience."

"*And* obedience." Surely the minister saying this must have been a Roman Catholic or a maybe a liberal, but not a reformational Christian minister. There seems to be only one way to hear these words. When once-confessional ministers who choose their words with care say that all saving benefits are had in baptism but can be forfeited by lack of faith *and* obedience, they have just told their congregation that works of righteousness do matter a great deal to our justification.

I'll leave the minutia of the theological arguments to the theologians, but I'm far more concerned with what the congregation hears, how words like these affect the minds and hearts of the flock. What is the inevitable reaction of the sheep to a baptismal homily in which they are told that they can have all the saving benefits of the gospel, but by their lack of faith and obedience—their good works—they will lose those saving benefits?

The answer requires no imagination. On two fronts words like these will turn the congregation away from the merits of Jesus. A homily like this points the flock not to the saving object of baptism and the One alone who gives sanctifying grace to obey, Jesus Christ. Rather it points them to the external means, baptism, and, in the same breath, to their faith *and* their good works. The congregation just heard the gospel get struck down by the sacrament-creep bus. I can't imagine a lyric extolling sacrament-creep, saving benefits that could be had and forfeited, singing very well: "You could have it, have it, have it, have it, down in your heart. Then forfeit, forfeit, forfeit, you could forfeit it," scarcely warms the heart. What the church has sung about these things goes more like this:

> The work which his goodness began,
> The arm of his strength will complete;
> His promise is yea and amen,
> And never was forfeited yet.[12]

Still more, when we hold the words of the baptismal homily up next to the confessional clarity found in the Heidelberg Catechism, we can more readily hear the sacrament-creep in the homily. The framers of the catechism are so careful to make plain that the outward washing of baptism in no

---

12. Augustus Toplady, "A Debtor to Mercy Alone" *Trinity Hymnal* (Atlanta: Great Commission, 1990), 463.

way washes away sin, "for only the blood of Jesus Christ and the Holy Spirit cleanse us from all sin" (Heidelberg Catechism 72).

What does a congregation take away from a message that makes the saving benefits of the gospel a conditional proposition? The sheep are left thinking that in their own baptism they had saving benefits but—watch your back—they could forfeit these by disobedience. What just happened? When a minister says things like this, he has put the sign on display, not the Savior.

Look to the Sign

While speaking at a conference in another state, I overheard two church officers discussing baptism. "The best thing I ever read on the means of grace," said one, "was from [he named a noted theologian scholar]; it went like this, 'They're not means of grace; they *are* the grace.'" I just about dropped my burger and potato salad. I realized that this was no mere wordplay; this was baptism on performance-enhancing drugs, the equivalent of elevating baptism to a sixth *sola*, baptism alone.

At Sunday afternoon dinner, there was a lively discussion about the means of grace, especially baptism. I began to realize that for this congregation the sacraments had taken on more and more importance. Like an overinflated balloon about to burst, the sacrament of baptism had become the main thing.

"When our eldest son was in rebellion and heading out the door," said the pastor's wife, "I reminded him of his baptism and that brought him back in the door." By the look on her face, she was convinced that her anecdote would convince me of the reformational orthodoxy of her counsel to her son. Theology birthed by anecdote is seldom helpful, but there was an unhappy epilogue to this anecdote: all three of her sons eventually rebelled, headed out the door, and kept going, their baptism notwithstanding.[13]

Sadly, it seemed that this ministry had allowed the means of grace to do the opposite of what means of grace were instituted by our Lord to do. Instead of being a signpost that pointed to Jesus, baptism had become an end in itself, the sixth *sola*. It had absurdly become a sign that pointed back to the sign.

To the Beach

Pointing our children to the means of grace instead of to what the means point to is not only futile; it's ridiculous. Doing so is like driving your family to the beach for a picnic, and when the sign appears next to the freeway with an arrow pointing to the beach, you pull the family van over onto the shoulder under the road sign. Cars and semitrucks whooshing past, you tell the kids to get out the picnic basket and the surfboards. We're at the beach.

Make no mistake about it: just as kids know the difference between the real beach and a road sign that only points to the beach, so must we make certain that our children know unequivocally the difference between the signs and seals and the One to whom they point. Disaster waits around the corner and all along the road if they begin to believe the Jesus-minimizing notion that "the means of grace are the grace."

The Enemy must be giddy at all this. The very means Christ gave to be yet another way of revealing his presence to us, we turn into an idol. The children of Israel did the same thing with the bronze serpent (2 Kings 18:4); the very sign given by God through Moses to point Israel to redemption in the coming Messiah, they turned into an idol, venerating the sign above

---

13. Though these three sons had thumbed their noses at all the outward signs of membership in the visible church, my prayer is that God by the gracious working of his sovereign Spirit would rend the heavens and regenerate their hearts; my prayer is that their parents would find their sons born again with new hearts, indelibly registered in the rolls of the invisible church.

the Savior it foreshadowed (John 3:14). We do no less when we prop up the idol of an overinflated baptism in front of our kids instead of Jesus. How tragic when the very means Christ instituted to point to him get distorted into U-turn signage that points away from the Savior and back to the sign.

Here again, reformational confessions of faith help us avoid the futility of expanding means of grace into the thing itself. "What is a sacrament? A sacrament is a holy ordinance instituted by Christ; wherein, by sensible signs, Christ, and the benefits of the new covenant, are represented, sealed, and applied to believers" (WSC 92). Wherever we live—Amsterdam, Edinburgh, Geneva, or your place or mine—when we point our children to the signs and seals instead of to Christ himself, the gospel will go flat.

Cheating our kids out of the real beach by parking under the sign to the beach will confuse and exasperate them. Inflate the means of grace beyond its biblical and confessional role and we should not be surprised that our children grow up hearing a deflated gospel, a limp, anemic message that diminishes the saving work of Jesus Christ.

How Presumption Destroys the Gospel

When the sacrament of baptism is injected with steroids, no one gets cheated more than our children. Joel Beeke observed the result when "parents overestimate their children's baptismal membership in the visible church." He warned of hypercovenantalism and "presumptive regeneration," teaching served up as standard fare in nineteenth-century Holland. Christian families in the Netherlands were also taught to point their children to the external means of grace, to presume that their baptized children were born again. The results could not have been more devastating.

Presuming on their children's conversion, parents stopped holding the gospel of grace before their families and stopped encouraging their children to repent and believe the gospel, to be born again. This error tragically worked against the gospel in Amsterdam; we should expect that it will do so today. "Though Kuyperian neo-Calvinists may not like to admit it," wrote Beeke, "religious life becomes grounded in external church institutions and activities rather than in the soul's communion with God."[14] William Young concluded, "A system for breeding Pharisees, whose cry is 'We are Abraham's children,' could hardly be better calculated."[15]

When we root salvation in an overfed covenantalism, a theology of the covenant in need of calorie counting and a membership at the gym, we can expect that our children will either fall in line as good religious moralists on the outside while reveling in covert sin when they think they're on their own, or they'll just go public, chuck it all and rebel. While some operate on theological autopilot, others—God be praised—will be regenerated by the sovereign grace of the gospel. Either way, our kids will likely leave the church of their youth: the rebels to wallow in the mire, and the truly regenerate to find a church that preaches straight-up, Christ-centered, grace-alone gospel.

For Discussion

1. Read 1 Corinthians 2:2–5 and discuss the various pressures and priorities in the modern world that distract us from the unchanging biblical truths summarized in confessions of faith.

   For I decided to know nothing among you except Jesus Christ and him crucified. And I was with you in weakness and in fear and much trembling, and my speech and my message were not in plausible words of wisdom,

14. Joel Beeke, *Bringing the Gospel to Covenant Children* (Grand Rapids: Reformation Heritage Books, 2010), 5.
   15. Ibid.

but in demonstration of the Spirit and of power, so that your faith might not rest in the wisdom of men but in the power of God.

2. Read Belgic Confession, article 21, and discuss how the best confessions of faith always keep Christ at the center of all saving benefits. How will being Jesus-centered like Paul affect us in the home as parents, children, and young adults?

Wherefore we justly say with the apostle Paul that we know nothing save Jesus Christ, and him crucified; we count all things but loss and refuse for the excellency of the knowledge of Christ Jesus our Lord, in whose wounds we find all manner of consolation. Neither is it necessary to seek or invent any other means of being reconciled to God than this only sacrifice, once offered, by which he hath perfected forever them that are sanctified.

3. How does presumption silence the message of the gospel? What results in our children's minds when signposts to grace become confused with grace itself?

Pray today for teachers in Christian schools and those who work with various ministries to children and young people. Pray for instruction that points to the Christ-centered, grace-alone gospel.

26

Confessing Our Unity

I HATE DISUNITY. There is nothing more soul killing than being at odds with the very people with whom I ought to have the most profound unity. I hate it. That's probably why Ephesians 2 is one of my favorite chapters of the Bible.[1] Christ himself has made peace through the blood of the cross. He is himself our peace "and has broken down in his flesh the dividing wall of hostility" (2:14). He has created the church to be one—not dozens or hundreds—his one body reconciled through his blood shed for his church on the cross (2:15–16).

As much as we long for unity, however, Satan is hell-bent on destroying that unity. He does this by disturbing the gospel, by insinuating corruptions into the message. This is the entire history of the church in a nutshell: one challenge to the gospel after another.

By Heresies Oppressed

In 1866, one stalwart Anglican vicar, Samuel Stone, ministering in the baddest part of town in London, planted his flag for the church's unity on the authority of the Bible. John Colenso, an Anglican bishop in Africa, had begun teaching that the Bible contained truth but was not the infallible, inerrant,

1. As Ephesians 2:11–22 is one of my favorite passages of Scripture, I have written a hymn on its theme of the unity of the body Christ, included in appendix A.

God-breathed revelation of the redemptive purpose of God in Christ. This was too much for gospel-loving Stone.[2]

Though he was an unimportant, nobody vicar, serving in an unprestigious part of London, he did what he could. He wrote a hymn, "The Church's One Foundation." Stone knew his Bible and he knew when and where to plant his flag. He knew that when men tamper with the meaning of the Bible, they will soon enough be tampering with its central figure, Jesus Christ. Stone knew that without Jesus there could be no salvation for sinners in his flock—and he cared deeply about his flock.

The story is told that Stone came upon several young toughs trying to hurt a little girl in his congregation. Stone, who had been a championship athlete in his university days, rolled up the sleeves of his clerical robe and punched the stuffing out of the boys. In another fashion, Stone rolled up his poetic sleeves and wrote a hymn to inflict blows on the Enemy of the gospel and his minions. But the hymn is not finally controversy centered; it is a glorious celebration of the unity of the invisible church: "Elect from every nation, yet one o'er all the earth." By the enemies of the gospel the beleaguered church he so much loved was "sore oppressed, by schisms rent asunder, by heresies distressed." Not only did Stone know there was a serious problem, he knew the solution, "Yet saints their watch are keeping."[3]

Pastors equipping their flocks to keep watch, to be vigilant in the pew, to search the Scripture as they listen is the only solution. Knowledge of the Bible's message as codified in confessions of faith is the great bulwark protecting the unity of what the church believes and preaches.

The Justifiable Slap

There truly is a war on, and the church must never lay down its arms when the gospel is under attack. The Enemy

2. Erik Routley, *Hymns and Human Life* (London: John Murray, 1952), 114.
3. Ibid.

does not want us to realize that it's a counterfeit of unity that gives the Enemy a place at the table. This side of the church's heavenly rest, enemies of the gospel will insist on a place at the table, all in the name of unity, but it's a cheap charade of unity. Where there is a discrepancy between the visible unity of the church and the truth of the gospel, the church must always find its unity, not around the name of a denomination or an individual minister, but around the pure doctrine of the gospel.

Though there are sad examples of churches splitting over paint colors, many of the church's divisions down through the centuries have been the result of faithful pastors and theologians holding the gospel line against the encroaching error of the enemies of the gospel. It is in the heat of these controversies that the church's greatest creeds and confessions have been forged. Without men standing for the unity of the truth, rolling up their sleeves and entering the fray of controversy, there would be no pure gospel message left.

One particular gospel-destroying challenge to the church's unity was confronted by the Council of Nicaea in the fourth century. This disturber of unity wasn't the color of the carpet. Ministers were denying the deity of Christ.

According to tradition (or legend), St. Nicholas got worked up listening to Arius blaspheme Jesus, saying that Christ is not the Son of God, the only Savior of sinners. Fed up with the blasphemy, St. Nicholas rose to his feet and slapped Arius across the mouth.[4]

Indiscreet as that may have been, out of the heat and blows of that conflict came the glorious credo, the Nicene Creed: "I believe . . . in one Lord Jesus Christ . . . God of God, Light of Light, very God of very God, begotten, not made, being of one substance with the Father, by whom all things were made."

4. Gene Edward Veith, "Putting St. Nicholas Back in Christmas," The Lutheran Witness, December 2011, http://witness.lcms.org/pages/wPage.asp?ContentID=1153&IssueID=61.

Where would the church be without this confession? Where would the unity of the gospel be without this glorious truth?

Why does this matter? For Reformer Ulrich Zwingli it mattered because there is no salvation outside the atoning sacrifice and imputed righteousness of Jesus Christ. "Who seeks or points out another door errs," wrote Zwingli, "yes, he is a murderer of souls and a thief."[5] Put it like that, and a slap on the mouth doesn't sound so out of place after all.

Unity of Truth

Historically, men who champion the drift away from the confession are often the same ones who are quick to declare all who disagree with them as schismatics disturbing the unity of the church. But doesn't it seem more logical that the divisive ones are those who want their individual interpretations, their pages of criticisms of the confession, to become the new articles of faith?

Loyalty to an individual (1 Cor. 1:12–13), to a celebrity preacher or a particularly learned one, may prove to be more of a setup for unity faking than for real oneness. Like artificial additives in your favorite meal, artificial unity is never good for the genuine unity of the body. Loyalty to an individual, sooner or later, erodes the church's larger unity around the pure doctrine of the gospel summarized in a confession of faith.

Some will always become enamored with new ideas, with new discoveries that lead to new ways of reading books of the Bible, with reconciling the Bible with science or modern psychology, and then they will set to work recasting the confession of faith in the image of the latest discoveries. The Enemy wants this to flourish, so he will help to shape the argument

5. Ulrich Zwingli, "The Sixty-Seven Articles of Ulrich Zwingli," in *Selected Works of Huldrich Zwingli*, ed. Samuel Macauley Jackson (Philadelphia: University of Pennsylvania, 1901), article 4, accessed May 1, 2014, http://www.chinstitute.org/index.php/eras/reformation/zwingli/.

in ways conducive to his object of corrupting and disturbing gospel unity. With careful handling from behind the scenes, the argument will proceed with the enticing wording of preferring a *biblical* theology to a *systematic* theology.

A convincing-sounding assertion. Who doesn't want to come down on the side of biblical theology? Though it seems to be an effective construction for taking the high ground in the discussion, there's a nagging problem. Men who use this argument are more than hinting that they no longer think biblical and confessional theology agree. Bear-baiting the confession and the Bible may be evidence that a minister no longer really believes the system of theology he once vowed he believed.

Here's how this may sound. In one minister's preaching, the doctrine of imputed righteousness was so increasingly absent that an elder finally asked him if he still believed the doctrine. "Well, *imputation* is not a biblical term," he replied. "I want a biblical theology, not a systematic one." Presumably many ministers who might make this kind of argument will, nevertheless, still believe in and use the word *Trinity*, which is also not a biblical term but one used in systematic theology. Wouldn't it make sense to go all the way and stop using the word *Trinity*? The selective application of this argument may reveal that, at the end of the day, what is at issue is not simply a preference for biblical language over confessional. Rhetoric may have become a smoke screen.

The gospel has been handed down to us in words, words that have been carefully defined and codified in our confessions of faith. When the plain meaning of those words gets toyed with, there's probably a reason. Saints keeping watch will sit up and listen when they hear this kind of doublespeak. Judging from the Enemy's schemes, the gospel is likely in the crosshairs. Hence, it is only "by being vigilant in our confession, [that] we can protect the church's unity."[6]

6. Michael Brown, "Schism and the Local Church," *Tabletalk*, May 2011, 25.

A Stream with No Banks

One ruinous counterfeit being substituted for the pure doctrine of the gospel and eroding unity may sound particularly appealing to families with kids. "Covenant faithfulness is the way to salvation, for the 'doers of the law will be justified' at the final judgment." As with all error, there is a miniscule kernel of truth here (a stopped clock is right twice a day). However appealing it may sound, point to our covenant faithfulness rather than to the steadfast faithfulness of the Savior, and all that remains is a counterfeit of the gospel. An attempt to swallow this kernel will demand a theological Heimlich maneuver to prevent death by choking.

Ministers who say these things to their congregations hasten to tack on that this faithfulness is all done in union with Christ. Then they hasten back to what seems to have become the main thing. I'm inclined to think that when we hear confusing messages like this, we've just heard the fine print. However vigorous the large-print affirmations of orthodoxy are, as with politicians and journalists, it's the fine print that reveals what someone really believes.

Although a message of salvation by covenant faithfulness erodes grace, advocates of this latest version of law-creep insist that their teaching is in the broad stream of the reformational confession of faith to which they still claim to ascribe. But to say that the way to salvation is by any degree of law-keeping faithfulness is nothing short of a reinvention of justification in the bland image of works righteousness—Rome without the bells and smells. If the banks of the confessional stream were this wide, we'd be looking at another worldwide flood, a confession with no boundaries at all.

Though I may be accused of being too meat-headed to grasp the intricate theological nuances, there's one nuance I do understand: what a message like this produces in the flock. It will nudge hearers back into the default mode of looking to their "covenant faithfulness," to their performance, to their obedience for their acceptance before God. Any teaching that does this will inevitably diminish in our minds and hearts the glories of the finished work of Christ in our place and will proportionately lessen our love and gratitude to Jesus for all that he has fully accomplished for us.

Favorite Sound Bites

Men who teach that "covenant faithfulness is the way to salvation" may also be ones who scour the literature of church history to unearth sound bites that appear to support their shifting ideas. Lifted out of context, these will then be used in an effort to normalize their aberrant views. For example, they may prefer to cite, and attribute to Augustine, the oft-quoted line, "Pray like everything depends on God. Work like everything depends on you."[7] These kinds of historical sound bites pair nicely with isolated Bible sound bites such as "a person is justified by works and not by faith alone" (James 2:24). And the hands are dusted and the discussion is over, as if the Bible and Augustine need no context and have nothing more to say on the topic.

Meanwhile, others attribute to Ignatius Loyola, founder of the Jesuits and mastermind of a movement designed to stamp out Reformation Christianity, the curiously similar admonition, "Use human means as though divine ones didn't exist, and divine means as though there were no human ones."[8] Good luck trying to find the original source on either of these, but

7. Variously attributed to Augustine and by some to Ignatius Loyola, though I was unable to find an original source for the quotation other than in the vast repositories of Christian clichés.

8. Though usually attributed to Ignatius Loyola, a form of the quotation appears in Spanish Jesuit Balthasar Gracian's *Art of Worldly Wisdom* (1637, maxim 251). In 1982, Joseph Jacobs translated the phrase as "Use human means as if there were no divine ones, and divine as if there were no human ones." See Balthasar Gracian, *The Art of Worldly Wisdom*, trans. Joseph Jacobs, accessed February 10, 2014, http://www.intellectualexpansionist.com/art-of-worldly-wisdom.pdf.

in your search you will discover, as I did, that these variously attributed lines are also favorites among some Mormons, even some Muslims—strange theological bedfellows, indeed.

I'm bewildered and saddened by ministers whose favorite quotations—whether from the Bible or church history—seem calculated to invite confusion about justification as a one-time act of God. The flock is in grave danger when its ministers discover a man-centered sounding nugget and then use it as authority to normalize their theological shift and to convince their flocks that their adjustments ought to be accepted as new articles of faith—grave danger, indeed.

How much worse when men misuse Scriptural proof texts to cast doubt on the freeness of gospel grace. Shakespeare must have observed this strategy among some of the clergy in his day:

> In religion,
> What damned error but some sober brow
> Will bless it and approve it with a text[?][9]

What's more, the Bard knew that even

> The devil can cite Scripture for his purpose.
> An evil soul producing holy witness
> Is like a villain with a smiling cheek,
> A goodly apple rotten at the heart.
> O what a goodly outside falsehood hath.[10]

Making large-print affirmations of doctrinal orthodoxy will always sound goodly on the outside; that's what they're meant to do. But what a preacher believes is always in the fine print, and we can be sure the fine print will always be backed up with a proof text.

9. William Shakespeare, *Merchant of Venice*, III.ii.77–79.
10. Ibid., I.iii.96–100.

Blessing confessional errors with proof texts never promotes the doctrinal unity of the church. Rather, these deviations and methods create a "perpetual guerrilla warfare within the church,"[11] waged to lend credibility to the latest confessional departure.

Unity about Forgiveness

An example of a corruption of the gospel insinuating itself into conservative Christianity that I referenced earlier is such a torpedo to the gospel that it requires further consideration here. "Justification—whatever else it is—is the forgiveness of sins. It is perfectly obvious that there is such a thing as temporary forgiveness because the Bible says there is. . . . Temporary forgiveness is a biblical datum." It takes little imagination to hear ministers in post-Reformation Amsterdam or Geneva saying similar things about justification.

However confidently asserted, this twenty-first-century minister's statement that the Bible teaches temporary forgiveness is not shared by a single reformational confession of faith. I doubt Luther would have thought a doctrine of temporary forgiveness was anything like entering the gates of paradise, as he referred to his conversion. Imagine Luther's glee at the discovery: "At last, I get it. Whatever else justification is, it is forgiveness, but only temporary forgiveness. O the joy! My burden is lifted—sort of, at least for the moment." Temporary forgiveness would be more like having your head smashed in the gates of paradise as they clanged shut.

Or imagine a hymn of praise to God about temporary forgiveness. The cry of the five bleeding wounds of the Savior in Charles Wesley's hymn would sound more like this: " 'Sort of forgive,' they cry, 'sort of forgive,' they cry; 'Maybe not let

11. Carl R. Trueman, "How Consumer Culture Fuels Change," *Tabletalk*, April 2010, 15.

that sort of ransomed sinner die.'" I can't imagine a doctrine of temporary forgiveness warming anyone's heart to praise.

Not only does it make for ridiculously bad hymn poetry, such a declaration is devastating to the central doctrine of justification by faith alone; if justification is about forgiveness of sins and the Bible teaches that you can be justified and have forgiveness of sins—and then lose or forfeit it—the entire structure of reformational theology crumbles.

It is precisely here that the confessional standards help Christians in every generation to continue to believe what the Bible teaches and what the wisdom of our theological forebears taught and believed about the gospel. In the Westminster Confession of Faith there is zero room for temporary forgiveness, a justification that can be had and then forfeited. "God did, from all eternity, decree to justify the elect, and Christ did, in the fullness of time, die for their sins and rise again for their justification. . . . God doth continue to forgive the sins of those that are justified" (WCF 11.4–5).

All the persuasive rhetoric to the contrary, what is a confessional datum on the irrevocability of forgiveness is so because it is a biblical datum: "If we confess our sins, he is faithful and just to forgive us our sins and to cleanse us from all unrighteousness" (1 John 1:9). The entire gospel depends on the faithfulness of God to do what he promised. It is the character of God himself that is at stake. God is unchangeable and so are his gifts. If forgiveness is changeable, then God himself is changeable. The central doctrine of justification is about something the immutable God has ordained and already accomplished, as Puritan Stephen Charnock so richly elucidates:

> What comfort would it be to pray to a God that, like the chameleon, changed colors every day, every moment? The immutability of God is a strong ground of consolation, and encourages hope and confidence. While we have Him for our

God, we have His immutability, as well as any other perfection of His nature. Let us also desire those things which are nearest to Him in this perfection: the righteousness of Christ that shall never wear out; and the grace of the Spirit, that shall never burn out.[12]

The ground of all comfort and confidence for sinners is that the immutable God justifies sinners based on the righteousness of his Son. He forgives my sins based on zero fitness in me, and he continues to forgive them based on zero fitness in me. He freely justifies sinners, as the Westminster divines put it, "for Christ's sake alone. . . . Faith, thus receiving and resting on Christ and His righteousness, is the alone instrument of justification" (WCF 11.1–2). The apostle Paul declares without equivocation that "the gifts and the calling of God are irrevocable" (Rom. 11:29). Whatever else that means, it clearly has to mean that the justifying gift of forgiveness of sins is irrevocable too. In fact, "God does continue to forgive the sins of those that are justified."[13]

I, for one, am counting precisely on this fact: the permanence and irrevocability of the forgiveness of my sins in the good news of Jesus Christ. Tamper with forgiveness and all that remains is abysmally bad news.

Confessing Our Unity

Whether from the various faces of law-creep or from the enervating error of temporary forgiveness, "by being vigilant in our confession of faith we can protect the unity that the Spirit has given us."[14]

Everyone has their theological boundaries; some are in the right place and protect the gospel from errors, while

---

12. Stephen Charnock, *The Existence and Attributes of God* (Evansville, IN: Sovereign Grace Book Club, 1958), 143.

13. Ibid., 11.5.

14. Brown, "Schism," 25.

others remove the ancient boundary stones and broaden the stream so as to enfold the latest new ideas and errors. "To talk theology at all is to talk boundaries and always has been."[15] The great danger in the church, however, is when we ignore the boundaries, when we arrogate our opinions over the enduring bulwarks of the gospel, and when we stop openly and honestly acknowledging and submitting to confessional boundaries.

The church will enjoy unity, walls of hostility broken down, peace and harmony, only insofar as it stands "firm in one spirit, with one mind striving side by side for the faith of the gospel" (Phil. 1:27). A confession of faith is the "open statement of the truth" (2 Cor. 4:2), so critical to maintaining the unity of the body.

The church of Jesus Christ, the city of God, is a glorious body, made so by its Head and Savior, Jesus Christ. Though the church is beset by corruptions of the gospel in every generation, the church's unshakeable foundation truly is Jesus Christ her Lord. We can take comfort that

> Soon the night of weeping
> Shall be the morn of song.[16]

Alas, when undershepherds set themselves above confessional unity, we should not be surprised when the flock soon has plenty of reasons for weeping, the sheep left defenseless, exposed to the ravages of encircling wolves.

For Discussion

1. Read Ephesians 2:14–16 and discuss obstacles to the church's unity.

15. Carl R. Trueman, "Why Do We Draw the Line?" *Tabletalk*, July 1, 2012, http://www.ligonier.org/learn/articles/why-do-we-draw-the-line/.

16. Samuel J. Stone, "The Church's One Foundation," *Trinity Hymnal* (Atlanta: Great Commission, 1990), 347.

For he himself is our peace, who has made us both one and has broken down in his flesh the dividing wall of hostility by abolishing the law of commandments expressed in ordinances, that he might create in himself one new man in place of the two, so making peace, and might reconcile us both to God in one body through the cross, thereby killing the hostility.

2. Read Belgic Confession, article 23, and discuss why our confidence is secure in a "foundation, which is firm forever," and not in covenant faithfulness or any merit in ourselves.

    And the same apostle says that we are justified freely by his grace, through the redemption that is in Christ Jesus.
    And therefore we always hold fast this foundation, ascribing all the glory to God, humbling ourselves before Him, and acknowledging ourselves to be such as we really are, without presuming to trust in anything in ourselves, or in any merit of ours, relying and resting upon the obedience of Christ crucified alone, which becomes ours when we believe in Him.

3. How does the certainty that justification is a one-time act of God, and that forgiveness is irrevocable, accurately reflect the character and attributes of God?

Pray today for those you've heard who speak publicly before large audiences. Pray for a clarity and purity of speech that allows them to call the church universal to unity around the pure doctrine of the gospel. Pray that they avoid sound bites that sow seeds of doubt in the unchangeable truths of the gospel and diminish the foundation Christ laid.

PART 7

Gospel Vigilance:
*Rediscovering the Gospel
Every Generation*

27

Never Yawn at Good News

WHEN I WAS LITTLE I was terrified of water. If I ever managed to work up enough courage to mount the diving board and creep out to the business end of the thing, I was the kid who would stand at the end of the board gnawing my lip in terror at the water, the line of jeering kids behind me growing longer and more vociferous. I was the quintessence of Isaac Watts' timorous mortal starting and shrinking and fearing to launch away.

The Gospel Is the Pool

To hear some ministers preach, we might think that the gospel is like that diving board and that when we are brought to living faith in Christ we take a good bounce and dive off the board. In this analogy, the board is merely what launches us into the pool of the Christian life. Observe, however, that in this metaphor you leave the diving board behind you. You no longer need it. You're in the pool. The diving board was just the means to become a Christian.

It's hard to imagine a more wrong-headed notion.

There is no greater tragedy than when preachers do this with the gospel: leave it behind. There seems to be the assumption that the flock has that gospel thing covered. Jesus and the gospel, in this mind-set, become a means to another end.

They seem to think that Jesus is the milk and the pool is where you find the solid food, the strong meat. The diving board is for the immature; the deep pool is for the mature. Jump into the pool; leave the gospel diving board behind you, and get on to the deeper things.

Some may return to Hebrews 6:1 for proof: "Let us leave the elementary doctrine of Christ and go on to maturity." They may equate Jesus and the gospel with "the basic principles of the oracles of God" (Heb. 5:12). Taken in its context, however, the basic principles the writer of Hebrews is urging us to leave behind are the veiled types and shadows gloriously pointing to and now revealed and fulfilled alone in Jesus Christ.

The gospel is the pool. We mature as we dive more deeply into the truth and beauty of the gospel, as we plumb the unfathomable depth of the love and grace of the Savior every day we live.

Group Yawn

What parent has not seen his or her teenage son or daughter do this in church or in family worship: let off a long, gleeking yawn. We know something is wrong when we see their eyes begin to glaze over, their mouths grow limp and sag open, their heads begin to lurch and bob. If we're honest, we may be irritated more because we're afraid others will see them and it will reflect poorly on our parenting skills. Our expert participation in covenant faithfulness is about to be unmasked. We're afraid our so-flawed covenant nurture will be exposed. So we try to be subtle as we prod our young adult children back to consciousness during the sermon.

Our kids may be becoming spiritually comatose because they are hearing the bland moralism of preaching that comes more from law-law land than from the land of pure delight. They may be taking on the spiritual *rigor mortis* that comes from hearing more about Moses than about Jesus. This may have occurred because the man in the pulpit has allowed, bit by bit, other distractions or interests to usurp the gospel in his message.

I am convinced that every symptom of decline enervating the church stems from our growing weary of Christ and his gospel, of our yawning at the majestic, at our becoming bored with what is indescribably glorious. Instead of being dazzled with Christ and his rescue operation in the gospel, we yawn, heave a sigh, and cast about for something more interesting.

Devilish Distraction

When the gospel stops quickening our pulse, when our kids are no longer agog at the Lion of Judah, the Enemy follows up by encouraging us to find something else about religion that will keep us thinking we are good Christians but that will further divert us from the wonder of the gospel.

He will applaud our efforts when we try to create a new program for growing the church, when we take the pulse of popular culture, when we recast our church in its exciting likeness. He will nod encouragingly when we take up a new theological conundrum, when we strain at a gnat and swallow a camel, when we begin to find scholarly stimulation in speculative theology, or when we decide to preach a sermon series or write a book about our latest discoveries. He's especially pleased with us when we point people to the learning and eloquence of the minister in the pulpit, when we parade the preacher more than the Prophet, Priest, and King he's supposed to be preaching about.

The Enemy is pleased when anything begins to occupy our attention besides the gospel. Handled carefully, soon enough the gospel loses its central place in the pulpit, in ministry, in counseling, in discipleship, in our reading of Scripture, our parenting, our worship, our giving, and in our service. Best of all, we won't even realize it has happened. The Devil doesn't let us in on his game.

All the while, we have become very busy; the Enemy likes us busy. But he wants us busy with other things, not gospel things. The key to success for him is that we turn incrementally away from the sufficiency of Christ and gradually more toward ourselves and what we're so busy doing. He likes it when we try harder, when we turn to self-discipline, when we find our identity more in what we are doing now than in what the Savior has already done.

Mobile Homes in Hurricanes

Meanwhile, what we believe about the gospel gathers dust. We begin to care less about what we believe and more about what we are being and becoming. It only takes a tiny nudge and we are focused on our sanctification, our holiness, our good works, but the pure doctrine of the gospel has faded in our minds and hearts. It's the diving board, somewhere back there behind us, and we're busy flailing around doing laps in the pool of the Christian life. Soon enough we forget what "history has shown time and again, a church that forgets its theology soon finds itself without any."[1]

But it's not just forgetting the theory of what we say we believe. Theoretical theology doesn't count for much. Theology that is declared but not believed, owned but not felt, isn't worth much either. Like a mobile home in a hurricane, one good blast and it's obliterated.

Gospel Central

Herein is the problem for those who make the obligatory confession that of course salvation is all of grace and not based on any of our good works but who lack a day-to-day practical embrace of those truths. Nothing erodes the heartfelt embrace of gospel truths more, according to Jerry Bridges, than when

1. Michael Horton, "Getting Past the TULIP," *Modern Reformation* 21, no. 1 (January/February 2012): 49.

"we have relegated the gospel to the unbeliever."[2] For all practical purposes, the gospel becomes the diving board we leave behind us; this is the real truncated gospel. "We have a truncated view of the gospel," argues Bridges when we "see it only as a door we walk through to become a Christian. In this view, the gospel is only for unbelievers. Once you become a Christian, you don't need it anymore except to share with people who are still outside the door. What you need to hear instead are the challenges and how-tos of discipleship."[3]

Bridges goes on to explain that this mistaken notion about the gospel leads many professing Christians to lead lives of quiet desperation. On the practical day-in-day-out of their lives, they fail to look to Christ and the gospel; they look to their performance for their identity and acceptance with God. When we're doing pretty well, no blatant scandalous sins to own up to, we can feel smug and expectant: God owes me blessings since I'm doing so well. Since practical theology is always what counts, what is the result of this kind of theology? It will always erode our understanding of how desperately we need the grace of the gospel every day of our lives.

Rather than hearing some new strategy for discipleship or hearing some new method of raising covenant children, "the one word that describes what we must continue to hear is gospel."[4] The gospel alone provides the proper motives for redeemed, regenerate sinners who want to please God, who want to walk with him, worship him, serve and obey him.

When we are urged to live the Christian life out of a sense of fear or to win or keep God's favor, grace always shrivels. "We are saved by grace, and we are to live by grace every day of our Christian lives."[5] But our default function is to shift

2. Jerry Bridges, *Disciplines of Grace: God's Role and Our Role in the Pursuit of Holiness* (Colorado Springs: NavPress, 2006), 19.

3. Ibid., 21.

4. Ibid.

5. Ibid.

from grace to something else for daily living. We're afraid that grace won't be a sufficient motivator for holiness; we're afraid that grace probably won't work; gospel might be all well and good for getting saved, but we need something more to produce holiness.

Slyly insinuated, this is yet another of the Enemy's lies to keep us from the freedom of the good news. He makes us think the gospel is too doctrinaire; "The indicatives of gospel theology are so impractical," he whispers in our ear. The imperatives of what we must do are so much more down-to-earth than what we're to believe. If you want holiness, avoid all that dull doctrine.

But the way to holiness, wrote Bridges, only comes as we hear "a continuous reminder of the gospel of God's grace through Christ."[6] Freed from anxiety and fear, our motives for holiness are now gospel motives: love because Jesus first loved us (1 John 4:19; 2 Cor. 5:14), and ineffable gratitude for the saving mercy of the gospel.

Dull Doctrine

Dorothy Sayers, acquaintance of C. S. Lewis and occasional presenter at debates on Christianity at the Socratic Club, is remembered for being one of the first women to earn an Oxford degree, for her defense of classical learning, for her creation of the Lord Peter Wimsey detective fiction series, and for being the foremost literary critic of the crime fiction genre. Some of us, however, may not think of her first as a doctrinaire, gospel-believing, theologically articulate Christian.

To pundits who have concluded that "churches are empty because preachers insist too much upon doctrine, 'dull dogma,' as people call it," she responds by warmly encapsulating the essence of the gospel. Too much dull doctrine?

6. Ibid.

The fact is the precise opposite. It is the neglect of dogma that makes for dullness. The Christian faith is the most exciting drama that ever staggered the imagination of man and the dogma is the drama. This is the dogma we find so dull, this terrifying drama of which God is the victim and the hero. If this is dull, then what, in Heaven's name, is worthy to be called exciting?[7]

How could my kids sleep through that? The Devil wants us to be thrilled with what should repulse us and be repulsed (or at least bored) with what should thrill us. And he does this by telling us lies, by making the terrifying drama of the cross seem tedious, by "par[ing] the claws of the Lion of Judah, certifying him 'meek and mild,' and recommend[ing] Him as a fitting household pet for pale curates and pious old ladies."[8]

Our way of infusing boredom into the gospel may be different in our place and time. We may have fewer pale curates and still fewer pious old ladies today. But we get distracted and enthralled with the wrong things every day. It should not surprise us that our kids do too.

Never Tire of the Gospel

My wife's wedding gift to me back in 1983 was the six-volume set of Dr. Martyn Lloyd-Jones' commentaries on Paul's epistle to the Ephesians. My wife has Welsh heritage, so she had an ethnic predisposition for the Welsh preacher. And she knew that I had come to appreciate reading him and listening to recordings of his preaching because of how clearly he conveyed the gospel to my heart. I have often felt as if he were speaking just to me. Others have felt the same way. When J. I. Packer first heard Lloyd-Jones, he said "he had never heard

7. Dorothy Sayers, *Creed or Chaos?* (New York: Harcourt, Brace and Company, 1949), 3.
8. Ibid.

such preaching." His words brought the greatness of God to Packer "with the force of electric shock."[9] If he was anything, Lloyd-Jones was a passionate herald of the wonder and glory of God displayed in the gospel. Commenting on Paul's words in Romans 6:22, Lloyd-Jones urges us never to grow bored with the gospel:

> The great Apostle delights in repeating these things, and our delight in repeating them also is the measure of our understanding of the faith. People who do not like these repetitions are very poor Christians, if they are Christians at all. One of the signs of the true Christian is that he never tires of [the gospel]. I can never understand the type of Christian[s] who . . . do not like to hear the gospel again! What a terrible state to get into, to feel and to say, "Ah, I know all about that; there is nothing there now for me." How unlike the great Apostle who delights in repeating these things! The true Christian cannot hear these things too often; he likes to hear the gospel, even in its simplest form, because of its central glory and because of its essential wonder.[10]

The Enemy wheedles away so that, deep within us, we scorn the gospel; we think it's too childish, too mundane. He wants to cover over the central glory of the gospel and to distract us from its essential wonder. Under his sway, we think the gospel is too unsophisticated, too childish, just for little ones. Augustine admitted this was once his attitude toward the Bible's central message. "I scorned to be a little one," he wrote. "Being swollen big with pride, I took myself to be a great one."[11]

9. J. I. Packer, cited in John Piper, *When I Don't Desire God* (Wheaton: Crossway, 2004), 77.

10. D. Martyn Lloyd–Jones, *Romans: Exposition of Chapter 6, The New Man* (Edinburgh: Banner of Truth Trust, 2003), 286.

11. Augustine, *The Confessions* (London: Burns, Oates and Washbourne, 1935), 3:52.

A few years ago I visited Westminster Chapel in London. I thought about the fruitful ministry of Pastor Lloyd-Jones, his pulpit in the heart of sophisticated London, only a short stroll from Buckingham Palace. But the glitter and urbane magnificence of London never made him ashamed of the gospel. In the light of the glory and grace of the good news, the things of earth had grown strangely dim for him. And time never dulled his passion but only made him more transfixed by the glory of the gospel of Jesus Christ.

We too must grow in grace and the knowledge of Christ, which is another way of saying we must remain in breathless wonder at the gospel. We must never relegate the gospel of Jesus to the status of the diving board and put it behind us— and then yawn at it. Without rediscovering a "robust and realistic theology grounded in the work of Christ,"[12] we will pass on to our children bland moralism, pedantic intellectualism, anemic religiosity. But we won't pass on to them the breathtaking wonder of saving grace in the gospel of Jesus Christ.

For Discussion

1. Read John 8:34–36 and discuss the difference between a slave and a son and how our sonship ought to astonish and fill us with wonder at the Savior.

   Truly, truly, I say to you, everyone who practices sin is a slave to sin. The slave does not remain in the house forever; the son remains forever. So if the Son sets you free, you will be free indeed.

2. How can we communicate the glorious reality of being made sons and heirs to our teens when they struggle

12. Mark Galli, "A Potentially Beautiful Day in the Neighborhood: Why Evangelicals Need the Young, Restless, and Reformed," *Modern Reformation* 21, no. 1 (January/February 2012): 49.

with temptation? How does Heidelberg Catechism 44 help us in this?

Q. Why is there added, "he descended to hell"?

A. That in my greatest temptations, I may be assured, and wholly comfort myself in this, that my Lord Jesus Christ, by his inexpressible anguish, pains, terrors, and hellish agonies, in which he was plunged during all his sufferings, but especially on the cross, has delivered me from the anguish and torments of hell.

3. Discuss ways we can better communicate the indescribably glorious wonder of our adoption into the family of God and help our children learn to rest in Christ.

Pray for yourself, your family, and the Christians you know, to be prepared to take your stand, plant your flag, and ready yourself for war. Pray for deep insights into the Word of God, equipping you with the belt of truth, the breastplate of righteousness, the shoes of the gospel of peace, the shield of faith, helmet of salvation, and the sword of the Spirit (Eph. 6:13–17).

28

Gospel Succession

CHURCH HISTORY IS, among other things, a chronicle of how little we learn from church history. "There is nothing new under the sun," wrote the author of Ecclesiastes (1:9), or put in modern parlance, "What goes around comes around." This probably has a great deal to do with how immune we imagine ourselves to be from the corruptions and defections of others. Remember how violently Peter protested that *he* would never deny Jesus? Sometimes the Lord graciously humbles us using the old switcheroo.

I was raised a Baptist. In college I began theological explorations that led me to become a Presbyterian (though many of my heroes are Baptists and the difference is not my hill to die on). When one of my sons went off to study architecture at the University of Washington, he eagerly became involved in and eventually joined a church that was not Presbyterian. It was Baptist. We talked a good deal in those days, and I had flashbacks of conversations I had had with my godly father when things were switched around (and some don't think God has a sense of humor).

Not Your Father's Church

I needed to check this out, so one Sunday evening I drove north to Seattle to visit my son and to go with him to his new church. Looking back, it would have been impossible for me to be fully prepared for what came next. Standing next to my son, I found myself in an urban warehouse, the walls painted black, garish lighting flashing around the stage and room. It was all so unlike the liturgy he had grown up with. My ears pounded, and I felt sick to my stomach as I watched the massive screen behind the band emblazoned with a giant close-up of the lead guitarist's fingers sliding up and down the neck of his instrument. We hadn't taken a wrong turn; this was church. Under the assaulting influence of the new nightclub liturgy, I was again bewildered and wondered if I was supposed to be singing something. There were 2,000 nineteen- to twenty-nine-year-olds in the room, but I could not hear anyone singing except the worship leader. His face was contorted with emotion and the well-meaning young man was groaning in a manner I felt uncomfortable attempting to emulate.

Yet he was singing a hymn, and I knew the words. But I was so distracted by the entertainment venue, the volume, and all the paraphernalia required by the band to pull off this kind of liturgy. I wondered how the underground church could ever make this happen without discovery by the authorities. It was so loud I couldn't sing, and I felt like I was in a state of shock induced by sensory overload. Curiously, most people around me didn't seem to be singing either. In this liturgy, participation in the actual singing didn't seem to matter. It was fine if you did, but it made no difference to what anyone else heard whether you sang or not.

Finally, I turned to my son, took a deep breath, and yelled, "Are we supposed to be singing?" He turned and hollered back in my ear, "I don't know!" No one around us was disturbed in the slightest by our yelling.

Fresh Message

After one final reverberating riff, things got quiet. The preacher greeted everyone and began his sermon. I'll admit it: everything I believed about sung worship had just been torpedoed. I readied myself for a sermon that would surely have hipster cool for an *entrée* with a garnish of therapeutic fluff, and a side of reclaim-the-city moralism. He wasn't five minutes into his sermon, however, before my assumptions were under siege.

I was hearing a straightforward, perceptive exposition, careful, imaginative, biblically sound and theologically solid sermon, one of the clearest gospel messages I had heard in a long time. I'll admit it, I was critical and looking for the worst, but there was nothing trite or superficial about this man's preaching. He laid out the ugliness of the bad news, and then he gave a winsome explanation of the beauty of the free grace of the gospel, an unabashed reformational message that winsomely heralded the glorious person and finished work of the Lord Jesus. It really was all about Jesus. I was blown away.

After the service, I asked my son why the new ministry appealed to him so much (I was afraid he'd say the music). He was quiet for a moment and then said his new pastor "doesn't try to make things all heady. He preaches straight-up gospel. I haven't really heard that growing up." His words were like blows in the pit of my stomach. I felt the way the father must have felt whose daughter asked him why they didn't hear much about the love of Jesus in their church. My son's words hurt all the more because I knew there was truth in them.

He went on about his new pastor. "And he assumes that if God has given me his grace in the gospel, he's also given me gifts, and those gifts need training, and he gives me that too. Then he puts me to work using my gifts in the church." Again he paused. "I never got a sense of that growing up. I was an observer. I never felt like there was a role for me in the church I grew up in."

What does a father do when he hears this from his son? I might be quick to say that college is a time of change and discovery and all those things were probably in place in the church he grew up in—he just didn't realize it—but now he has a fresh perspective. I tried this line of reasoning with myself, but it wasn't working.

I told him how much I loved him, Presbyterian or hipster Baptist, and encouraged him with my blessing. I'm in for the long haul with my children; how could I not support him when he was hearing biblically clear, theologically passionate gospel preaching and being so intentionally equipped for service in the body of Christ? He went on to complete extensive leadership training and was asked to participate in planting another church elsewhere in the city. Now married with children, he continues active in ministry in another urban church plant, and we continue to have rich fellowship around Jesus and the gospel.

Was My Son Right?

I was forced to think deeply about what my son had said. In many ways he was right. Ministry was largely done for us, performed with expertise by the experts. And the congregation was mostly passive. On the one hand, few things are more devastating to the youth of a church than to realize this. On the other hand, realizing it may be the way to begin fixing it.

Imagine how impoverished the church would be if John Gifford had not cultivated the gifts of John Bunyan and given him a role in the church in Bedfordshire in the seventeenth century. And it may do us some good to recall that peasant-laborer Bunyan not only didn't go to seminary, but he also had no formal education past grammar school. We must take church leadership seriously, but in our zeal for a well-trained ministry, we must never give our young people the ghost of an impression that they don't have gifts given by God. The church absolutely must have those gifts to function as the body of Christ.

Old and Young

My children were not alone. I began seeing more of the college-age young people either rebel, passively conform and slouch their way through church, become self-righteous Pharisees, or I have seen them rediscover the gospel and catch fire—a growing number deciding to go elsewhere to church, where they were needed, where their gifts and energy were wanted.

Nevertheless, there is a resurgent youth culture shaping the contemporary church that makes many parents and church leaders understandably concerned. There's a new normal that at times makes it feel like it's a sin to have white hair or wear a tie. We may think this is uniquely a contemporary phenomenon. It's not. For as long as old people and young people have shared the planet, and shared their place in the church, there have been generational problems to overcome.

Calvin must have faced it in Geneva, and on his deathbed offered timeless advice to youth. "You younger men, be humble and seek not to achieve greater things, for youth is seldom void of ambition and tends to despise the opinions of others."[1] We nod sagely and feel like Calvin nailed it. We hope our sons are listening. Hearing impaired though they may be, they need to hear this. And we parents need to help our sons and daughters understand this generational ambition to take over, to despise the past, and recast the church in the image of the latest thing.

But Calvin wasn't finished. He went on and addressed the corresponding danger for older folks in the church. "Let the old not bear envy towards the young for the grace they may have received, but let them rejoice and bless God for having bestowed it on them."[2] Calvin did nail it. Our zeal for biblical worship and maintaining the truth may be a thin disguise

1. John Calvin, *Letters of John Calvin* (Edinburgh: Banner of Truth, 1980), 256.
2. Ibid.

for cronyism, keeping hold of the reins of power. When this is the case, our young people will see through our motive like a ladder.

I think Calvin understood that one of the reasons churches atrophy is their desire to control the behavior of their youth, to keep them in their place. Most of them will stay in their place—until they're older. Then they'll take the grace they have received elsewhere. They will go to church where they are needed, where their energy and zeal are valued. However careful a church is to have qualified elders, it must never exasperate its young people and make them feel useless in gospel ministry. "Do not discourage one another," said Calvin to young and old. "Be not an obstacle to one another."[3]

God *has* bestowed gifts and graces on our regenerate children. Far from being obstacles exasperating our young people, we ought to be giddy with pleasure—and guide and equip them for ministry, and give them a meaningful place to serve in the body. Just as a youth-culture church is significantly incomplete, so is the church without the active, joyful, gifted contribution of its young people.

Podcasts in France

My personal journey to rediscover the grace of the gospel continued. Because of her interest in missions, one of my daughters wanted to study French—in France. I'll admit I was anxious and prayed a lot that year. I was not so worried that she would rebel and gorge herself on European hedonism, but still I prayed a lot. She and her friends would listen to podcasts of sermons every week. "We listen to R.C. Sproul," she told me on the phone, "John Piper, Tim Keller, Ravi Zacharias, and Mark Driscoll." She went on to say that she also listened to the sermons of another minister.

3. Ibid.

I encouraged her to keep doing this. When she came home for Christmas, we had a long talk. With tears in her eyes, she said, "Daddy, there's such a big difference." I reassured her that different men had different gifts, and she should expect them to have different preaching styles; few men will have the remarkable gifts of these men, and we should never allow that to make us discontent with God's ministers with more ordinary gifts. "That's not what I mean." She went on to explain that she often listened to each of these men preach from the same book of the Bible. "At first I thought it was just different delivery style. But that's not it," she insisted.

I pressed her. I needed to know what the difference was. "While Dr. Sproul and the others point me to Jesus and the gospel of grace—" I felt numb as I anticipated what she would say next. Naming the other pastor, she said, "He takes us to our works—every time. They preach what Jesus has done by his grace; he preaches what I must do by the law."

I knew she was right. Like hammer blows, my son's words echoed in my head: his new pastor "preaches straight-up gospel. I haven't really heard that growing up." My other children were saying similar things. I had so hoped that my efforts to fill in the blanks, to compensate for what they had been hearing would work. It hadn't.[4]

Playing Ape

Some tell us to teach our kids to move their hands, feet, and lips, and their hearts will follow. But the danger is that when our children do things without the heart they settle into a routine of religiosity and moral behavior; pretty soon the external conformity of their behavior helps them forget altogether the need for the heart. "The moving of the body

---

4. My adult children have been led along by grace, sometimes through thorny pathways, to rediscover the gospel and walk with Jesus.

outward," wrote Scots Reformer George Wishart, "without the inward moving of the heart is naught else but the playing of an ape and not the true serving of God."[5]

Though it looks like good self-discipline, doing before feeling is dangerous.[6] And it may ruin us and our children. But we'll have lots of company: Pharisees were great doers without the movement of the heart. We can never be satisfied with changed behavior without a changed heart. Changes motivated by guilt and fear are not yet gospel-motivated changes. Self-discipline and child discipline must always have as their goal the heartfelt motivation of love for Jesus, who first loved us, and gratitude for the great mercy he has shown us and continues to show us in the gospel.

It's not only our good works that must flow from love and gratitude, but also our worship as well. The more we engage in the habit of public worship without believing and loving, the less we will believe and love. This is the great danger of solemnity and formality. It's so easy to do it without heart. The church needs the new generation each generation to re-enliven its worship with a renewed passion for the gospel and for Jesus Christ.

We must guard against accepting all counterfeits. Insisting on worship that's only new and hip or on worship that never deviates a whisker from the way we've always done it—both will miss the mark. A liturgy dictated by the trend machine will eventually devolve into irrelevancy. And a formal liturgy that encourages the playing of apes, but that does not intentionally root worship in the centrality of Christ's finished work in the

5. George Wishart, cited in Eustace Percy, *John Knox* (London: James Clarke, 1964), 54.

6. Of course, when our children are infants and small children—even at times as they get older—we do restrain their external behavior. We don't let our toddler play in the freeway, even though in his heart he really wants to play with the semitrucks whizzing by. But we must never be satisfied with modifying their external behavior without nurturing their hearts with the gospel. This begins in the cradle and persists throughout their lives.

gospel, will send our believing young people on a quest for a church that does.

Heart and Head

I promised that this book would not offer a simplistic solution to the decline of the church. I will, however, distill it down to its most basic habit. And it's first a habit of the heart, not a habit of the hands, or mouth, or feet. We must be daily thrilled with Jesus and the depth and richness of his electing love for us in the gospel. Only then can we nurture our children in the beauty of the gospel, bathing them in our own wonder at the Savior.

Moms and dads enraptured by the Son of God will speak more to their children's hearts than to their heads. We must pray earnestly for the other voices speaking into their lives, especially their pastor's. "When you ascend the pulpit," wrote Toplady, "leave your learning behind you: endeavor to preach more to the hearts of your people than to their heads."[7] Pray earnestly that your pastor's wonder at the gospel of Jesus will be fresh and that he will convey his wonder to the hearts of your children. If this is not happening, ready yourself for rebellion or glazed-over conformity, or for them to discover the grace of the gospel and find another church.

It will happen to us, and when we think it won't, we may be putting our faith more in our parenting than in the gospel. The grace of the gospel alone speaks to the heart and renews the mind. Anything short of this will work our children into a perpetual state of spiritual pride, lethargy, or worse.

Sing Your Theology

There are few better ways to re-enliven our sense of the gospel than to join our voices with what Christians have been

7. Toplady, *Diary and Hymns*, 54.

singing for centuries. Singing gets closer to the heart. Singing the riches of the gospel, praising the Savior for being our surety before the throne of his Father, praising him because

> My name is graven on His hands,
> My name is written on His heart[8]

will direct our children away from vacuous formality in worship and from its counterpoise, affected emotionalism.

Singing psalms and hymns, however, is not enough. Traditional Welsh choirs still sing hymns, and so did Elvis. It's critical how we sing. Our children must never think we sing hymns out of tradition, just because. Singing—real singing—is the audible overflowing of a joyful heart. But it is joy based on substantive doctrinal truth. Choose meaningful lyrics with the depth and richness of the Psalms; avoid vain repetition; cultivate appreciation and understanding of poetry that imaginatively adorns the theological reasons for the praise. Pause and consider what you have just sung. Reread key phrases and ask your children what they mean; help them find passages of Scripture the hymn writer might have been meditating on while creating lines like these:

> Because the sinless Savior died
> My sinful soul is counted free.
> For God the just is satisfied
> To look on Him and pardon me.[9]

Never just sing those words. Halt in your tracks, astonished, and consider what you've just sung. And never neglect the Psalms. One of the ways to disabuse our children of the urge to think the church is irrelevant and obsolete is to move

8. Charitie Lees Bancroft, "Before the Throne of God Above," 1863, last modified December 26, 2010, http://www.hymntime.com/tch/htm/b/e/beforetg.htm.
9. Ibid.

their hearts with inspired poetry penned three thousand years ago and sung and danced to by generations of believers and worshipers ever since. Join those joyful generations in your family's worship together.

Worldliness encourages our children to think that the church is the "dry and weary land where there is no water" (Ps. 63:1), when it's the reverse. When our kids' affections have been trained by virtual pleasures, by artificial thrills, by stunning special effects, they will believe the lie. Fed daily on what the popular culture serves up, our kids will yawn at what should fill them with wonder: the redemptive purpose of God in Christ. The latest films, music, sports, technology—all these seem so exciting and impressive. A message of bland moralism, therapeutic religiosity, anemic self-help, or even erudite shock and awe can never compete. Only one thing, one Person, can invoke and sustain heartfelt wonder.

Nurture your children on oral reading of the Bible, pausing, asking them questions, explaining, discussing, having them read and own the Word of God. And nurture them in the great confessional catechisms so that they know what they believe and why they believe it. Once again, never do any of these things without the heart; don't teach them to be apes. Look up the Scripture proofs and engage them in vigorous discussion of the sources for these timeless confessional summations of gospel truth. Do all this with the goal of enthralling their imaginations with the story of redemption and with the loveliness of the Redeemer himself.

The normalization of the stupendous is the Enemy's great strategy with our children—and with us. The disciplines of the Christian life—prayer, reading the Scriptures, singing praises, learning Bible doctrine in the catechism, corporate worship—all these must be daily refreshed so that they remain and grow as disciplines joyfully engaged in by grace alone. We must often remind ourselves, it's never our spiritual good habits that work.

Do all this with the goal of putting Christ on display before your children, of enthralling them with the beauty of the Savior and his grace. Grace alone is what brings the Savior near.

All the while, the Enemy will be at his tricks. When he fears he may be losing us, Satan has a particularly entertaining card to play. When we discover the riches of the gospel of free grace and are earnest in the training of our children, he makes us proud of how well we're doing; look at how much more our children know about God than all the other kids out there with lesser parents.

If he plays his hand carefully—and he will—he'll have us patting ourselves on the back for our newly discovered doctrinal knowledge, proud of how much more our kids know about total depravity and the freedom of God's grace. Careful to keep us from seeing the monstrous irony, he'll have us rolling our eyes in disgust at all the ignorant Christians who aren't smart enough to believe as we do about the doctrines of grace. "Self-righteousness can feed upon doctrines," cautioned John Newton, "as well as upon works."[10] When our children get orthodoxy in their heads but not in their hearts, they can become theological Nazis to put the most radical ideologue to shame. Rattling off their Bible verses and catechism and swaggering at their vast doctrinal understanding, our kids will have forged doctrine into an iron club with which to bludgeon the uninitiated. As we put them on display, preening ourselves for our skillful parenting, we'll have helped them do it.

Prayer

What is our only defense against all the Enemy's twisted strategies? For spiritual disciplines not to devolve into yet another angle on legalism, we are utterly dependent on prayer, on earnest and familiar communing with God. Prayer brings God near to us and us near to God, into his very courts. "Blessed is the one you choose and bring near, to dwell in your courts!

10. Newton, *Selected Letters*, 115.

We shall be satisfied with the goodness of your house, the holiness of your temple!" (Ps. 65:4). Pray not as an exercise of self-discipline, because you feel like you have to; pray because you *have* to, because you're desperate.

Help your children understand that if they exhaust themselves trying to find satisfaction in the counterfeit splendors of the temporal world, they will come up empty. Only the goodness and holiness of Christ satisfies; the steadfast love of the Savior alone is better than life itself (Ps. 63:3). Dazzle yourself, dazzle your children with the wonder of being chosen, brought near, into the very courts of the King of Kings! Bring them to their knees so they realize what Newton understood:

> Solid joys and lasting treasure,
> None but Zion's children know.[11]

For Discussion

1. Discuss how Christ's finished work for and in our children enables us to encourage them to participate in the work of the kingdom now. Reflecting on the chapter, outline the pattern Paul used in speaking with a young man in 1 Timothy 1:14–17:

   And the grace of our Lord overflowed for me with the faith and love that are in Christ Jesus. The saying is trustworthy and deserving of full acceptance, that Christ Jesus came into the world to save sinners, of whom I am the foremost. But I received mercy for this reason, that in me, as the foremost, Jesus Christ might display his perfect patience as an example to those who were to believe in him for eternal life. To the King of the ages, immortal, invisible, the only God, be honor and glory forever and ever.

11. John Newton, "Glorious Things of Thee Are Spoken," *Trinity Hymnal* (Atlanta: Great Commission, 1990), 345.

2. Discuss how Heidelberg Catechism 55 gives us perspective on how we should view our young people and their gifts in the body of Christ.

Q. What do you understand by "the communion of saints"?

A. First, that all and every one, who believes, being members of Christ, are in common, partakers of him, and of all his riches and gifts; secondly, that every one must know it to be his duty, readily and cheerfully to employ his gifts, for the advantage and salvation of other members.

3. Read Ephesians 4:11–13 and discuss the danger when young adults begin thinking that ministry is largely done for them and that their gifts are not needed in the church.

And he gave the apostles, the prophets, the evangelists, the shepherds and teachers, to equip the saints for the work of ministry, for building up the body of Christ, until we all attain to the unity of the faith and of the knowledge of the Son of God, to mature manhood, to the measure of the stature of the fullness of Christ.

Pray today for your pastor and elders that they will have shepherds' hearts toward the souls of the youth in your church.

29

All Else Fails, but
Grace Works

LOOKING INTO the anguished face of the mother, I saw a heart that was breaking. There was profound disappointment and sadness in her features; there was hurt and an edge of bitterness in her eyes.

This dear woman and her husband had raised their daughter in the church, and not a liberal church; it was one that considered itself to be orthodox, maybe even the most orthodox. They weren't marginal folks living scandalous lives during the week and dragging themselves bleary-eyed to church on Sunday morning. They'd attended regularly, encouraged their children to participate in the activities and programs the church offered, even sent their children to the church's Christian school.

But something had gone wrong, badly wrong. Something hadn't worked. Their adult daughter had come to think of the church as an infectious disease and wanted nothing to do with it. I wish this story was an isolated one, but honest Christians know it's not. Perhaps every church has its exposed underbelly, its casualties, its visible members who have defected. But nothing grieves Christian parents more than when it's their children who have rebelled and walked out the door, leaving behind the "solid joys and lasting treasure"[1] for the "gilded toys of dust,"[2] the counterfeit baubles the world offers.

History doesn't equivocate; this happened in Amsterdam, and in Geneva, and in Edinburgh, and in Northampton, and no doubt it is happening in many of our churches in this generation. But why does this happen?

Performing Orcas

We will never be enthralled with the love and grace of Jesus—the grace alone that works—until we see and own up to what great sinners we are, how desperately lost we are, and just how badly we need rescuing. What's true for us is true for our children. They will value grace in exact proportion to how much they know they need it; self-righteous moralists don't think much of grace. Hence, when the church places a greater priority on external conformity than on the inward realities of our union with Jesus Christ, we lose the right to feel cheated when our kids rebel, when they thumb their noses at the gospel and wander into the far country.

We have to get this into our heads and into the deepest recesses of our hearts: moralism is ugly. To put it the way Jesus did in Matthew 23:27, moralism—external law keeping and conformity—is like whitewashed tombs, like worm-infested graves below the grassy knolls in a cemetery; things may look good on the outside, but inside, where it counts, it's rotten and it stinks. And our kids will pick up on the odor.

When our children begin to realize that we are finding our identity, even to the smallest degree, in our performance instead of in our position, they start smelling something fishy.

1. John Newton, "Glorious Things of Thee Are Spoken," *Trinity Hymnal* (Atlanta: Great Commission, 1990), 345.

2. Mary D. James, "All for Jesus," *Trinity Hymnal* (Atlanta: Great Commission, 1990), 565.

When they detect that we find our confidence and assurance in our duty-doing good works more than in the wonder of Christ's work for us, the smell gets stronger.

Few things encourage this more than preaching that turns us back in on ourselves, on our performance of external duties, on the bare institution of the church, on our visible identity in the sacraments of the church. When a genera- tion is suckled on a message that tells them that they can have confidence in the favor of God by their conformity to all his commandments, our children will begin to hold their noses. When they hear a message that gives their parents confidence in their children's salvation based more on the parents' faithfulness than on the sovereign faithfulness of the gracious purpose of God in the gospel, they will start groping for a gas mask. When preaching spends more time on the demands, on the imperatives, than on the indicatives, the glorious truths of the saving love of the Father in his Son, the strangulation is nearly complete.

A message that does not make indelibly clear to our chil- dren how desperately they need the gospel every day of their lives will produce one of three reactions in them. Clutching at their noses, they will rebel and bolt out the door. Or they will become like the performing orcas at an aquarium, jumping through the hoops, nodding and bowing on cue, externally conforming to the prescribed expectations—and feeling pretty good about themselves for doing it—until the unresolved sin inside of them finds expression in the crushing ugliness of a double life. Or, drawn sweetly by the grace of the gospel, they will find another church where grace and Christ are the center of the message.

I wonder if Satan's favorite option above is the middle one, the one that takes the gradual road to hell, the one without signposts, without sudden turnings, the one that puts our kids in a law-law land stupor.

Tainted Purity

"Satan's stratagem," wrote Calvin, "is that he does not attempt an avowed destruction of the whole gospel, but he taints its purity by introducing false and corrupt opinions."[3] And he's so clever about it. He understands our default setting. "We all automatically gravitate toward the assumption," wrote church historian Richard Lovelace, "that we are justified by our level of sanctification."[4]

It is this automatic setting in our minds and hearts that makes the Enemy's work of corrupting the gospel so routine. There is no more productive way for him to taint the purity of the gospel than by making our growth in holiness and obedience a conditional activity that sweeps over justification. He's subtler about it than this, but I imagine he insinuates it like this: "You'd better shape up and obey—or God'll take your justification away." I imagine the Enemy gets an especially perverse delight out of encouraging us to run around doing holy activities (ones he would hate if they came from the heart) and then by directing us to gaze on our good works; he sets us to preening ourselves because of how faithful and obedient we're being—when we're really not.

But what is the ultimate result, the one that most enduringly taints the purity of the gospel's message? When we allow things to get flip-flopped, "it inevitably focuses our attention not on Christ but on the adequacy of our own obedience," wrote Lovelace. "We start each day with our personal security resting not on the accepting love of God and the sacrifice of Christ but on our present feelings or recent achievements in the Christian life."[5] A gospel that diverts us in the slightest from Christ is already tainted; the Enemy's strategy has already worked.

3. John Calvin, *Commentary on Galatians*, trans. and ed. John Owen (Grand Rapids: Eerdmans, 1974), 97.

4. Richard Lovelace, *Dynamics of Spiritual Renewal* (Downers Grove, IL: InterVarsity Press, 1979), 101.

5. Ibid.

Semper Reformanda

Most Christians, regardless of their theological and denominational background, will confidently affirm that they don't initially earn the favor of God by their good works. But as Billy Graham's grandson puts it, "I haven't met one Christian who doesn't struggle daily with believing—somehow, someway— that our good behavior is required to *keep* God's favor."[6]

Intractably predisposed to think we keep God's saving favor by something we do, we then hear moralistic preaching that fuels our inclination by explicitly pointing us to our performance—and the daily struggle grows worse. Coupled with our doubts about the free promises of the gospel, we hear someone tell us that true faith in God requires us "to know all of the commandments of your God and the regulations of his word" and that this knowledge "makes you determined then to obey them all and confident that in obeying them you will have your reward both now and forever." This kind of message is like pushing the launch button on a nuclear warhead zeroed in on the gospel.

Little wonder R.C. Sproul maintains the church is caught in yet another crisis in justification.[7] In some respects the sixteenth century was better off: they had only one overarching source of gospel corruption, the medieval church. Today the enemies preaching conditional justification are within the Protestant gate. Some use the rallying cry, *semper reformanda* (short for "the church always reformed"), as an appeal to move beyond reformational boundaries. Using the axiom as fuel for innovation, these men seem to think the church needs to be always reforming because the latest scholarship has rendered the old confessional doctrines out of date and passé. But this is

6. Tullian Tchividjian, *Jesus Plus Nothing Equals Everything* (Wheaton: Crossway, 2011), 49.

7. Sproul, "Molehills out of Mountains," *TableTalk*, May 1, 2010, http://www.ligonier.org/learn/articles/making-molehills-out-mountains/.

a distortion of the original meaning; *semper reformanda* meant the church must always return to the root, *sola Scriptura*. That is, we must rediscover and reaffirm every generation the gospel of free, justifying grace taught in Scripture; we must always be reforming because attacks will always be launched against the pure doctrine of the gospel. Hence, concern over going back to the root and getting justification right in our generation "is not a tempest in a teapot;" according to Dr. Sproul, "it's one by which salvation itself is defined."[8]

Work Out Your Salvation

But wait a minute, you might be saying. Doesn't the Bible command us to do good works? Aren't we supposed to be striving, exerting great effort, running the race, beating the air, making our bodies our slaves? Doesn't the Bible even tell us to work out our salvation, even with fear and trembling?

It does, indeed, say these things. However, none of these verses are understood aright if they are turned loose like pit bulls on justification. When selective texts are used as attack dogs to shred the certainties of justification by grace alone, through faith alone, in Christ alone, we can be pretty sure that the one handling the dog and managing the tension has an agenda, one that will eventually mangle the gospel message.

Here's what Paul wrote to the church in Philippi: "Work out your own salvation with fear and trembling, for it is God who works in you, both to will and to work for his good pleasure" (Phil. 2:12–13). We are most certainly called to diligent work, but immediately Paul reminds us that it is God who is enabling us to work, to obey; it is God who is at work in us doing his will and pleasure. Moreover, there is a clear theological consensus on this among the heroes of church history. "As the effect is in the cause," wrote John Owen, "the fruit is

8. Ibid.

in the root."[9] The effect, our good works, has a divine cause, the grace of God in the gospel, and so the fruit of our good works springs from the root of justifying grace working in us, as promised—no bargains, no conditions.

But this is no isolated text on good works. And the theological greats knew very well the unrelenting determination of the Enemy to prey on the gospel. Puritan Samuel Bolton wrote, "Just as 'without me ye can do nothing' (John 15.5), so 'I can do all things through Christ which strengtheneth me' (Phil. 4.13). A weak Christian and a strong Christian shall be able to do all. Nothing will be too hard for that man who has the strength of Christ to enable him, and the Spirit of Christ to work with him."[10]

Describing the twofold debt that we owe to God of sin and the debt of service, Bolton wrote, "These two were both transferred to Christ, and He has fulfilled all righteousness for us, both the obedience and the suffering, so that we are now said to be 'complete in him'" (Col. 2.10).[11]

Confusing the sheep with a message that gives the impression their obedience is a condition of their justification, creates a spirit of bondage incompatible with the freedom of the gospel. Trembling, the sheep cast about, wondering if we've been obedient enough, if we've crucified the flesh enough, if our faithfulness is faithful enough. Hear the contrast in Bolton's liberating message:

> We are freed from a state of bondage, a spirit of slavery in service, and brought into a spirit of sonship and liberty in service. As Christ by His blood redeemed us from being slaves, so by His obedience and Spirit He has redeemed us to be sons. Now we are drawn to service, not with cords of fear, but with

9. John Owen, *The Works of John Owen* (Edinburgh: Banner of Truth, 2007), 5:73.
10. Samuel Bolton, *The True Bounds of Christian Freedom* (Edinburgh: Banner of Truth, 1994), 41.
11. Ibid., 42.

the bands of love; not by compulsions of conscience, but by the desires of nature (2 Peter 1.4). As the love of God to us was the spring of all His actions to us, so our love to God is the source of all our obedience to Him.[12]

When we are trying to keep the favor of God by our obedience, we are being drawn with cords of fear, not love, and compulsion, not heartfelt desire. Like Bolton, the Westminster divines thrill us with confidence in God's promise, grounding our obedience in the certainty of the Spirit's enabling grace working in us. "The grace of God is manifested in the second covenant, in that he . . . promiseth and giveth his Holy Spirit to all his elect, to work in them that faith, with all other saving graces; and to enable them unto all holy obedience, as the evidence of the truth of their faith and thankfulness to God" (WLC 32).

The grace of God in the new covenant is freely given to us by Christ the Mediator, the promise of the Holy Spirit to all the elect, "to enable them unto all holy obedience," not as a contingency to justification but as the evidence of true faith expressed in gratitude to God, all based on God's gracious appointment for our salvation. There's nothing contingent or uncertain about this grace. It's real grace, given by God, and it has its real effect in us. It really does work. It produces the fruit of grace in us: heartfelt, grateful obedience; good works flowing from love, our love for the Savior who first loved us.

We rest in peace, we draw nigh to our heavenly Father with confidence because he has ordained and fully accomplished salvation, justification, and sanctification, and all saving benefits, for us. The gospel according to Isaiah makes this brilliantly clear. "O LORD, you will ordain peace for us, for you have indeed done for us all our works" (26:12). Any message that allows sanctification to backwash and erode justification

12. Ibid., 48–49.

destroys that peace, enervates our walk, and turns us to hand-wringing, moralistic self-improvement. This kind of law-creep dilutes the gospel. And a diluted gospel never works.

The Gift of Good Works

The church in Amsterdam lost sight of a nonnegotiable fact: the antidote to law-creep is to keep Jesus Christ at the center of everything, everything we believe and teach, and everything we do and practice. "The more [we] study Christ," wrote Puritan Richard Sibbes, "and the fullness that is in Christ, and all comfort in him alone to be had—'wisdom, righteousness, sanctification, and redemption' (1 Corinthians 1:30)—the more men grow up in the knowledge of Christ, the more they grow spiritually."[13]

We find all our comfort in Christ, who is not only our justification but also our sanctification. I suspect the Enemy wishes he could forever bury men such as Sibbes. Believing that Christ is also our sanctification is a corrective to all corruptions of the gospel, but especially ones that attempt to deceive us into thinking that our good works in some way contribute to our final justification.

The Law Cannot Sanctify

There's no need for confusion on this critical understanding, yet the Enemy levels his guns here in every generation. Charles Hodge, after making the point that the effects of grace are also gifts of God, appeals to the entire message of Scripture for evidence: "[That] sanctification is a supernatural work is proved from the fact that it is constantly referred to as God as its author. It is referred to God absolutely."[14] And then he gives a

13. Richard Sibbes, *The Works of Richard Sibbes* (Edinburgh: The Banner of Truth Trust, 1983), 4:215.
14. Charles Hodge, *Systematic Theology: Soteriology* (Peabody, MA: Hendrickson, 2003), 3:215–16.

representative sampling of the Bible's relentless message about God in Christ working his sanctifying will and promise in us.

"Now may the God of peace himself sanctify you completely. . . . He who calls you is faithful; he will surely do it" (1 Thess. 5:23–24). "The God of peace, that brought again from the dead our Lord Jesus . . . make you perfect in every good work to do his will, working in you that which is well pleasing in his sight" (Heb. 13:20–21 KJV). And referring to Christ, he "gave himself for us, that he might . . . purify unto himself a peculiar people, zealous of good works" (Titus 2:14 KJV). Again Christ "loved the church, and gave himself for it; that he might sanctify and cleanse it with the washing of water by the word, that he might present it to himself a glorious church, not having spot, or wrinkle, or any such thing; but that it should be holy and without blemish" (Eph. 5:25 KJV). Hodge could have added, "Work, for I am with you, declares the Lord of hosts" (Hag. 2:4), and many other like texts spread throughout the pages of the Bible.

After urging us to work and be diligent in our sanctification, Peter sums up the message of his letter telling us to "grow in the grace and knowledge of our Lord and Savior Jesus Christ" (2 Peter 3:18). He does not tell us to grow in law and our knowledge of law. John Piper put it this way, "Not only can the law not justify, but it cannot sanctify either."[15] This is a crucial point, a point all Christians must get right if we're going to get the gospel right.

Some are quick to dismiss what Piper is saying here, but he is speaking in a manner consistent with the confessional understanding of his Presbyterian brethren. "The principal acts of saving faith are accepting, receiving, and resting upon Christ alone for justification, sanctification, and eternal life, by virtue of the covenant of grace" (WCF 14.2). Not by a cov-

15. John Piper, "The Law" (sermon, Bethlehem Baptist Church, Minneapolis, MN, November 11, 2001).

enant of law, but by the covenant of grace, wherein we rest alone on Christ for all saving benefits—including sanctification. But because we persist in eroding this grace-saturated understanding of the gospel with law-creep, we need constant reminders. Paul Tripp cautions us that when we look to the law for our sanctification we're "asking the law to do what only grace can accomplish."[16] However zealous for holiness our motives are, law doesn't produce holiness. "The law is not of faith" (Gal. 3:12), and faith alone produces holiness. Therefore, law won't work, because it can't work. Only grace works.

Grace Is Not a Thing

Why do the Scriptures and the best theologians throughout the ages always point us to grace for our sanctification? Because looking anywhere else will undermine justification. Church history ruthlessly proves this. Second, we look to grace for sanctification because grace alone produces good works in us.

The Enemy wants us to flip all this on its head. He wants us to make the Bible's admonitions to work, to be diligent, to examine ourselves the sum of its message about sanctification and assurance. Satan then wants us to subsume grace under works, to shout down the indicatives with the imperatives, to set grace and good works against each other, and then to make us suspicious of too much grace. "It doesn't help my flock to just hear grace, grace, grace," said one minister. He seemed to fear that grace wouldn't work; grace wouldn't produce the moral improvement he longed to see in his flock.

So often we speak about grace as if it were some kind of commodity. We make it sound as if there's a thing called grace, and, like the thing called pizza, too much of it isn't good for us. Doing this reveals a vital misunderstanding of what grace is. "There is no 'thing' that Jesus takes from himself and then

16. Paul Tripp, "Wednesday's Word," (e-letter), August 8, 2012.

hands over to me," said Sinclair Ferguson. "It is not a thing that was crucified to give us a thing called grace. There is only Jesus himself."[17] So what happens to the statement of the preacher who thought too much grace wasn't good for his flock if we substitute Jesus for the word *grace*? "It doesn't help my flock to just hear Jesus, Jesus, Jesus." It doesn't? I think all true preachers of the uncorrupted gospel know deep down that Jesus is in fact the *only* thing that will help their flock.

The only reason grace works for our salvation is because grace is "Christ clothed in the gospel,"[18] as Calvin put it. I find it immensely helpful to think of the *solas*, the "alone" declarations of the Reformers, as five ways of saying one thing: *solus Christus*, Christ alone. In our justification and in our sanctification, we don't look to grace as a salvation commodity in itself. First and last, we look to Jesus Christ.

We do this because only Christ creates holiness in us. Union with Christ always produces genuine effects in us. "There will be three effects of nearness to Jesus," wrote Spurgeon, "—humility, happiness, and holiness."[19] Sanctification and holiness don't come about by a manifestation of the law to us. Humility, happiness, and holiness are the result when Jesus unfolds the wonder of his presence to his children. Spurgeon calls this "paradise in embryo"[20] when we are drawn near and draw near to the personification of grace, Jesus Christ himself.

The Law of Christ

On the one hand, when we look to Christ, when we know him and the power of his resurrection, we will delight in his Word, his will and ways, in the law of Christ. True faith will

17. Sinclair Ferguson, "By Grace Alone," *Tabletalk*, February 2010, 81.

18. John Calvin, cited in the above.

19. Charles Haddon Spurgeon, "Morning, May 12," *Morning and Evening: Daily Readings, Christian Classics Ethereal Library*, accessed January 14, 2014, http://www.ccel.org/ccel/spurgeon/morneve.html.

20. Ibid.

embrace and revel in his law from the inner man, from hearts transformed by the grace of the gospel. Devout religious leaders in Jesus' day, on the other hand, proved beyond a doubt that looking to the law not only does not justify, it does not sanctify either.

After a terrorist threat and a chaotic rescheduling of flights, I had a memorable demonstration of this. In the middle of the night, I finally managed to get a seat on a flight back to Seattle. Sitting next to me was a man wearing a *yarmulke*, a prayer shawl, and fingering the pages of a copy of the Torah on his lap. Weary as I was, I sensed this was another providential appointment, and so I began a conversation with him. In moments we were talking about the law of Moses—his favorite topic—but he refused to let me read from the New Testament. "I never have nor ever will read anything from that book," he said with conviction. I tried to explain to him that he actually had read many things from the New Testament because Jesus, who claimed to be the fulfillment of everything written in the law, was almost constantly reciting from the Old Testament. I read from Psalm 22 and later from Isaiah 53. He listened patiently, but it was clear he wanted to get back to what was really important to him, the precepts on the pages of his copy of the Hebrew law.

This devout Orthodox Jew delighted in the law; it was his whole life; he loved it and meditated upon its rules day and night. But he had nothing but restrained condescension for the Messiah, Jesus, the better High Priest who alone fulfilled all righteousness for sinners. For him it was the precepts, not the Person, that could make him holy. This man would have completely rejected any notion that the law can't sanctify him. He had an undoubting faith in the law and in his ability to keep it. And of corresponding necessity, he had no faith in the finished work of the Savior who bore the curse of the law, by whose righteousness alone a sinner can be justified *and* sanctified. As did the Pharisees, this sincere man wanted nearness to the law—but not nearness to Jesus.

Legalism is no respecter of ethnicity, however. Because Pharisaic legalists looked to the law for their sanctification, we should never allow their abuse of the law to drive us from it. True Christians love the Bible, the law, the revelation of the will and way of Jesus to us. We meditate on it day and night and delight in the law as a gracious means by which our High Priest sanctifies us.

Just as grace is not a thing, so Christ's law is not a thing outside of and disconnected from his person. His law, his Word, is Jesus' love letter to us—all of it, the Law, the Prophets, the Psalms, the Proverbs—every word is the word of the Savior to us, Jesus in every part of speech, on every page. And because we love our Savior, we will love every jot and tittle of his Word to us. Only when we gaze upon the loveliness of Jesus, then, and only then, will we truly delight in God's law from hearts united with Jesus the living Word of God himself.

Ten Looks at Christ

Knowing how deceitful above all things our hearts are, how desperately wicked we are, root and branch (Jer. 17:9), Scottish pastor Robert Murray McCheyne offered one of the most helpful axioms for keeping the gospel straight. "For every look at yourself, take ten looks at Christ."[21] We look to Christ because there is no other hope; his grace alone works to justify *and* to sanctify us.

When Augustine opened a Bible in his garden in Milan, he placed his finger on the words, "Put on the Lord Jesus Christ, and make no provision for the flesh, to gratify its desires" (Rom. 13:14). Paul did not write, "Put on the law." He tells us to put on Christ, to turn from self and sin to Jesus; it is only

21. Robert Murray McCheyne, *Memoir and Remains of the Rev. Robert Murray McCheyne* (Philadelphia: Presbyterian Board of Publication, 1844), 293.

by the power of the sinless Savior that we are freed from the lusts of the flesh.

We joyfully affirm with the psalmists that the law is good, that the will and way of our Lord is lovely and delightful, that the law is given as a pure guide to our gratitude and defines our adoring obedience. Saying, however, that law sanctifies us is like praising the violin instead of the musician or hailing the chisel instead of the woodcarver. When we say law sanctifies us, we are giving credit to the means, the schoolmaster whose role is to lead us to the Divine Object, Christ himself (Gal. 3:24).

Preaching that does this won't work. However zealous for good works a preacher may be, when he fails to point his flock to the indelible benefits of their union with Christ, his message will not produce gospel holiness. Pointing the flock to law and not to grace is to direct us inward; we can't have it both ways; looking inward directs us away from Christ. Only in Christ can we do all things (Phil. 4:13), without him we can do nothing (John 15:5).

Grace works because grace is Christ's work, the work of the steadfast love of the unchanging Son of God in us. Any message that makes us begin to doubt this about the grace of the gospel is a counterfeit. It's not merely the same message, different emphasis. It's a distorted message and is, therefore, no longer the gospel. Paul reserves his most vitriolic language for preachers "who trouble you and want to distort the gospel of Christ" (Gal. 1:7). He doesn't try to be nice; the souls of men are at stake. If anyone preaches "a gospel contrary to the one we preached to you," he wrote, "let him be accursed" (1:8). It was a distorted gospel creeping in that was plaguing the church of Galatia in Paul's day, and it was a corrupted gospel message that produced spiritual disaster in Amsterdam, Geneva, Edinburgh, and Northampton, all once paragons of gospel triumph. A distorted gospel will have the same effect today.

At the last, we will hold fast to the pure doctrine of the gospel only when we acknowledge that this grace-corrupting cancer can and will happen in our churches, in our families, in our children, in our own hearts. Knowing this, we will joyfully rediscover afresh the steadfast love of the gospel every generation. And there is only one way to do that. "Learn much of the Lord Jesus," as McCheyne wrote.

> He is altogether lovely. Such infinite majesty, and yet such meekness and grace, and all for sinners, even the chief! Let your soul be filled with a heart-ravishing sense of the sweetness and excellency of Christ and all that is in Him. Let the Holy Spirit fill every chamber of your heart; and so there will be no room for folly, or the world, or Satan, or the flesh.[22]

Solus Christus

For Discussion

1. Read John 15:15–16 and discuss the source of fruit bearing as understood by John Owen when he wrote, "As the effect is in the cause, the fruit is in the root."

   No longer do I call you servants, for the servant does not know what his master is doing; but I have called you friends, for all that I have heard from my Father I have made known to you. You did not choose me, but I chose you and appointed you that you should go and bear fruit and that your fruit should abide.

2. According to the author, we and our children will value grace in the exact proportion to what? What are other obstacles to valuing grace?

22. Ibid.

3. Read Heidelberg Catechism 58 and discuss the role our future hope has in our present worship and service motivated by love and gratitude by the free grace of the gospel of Jesus Christ.

Q. What comfort takest thou from the article of "life everlasting"?

A. That since I now feel in my heart the beginning of eternal joy, after this life, I shall inherit perfect salvation, which "eye has not seen, nor ear heard, neither has it entered into the heart of man" to conceive, and that to praise God therein for ever.

4. Discuss what Calvin meant when he wrote that grace is "Christ clothed in the gospel."

Pray for the readers of this book and for their children, that they will make much of Christ, recognize his holy work in their lives, and live in awe and gratitude as they understand more and more the magnitude of Christ's finished work in the free grace of the gospel.

Appendix A

We Worship Christ

I WAS INCLUDED in the loop of a series of e-mails from church musicians who had attended a music symposium in Florida. They all seemed to agree that there was a dearth of hymn poetry on the theme of unity and oneness in the body of Christ as explored by Paul in Ephesians 2:11–22.

I began reading the passage, cross-referencing, and gathering phrases, words, and ideas. In December of 2009, when what the Bible means about confessional unity had been wrenched from the theoretical to the wincingly real and immediate in our lives, the following lines came together as if I had been given a poetical-theological spinal block—painlessly—at least while writing the hymn.

> We worship Christ, the Cornerstone,
> Who made us one in him alone!
> Not Jew nor Gentile, bond nor free,
> This commonwealth of unity.
> Our Lord has from the two made one,
> And with his blood our peace has won.
>
> Brought near in Christ, the Prince of Peace,
> Our envy, strife, and warfare cease;
> For tribes and tongues, and strangers all,
> Our Peace has broken down the wall;

New covenant mercy he extends
To us, his fellow heirs and friends.

One faith, one hope of heav'n above,
A unity of holy love;
One body made of many parts,
A unity of loving hearts;
One temple built of cast-off stone,
Made holy by the Holy One.

To Jesus Christ we lift one voice—
The household of our Father's choice—
Whose love makes ours for others grow
And makes the watching world to know
That our abiding Cornerstone
Has made us one in Christ alone!

Douglas Bond © December 2, 2009

Appendix B

A Hymn If Grace Doesn't Work

I'VE LONG THOUGHT that one of the significant problems with synergistic theology is that it doesn't sing very well. "Jesus paid it all," would have to sound something like, "Jesus paid most of it; most of it to him I owe," which of course is far worse than just bad poetry.

What I've observed is that whatever their declared theology, when hymn writers set their quill to paper to write a hymn of praise to God, they feel constrained to extol the free mercy of God in Christ. But I have long wondered what a hymn would sound like written by someone who believes that God and man are in a responsible partnership in salvation, where we determine our destiny by our faith and our obedience. So I attempted to project myself into the theology of synergism (which is actually so much easier than any of us really wants to admit) and out came this:

> I praise and worship Father thee
> Since I have chosen free
> To bow before your majesty
> By my own liberty.
> O God of fairness, with my voice,
> I praise you for my choice!

The Father leaves us, every man,
To choose him if we can;
My will he never violates
But passive sits and waits.
O God of fairness, with my voice,
I praise you for my choice!

The Son who did his best for all
Leaves me alone to call;
Along with all the human race,
I'm left to choose my place.
O God of fairness, with my voice,
I praise you for my choice!

The Spirit draws—but not too much;
My will he'll never touch,
But leaves me free to choose my faith,
The captain of my fate.
O God of fairness, with my voice,
I praise you for my choice!

It would not make a bit of sense
To earn my recompense,
If I don't have ability,
My free will and my liberty.
O God of fairness, with my voice,
I praise you for my choice!

Douglas Bond © January 29, 2012 (with apologies)